Three Strikes Laws

Three Strikes Laws

Jennifer E. Walsh

Historical Guides to Controversial Issues in America

GREENWOOD PRESS
Westport, Connecticut • London

345.077 WALSH 2007

Walsh, Jennifer Edwards.

Three strikes laws

Library of Congress Cataloging-in-Publication Data

Walsh, Jennifer Edwards
   Three strikes laws / Jennifer E. Walsh.
      p. cm. — (Historical guides to controversial issues in America, ISSN 1541–0012)
   Includes bibliographical references and index.
   ISBN 0–313–33708–X
   1. Mandatory sentences—United States—History   2. Life imprisonment—United
States.   3. Recidivists—United States.   4. Mandatory sentences—California.   5. Life
imprisonment—California.   I. Title.
   KF9685.W36   2007
   345.73'077—dc22   2006035283

British Library Cataloguing in Publication Data is available.

Library of Congress Catalog Card Number: 2006035283
ISBN-10: 0–313–33708–X
ISBN-13: 978–0–313–33708–6
ISSN: 1541–0021

First published in 2007

Greenwood Press, 88 Post Road West, Westport, CT 06881
An imprint of Greenwood Publishing Group, Inc.
www.greenwood.com

Printed in the United States of America

The paper used in this book complies with the
Permanent Paper Standard issued by the National
Information Standards Organization (Z39.48–1984).

10 9 8 7 6 5 4 3 2 1

For Greg, my Barnabas
2 Corinthians 4:5-6

Contents

Illustrations

TABLES

FIGURE

Preface

More than a dozen years have passed since the Three Strikes movement swept through the nation, imposing harsher criminal penalties on recidivists and reframing the debate on how crime should be managed. Rising crime rates coupled with media reports about atrocities committed by repeat offenders convinced many that tougher sentencing laws were necessary to protect public safety. As a result, Three Strikes measures were quickly endorsed by leading politicians on both sides of the political spectrum, including President Bill Clinton, a Democrat, and California governor Pete Wilson, a Republican. They were also overwhelmingly supported by the citizenry. Consequently, Three Strikes laws were quickly adopted by half the states and by the federal government.

Shortly after the adoption of Three Strikes policies, crime rates began to fall rapidly across the nation. This decrease in crime convinced many that the new laws were working to safeguard the public. However, subsequent reports about offenders being sentenced to life in prison for minor felonies coupled with a scholarly skepticism over the effectiveness of the laws led some to suggest that the laws were unjust and a waste of taxpayer resources. Since then, the dispute between Three Strikes supporters and opponents has exploded into a political firestorm that has ignited debate in other policy arenas, including the management of overcrowded prisons, the sentencing of other types of offenders, and the prioritization of state spending in a fiscally restrictive climate.

As is common in policy debates like these, those in the middle are often left to sort out the various pro and con arguments raised by advocates on both sides of the issue. This publication will prove to be a valuable resource for those who wish to explore this important and controversial issue. Students in history, political science/public policy, and criminal justice, as well as members of the public, will benefit from the objective overview and analysis presented throughout this volume. In the introductory chapters, the Three Strikes movement is explained in the broader context of sentencing reform that began in the mid-1970s and continues through to the present day. Instructors who teach introductory courses in public policy, criminal justice, and corrections will find this overview helpful for students who have a difficult time keeping track of the many changes that were adopted in the latter half of the twentieth century. In chapter 2, the factors contributing to Three Strikes laws are reviewed, including the media coverage of the kidnapping and murder of Polly Klaas and the attention given to crime and justice issues by politicians competing for election. Chapter 3 describes the particulars of California's Three Strikes policy and explains the reasons for its controversy. This chapter will be particularly useful for readers because much of the Three Strikes debate focuses on issues related to this one law.

Constitutional challenges to Three Strikes laws, including an analysis of the 2003 U.S. Supreme Court rulings, are analyzed in chapter 4. Chapter 5 overviews many of the concerns that were raised when the laws were first implemented, and chapter 6 explains the various research studies that have analyzed the effectiveness and the efficiency of Three Strikes sentencing laws. This chapter will be most helpful to those who find it difficult to sort through the numerous scholarly studies that appear to produce contradictory results. Finally, the last chapter describes the recent attempts to reform Three Strikes laws, including a detailed discussion of Proposition 66, a reform initiative that California voters defeated in November 2004. It also includes a discussion of reform efforts that are pending at the time of this publication.

This work represents a culmination of more than a decade of research on the history, development, and implementation of the nation's Three Strikes laws. Many thanks are owed to those who made this cumulative research possible. In particular, I am indebted to Joseph M. Bessette, Alice Tweed Tuohy Professor of Government and Ethics at Claremont McKenna College, who has been an ongoing source of support and help throughout various stages of this research. Special thanks are also extended to the Henry Salvatori Center at Claremont McKenna College for sponsoring prior segments of my Three Strikes research; James A. Ardaiz, Presiding Justice, California Fifth District Court of Appeal; the California District Attorneys Association; and many of the individual California district attorneys who have graciously given their time (and data) to further my understanding of the Three Strikes phenomenon.

Introduction

In 1976, researcher Robert Martinson declared that "the history of correction is a graveyard of abandoned fads."[1] In the United States this has certainly proven to be true. Since our founding, we have experimented with various ways of censuring those who violate the social contract and threaten the order of our society. Early policies, which have since been disavowed as primitive, used public shaming, church expulsion, pain, mutilation, and exile to encourage obedience. In more recent times, policy makers have tried to correct misbehavior by placing offenders in psychological therapy, education, and job training programs and by subjecting them to intensive supervision and imprisonment. Yet, even these so-called enlightened policies have proven to be unsuccessful in eradicating crime once and for all. Because human behavior remains unpredictable and sometimes impervious to correction, the search for a better, more effective crime policy continues to the present day.

Despite the variations that crime policy might entail, our choices in dealing with criminal behavior can be separated into four different options. First, as a society, we have the option of overlooking bad behavior and choosing not to pursue retribution against the offender for his violation of the social contract. Political philosophers have suggested, though, that this strategy is problematic. When there is no respect for law, and when vengeance against wrongdoing is accomplished through personal retribution, society will dissolve and anarchy will ensue. We will once again live in a state of nature wherein the strong will prey upon the weak.

Assuming that this is an unacceptable alternative for modern society, a second option is to pursue reconciliation with the offender after his first contravention of the social contract. The premise of the social contract is that members of the community come together to form a civil government that is based on the consent of the governed. All members of society are presumed to be valuable; therefore, restoring the offender to a right relationship with others in the community is usually the preferred course of action. Reconciliation could be accomplished by reasoning with the offender, requiring some form of restitution for the victim, imposing some form of societal or spiritual chastisement to produce repentance, or any combination of these. It could also be sought through modern rehabilitation-based treatment programs that aid the offender in restoring his relationship with others and society at large.

A third option is to expel an offender from civil society, either through physical exile or by isolation through incarceration. In the past, this option has been used against those offenders who have repeatedly transgressed and have resisted attempts at reconciliation or who have shown no signs of repentance or rehabilitation. Pursuing a policy of isolation is often considered necessary because repeated violations of the social contract undermine the stability of civil society and threaten the well-being of all who are in the community. Removing the offender from society may be the only practical way to restrain the offender so that he does not misbehave again. It also sends a message to other would-be offenders that violations of the social contract will result in severe consequences. Today, physical exile is no longer viable, but the invention of the modern prison has made segregation and isolation through incarceration a feasible, yet expensive, alternative.

A last option is to permanently expel the offender from human society through execution. Previously, execution has been used to incapacitate those who sinned repeatedly against society, but since the advent of the modern prison system, it has been reserved for offenders who commit particularly heinous crimes. Execution serves to punish the offender for his crime under a proportionality principle: severe wrongdoing necessitates severe consequences. Execution also allows the state to exact retribution and recompense on behalf of the victims' families.

Over the last two hundred years or so, policy makers in the United States have used all of the last three options to circumvent and curtail crime. By simultaneously pursuing reconciliation, isolation, and execution, our political leaders have tried to eliminate crime—or at least minimize its occurrence. For much of the twentieth century, lawmakers pursued policies of reconciliation through rehabilitation because developments in the area of human psychology and social behavior convinced many that offenders could be cured of their criminal tendencies. However, rising crime rates during the zenith of the rehabilitation era forced many to lose faith in this strategy. As a result, policy makers began to reconsider more restrictive and punitive policies instead.

The modern get-tough movement, which emerged in the mid-1970s, came about as confidence in our nation's social structures declined and the nation's crime rate began to climb. Although the increase in crime was blamed on many factors, including gangs, drugs, and rising unemployment rates, many court observers believed that an overly lenient judicial system was also responsible. Research findings cast doubt on the usefulness of rehabilitation programs, and recidivism rates indicated that strategies of reconciliation were not effective. Consequently, many described the prison system as a revolving door, releasing prisoners only to have them return to a life of crime.

Policy makers responded to public concern over escalating crime by enacting a series of sentencing reforms that were designed to make prison sentences longer and more certain. For example, sentences were stiffened for drug crimes, gang crimes, and gun-related crimes; probation was eliminated for many felony offenses; and judges were stripped of their sentencing discretion by the enactment of numerous mandatory penalties. On the heels of these reforms, the federal government and half the states enacted laws requiring tougher sentences for repeat felons. Identified by the "Three Strikes and You're Out" slogan, these laws attempted to isolate career criminals by imposing on them lifetime or near-lifetime sentences once they had been convicted of a third offense. Although the specific details of Three Strikes laws varied from state to state, the goal of isolating and incapacitating repeat offenders through long prison sentences was the same.

Since their enactment over a dozen years ago, Three Strikes laws have generated much controversy. Opponents maintain that the laws are unfair because they can result in sentences that are disproportionately severe when compared to the current (triggering) offense. They also argue that Three Strikes laws are largely ineffective at reducing crime and are responsible for incurring negative side effects on the criminal justice system, such as courtroom backlog and jail and prison overcrowding. They also contend that policies of incapacitation are wasteful because valuable tax revenues are spent warehousing inmates who no longer present a threat to society.

Despite these concerns, Three Strikes laws remain popular with the public and with policy makers. Supporters believe that the policies are largely responsible for the dramatic decrease in crime that occurred in the late 1990s. They maintain that the laws have kept millions of Americans from becoming crime victims and that the reduction in crime has produced a savings in both social and economic costs. Three Strikes supporters also contend that the law has made members of the public feel safer in their communities.

The Three Strikes movement is a controversial, multifaceted phenomenon that has piqued the interest of academics, policy makers, students, the media, and members of the public. Because of this complexity, a thorough understanding of the law requires thoughtful analysis in a number of key areas. In chapter 1 of this book, the historical origin of the Three Strikes movement is reviewed in detail. In particular, this section explains the context for the Three Strikes movement through a discussion of critical background issues, including rising crime rates, faltering confidence in the rehabilitation model of punishment, and high rates of offender recidivism. Furthermore, this chapter presents an overview of policy makers' previous attempts to get tough on crime through reforms that produced sentencing guideline systems, determinate sentencing policies, and mandatory minimum penalties.

Although Three Strikes laws developed as part of this broader get-tough movement, the enactment of the specific policies came about suddenly in response to a series of high-profile crimes that captivated the American public and sparked their interest in lengthy sentences for dangerous repeat offenders. Chapter 2 reviews these cases and explores the role of the media and the influence of election-year politics on the development of Three Strikes policies. This section also includes a review of the various Three Strikes laws that were implemented across the nation during this period.

Although 26 states and the federal government have now implemented a type of Three Strikes law, California's version is by far the most controversial. Critics of the California Three Strikes law argue that the law is too broad because it allows offenders to be sentenced to 25 years to life in prison for a low-level felony. They also point out that California uses its law much more frequently than other states, thereby exposing many more of its offenders to mandatory sentences. Proponents of the law respond that the law incorporates a substantial amount of discretion that can shield less-deserving offenders from the full effect of the law. Chapter 3 highlights the features of the California law and analyzes the arguments on both sides of the various controversies.

Offenders subject to Three Strikes laws have argued that the lengthy mandatory penalties are unconstitutional. Some contend that the laws violate the Constitution's prohibition against double jeopardy while others allege that they constitute cruel and unusual punishment in violation of the Eighth Amendment. Chapter 4 discusses the various arguments related to the constitutionality of Three Strikes policies and presents an overview of the U.S. Supreme Court's response to these claims.

After the Three Strikes laws were enacted nationwide, criminal justice scholars and other court observers predicted that the system would suffer from a variety of negative side effects, ranging from severe case backlog from an increased number of jury trials to universal prison overcrowding. Although the systems in some states did experience noticeable side effects at first, most of the initial predictions failed to come true. In Chapter 5, issues related to implementation are discussed and various theories are presented that may help to explain why the impact of the policies has been much less than what was originally predicted. One of these theories suggests that the steep decline in the nation's crime rate shortly after the laws were implemented is responsible for the lower Three Strikes case volume. Supporters of the Three Strikes laws were quick to claim credit for the decline in crime while opponents presented evidence to refute the conclusion that the new policies had caused the reduction. To assess whether Three Strikes is responsible for reducing crime, chapter 6 reviews the various empirical studies that have examined the efficacy of the laws.

In 2003, U.S. Supreme Court justice Anthony Kennedy publicly questioned the wisdom of mandatory sentences and urged lawmakers across the nation to repeal these measures. This appeal for reform has sparked a public debate about the harshness of our nation's sentencing laws and has called into question the appropriateness of Three Strikes legislation. Although no state has yet to formally repeal or substantially reform its Three Strikes law, a number of efforts have proposed to do just that. These attempts, described in the final chapter, have not yet been successful, but additional efforts that are currently under way may result in substantial changes to these policies.

The Three Strikes movement is more than just the sum total of the various laws that were passed during the mid-1990s. Rather, it represents a substantial—and perhaps permanent—shift in how we think about crime and the problem of repeat offenders. Voters sent a clear message to lawmakers that the status quo would no longer be tolerated, and this message still reverberates in the legislative chambers today. Although crime has declined in recent years, recent criminal justice policies still emphasize a get-tough approach. It is possible that this will change in the future, but for now, it appears more likely that the effects of the Three Strikes movement will continue to impact policy for decades to come.

NOTE

1. Robert Martinson, "California Research at the Crossroads," in Rehabilitation, Recidivism, and Research, ed. Robert Martinson, Ted Palmer, and Stuart Adams (Hackensack, N.J.: National Council on Crime and Delinquency, 1976), 64.

1

Rising Crime Rates and the Get-Tough Movement

In 1992, the phrase "three strikes—you're out!" was known only as an umpire's call that sent a dejected baseball batter back to the dugout. Within five years, however, the phrase "three strikes" was better known to the public as a moniker for tough new sentencing laws implemented by the federal government and half of the states. While many observers were surprised by the fervor with which these reforms were embraced, these laws could be viewed as just another phase of the "get tough" movement that began in the mid-1970s. As crime rates began to soar, public sympathy for wayward offenders quickly dissipated and voters began to urge policy makers to abandon rehabilitation programs and instead adopt harsher criminal penalties. By the mid-1990s, the nation's criminal justice system had been completely transformed from a system based on the philosophies of rehabilitation and renewal to one based on the philosophies of deterrence and incapacitation.

IDENTIFYING THE PURPOSE OF PUNISHMENT

At the heart of every penal policy is one practical goal: to prevent people from committing crime. Suggestions about how this should be done vary, but they typically correspond with one of four philosophical approaches. Rehabilitation, the first approach, tries to discover and correct the underlying causes of crime in order to prevent crime from occurring in the future. The rehabilitation model has been compared to a medical model, wherein doctors identify the cause of bodily dysfunction or disease and prescribe a course of treatment or remedy. Similarly, criminologists who adhere to the rehabilitation philosophy often attribute crime to the presence of negative social, economic, psychological, or physiological conditions or dysfunctions. They believe that people break the law because of external influences or internal impulses; therefore, government should try to uncover the cause of crime for the individual offender and then apply the appropriate therapy or treatment. The criminal justice system, in its attempt to stop crime, can treat the offender—and those in the community who are at risk for committing crime—with state-sponsored programs that emphasize psychological counseling, parenting skills, educational and vocational training, or substance-abuse treatment.

Deterrence, the second philosophical approach to fighting crime, stems from the belief that people commit crime because it gives them some sort of benefit. A person might, for example, hold up a convenience store because it would give him more cash than he could earn in a day through legitimate employment. Another person might use illegal drugs because of the physiological highs they produce. Deterrence theorists believe, however, that the attractiveness of a crime can be diminished when the associated costs or consequences are increased, such as in the form of increased punishment or increased certainty of apprehension. A person might think twice about robbing a convenience store if he knew that he would definitely be caught by police and sentenced to prison. Similarly, a person might forgo a drug-induced high if she knew that it would lead to a lengthy jail sentence.

Even though we may not realize it, much of our criminal law is based on the theory of deterrence. For example, we often obey traffic laws out of fear of what will happen if we get pulled over by a traffic officer. Motorists choose to observe the speed limit or obey traffic signals when apprehension is likely and when the associated penalties are sufficiently high. Although many assume that deterrence theory prescribes harsh punishments for breaking the law, it only requires punishment to be *severe enough* to keep people from disobeying. For example, the fine for excessive speed need not be as high as $4,000 to be an effective deterrent; for most people, a fine of $400 is steep enough to keep them from driving too fast. With regard to traffic offenses, additional related consequences, such as increased car insurance rates, suspended licenses, or even social stigma or shame, also work to increase the cost of the offense. Similarly, traffic officers need not be present at all times to keep drivers fearful of detection and apprehension; rather, officers just need to be visible enough to keep the possibility of being pulled over present in the minds of motorists.

Retribution is a philosophical view that often operates in conjunction with deterrence. It proposes that offenders receive punishment as a form of recompense for their misdeeds. While historically this approach was used to impose some form of vengeance on behalf of the victim, the American system of justice has embraced a more moderate version of retribution under the title of "just deserts." This interpretation of retribution argues that government should impose punishment on the offender because it is what he justly deserves for having broken the social contract. Typically, punishment is measured in proportion to the harm that has been committed. Similar to the ancient eye-for-an-eye argument, which placed limitations on the amount of vengeance that could be extracted by a victim, the government must restrain itself and not impose a punishment that is more severe than the crime that has been committed. Correspondingly, some theorists believe that only serious offenders should be sentenced to prison and that the majority of prison terms should be just a few years' duration. Offenders who commit nonserious crimes should receive alternative punishments, such as fines and weekend jail time, instead of prison time.[1] Although criminologists who endorse this perspective argue that punishment should primarily serve a moral purpose—not a practical one—secondary practical effects, such as deterrence or even rehabilitation, can be encouraged at the same time.

Incapacitation is the fourth philosophical approach commonly seen in punishment policies. Criminologists who subscribe to this position claim that some people are incorrigible; therefore, they should be isolated from the rest of society in order to prevent them from committing additional harm. In its most extreme form, incapacitation can be accomplished through execution—which could be described as the ultimate form of societal segregation. Today, however, incapacitation usually takes the form of extended imprisonment and is used to justify policies that impose lengthy sentences on those who appear to be incapable of conforming to the requirements of the law. Thus, the prison system becomes the incapacitating agent by separating such criminals from potential victims.

How society determines who is incorrigible has been an issue of great debate. Certainly, one could argue that anyone who has ever broken the law has the capability to do it again. Yet, incapacitation would likely be inappropriate for all first-time offenders since a sizable percentage of them will not commit a second, third, or fourth offense. A number of first-time offenders, however, will go on to commit additional crimes, and lawmakers often try to target these repeat offenders with incapacitation-based penalties. The key to an effective incapacitation law is the ability to predict which offenders are incorrigible. Hindsight will reveal who the high-risk offenders were, but identifying these offenders in advance has proven to be a difficult task. That has not stopped policy makers from trying, though; the crime-control benefit of segregating the right group of offenders is too valuable for legislators to ignore.

Lawmakers were first made aware in the early 1970s of the impact that repeat offenders can have on the cumulative crime rate. Sociologists Wolfgang,

Figlio, and Sellin studied a cohort of nearly 10,000 Philadelphia youth, ranging between 10 and 18 years of age. By examining the educational and criminal records of these boys, they found that 18 percent of the group could be considered chronic offenders; each of these 627 boys had committed five or more offenses apiece. Combined, these boys were responsible for more than half the crime committed by the entire cohort. Furthermore, the study revealed that as the number of offenses committed by the youth increased, the severity of the criminal activity increased as well.[2]

RISE OF THE REHABILITATION SYSTEM

Although some penological theories, such as deterrence, have been consistently used in our criminal justice system, others, such as rehabilitation and incapacitation, are relatively new. For example, during the colonial period and the first hundred years of our nation's history, most offenders were punished for the purpose of deterrence and retribution. Sentences were typically corporal in nature and included such punishments as confinement in the stocks, whipping, branding, and hanging.[3] Jails existed, but they were reserved for detaining offenders until the time of trial. Sentences were usually carried out promptly in order to maximize the deterrent benefit of the punishment, and legal appeals before sentences were carried out were rare.

The movement away from a retributive system of justice to one that emphasized a new theory of rehabilitation began in the 1870s. Developments in the field of sociology had convinced many social reformers that crime was merely a by-product of a dysfunctional society. Immigrants, juveniles, and newly freed slaves were thought to commit crime because they lacked education, proper social skills, and appropriate moral training. Reformers believed that it was wrong to simply punish these offenders and send them on their way. Instead, they proposed that these offenders be kept in a secure location and properly educated and socialized so that they could be redeemed and made fit for civil society. Later, developments in the fields of psychology and psychiatry encouraged reformers to "treat the criminal, not the crime," and mandatory counseling programs and psychiatric drug therapies were added to the list of rehabilitative programs offered by the state.[4]

Prisons and other secure institutions were used to facilitate the treatment of miscreants. Juveniles were adjudicated under special circumstances, and, when found to be delinquent, they were kept in group homes wherein they were educated, socialized, and often physically disciplined.[5] Adults were usually kept in separate facilities that resembled our current prisons, although in these particular institutions, the emphasis on the detention process was restoration, not retribution. Throughout the course of their stay, offenders were individually assessed and treated under a medical model approach that equated the prison with a quasi hospital that offered individual therapeutic programming instead of punishment.[6]

To facilitate this new emphasis on reformation and rehabilitation, states began to adopt indeterminate sentences and formal systems of parole. Beginning with the New York Elmira Act in 1877, states replaced fixed or determinate punishments with indefinite or open-ended sentences. Rehabilitation advocates encouraged these reform efforts because the new emphasis on offender rehabilitation made it impossible to stipulate in advance precisely how long a person should be held. Some offenders might be rehabilitated in a comparatively short period of time, while others would require longer periods of treatment in reformatory institutions. Thus, they believed that the ability to tailor sentence lengths to individual needs was one of the key components of rehabilitation success.[7]

Although state lawmakers were generally supportive of the indeterminate sentencing model, most insisted that they retain some control over sentence lengths. Some states, like New York, identified a maximum period of time that an offender could be held in custody, whereas other states, like Ohio, Michigan, Minnesota, and Illinois, identified both a minimum and maximum term of imprisonment. Indiana chose to give the individual sentencing judge authority to establish minimum and maximum limitations.[8]

At the same time that states were moving toward a system of indeterminate sentencing, lawmakers also began to formalize their procedures for parole. Since the early 1800s, prison officials had offered inmates the possibility of early release if they worked hard and behaved well; however, most states did not formalize this practice until the late 1800s. In most states, the two new systems, indeterminate sentencing and parole, were combined.[9] Prison reform advocates encouraged this merger since it simultaneously served two critical functions. First, it helped to control the behavior of inmates in prison because the possibility of early release gave them an incentive to cooperate with prison authorities. Second, it gave prison officials the opportunity to review inmates' rehabilitation progress. Offenders who were considered to be appropriately reformed could secure release, whereas those who needed more treatment could be kept in prison until the maximum allotted time had been served.[10]

By 1922, the rehabilitation revolution that prompted the makeover of the nation's criminal justice system was complete. Forty-four states, the federal government, and the federal territory of Hawaii had implemented a system of parole. Of these, 37 states had combined parole with a system of indeterminate sentencing; only four states were without either type of reform.[11]

ABANDONING THE REHABILITATIVE IDEAL

Although the move to a rehabilitative-based penal system was nearly universal by the 1920s, states grew disenchanted with the new system after just a few decades of use. Concerns about the coercive nature of rehabilitation, the fairness of indeterminate sentencing, the appropriateness of open-ended punishment, the effectiveness of corrective programming, and, above all, the failure to curb rising crime rates prompted lawmakers to examine their support of treatment-oriented sentencing. By the end of the 1970s, states that had once embraced all facets of the rehabilitative ideal, such as indeterminate sentencing, systems of parole, and rehabilitative therapies, were now quickly adopting alternative approaches that promised to get tough with offenders.

One of the first criticisms of rehabilitation focused on its potential for inmate coercion. Because offenders were placed in reformatories as a result of their misdeeds—and not as a result of their voluntary choice—their participation in therapeutic programs raised thorny ethical questions. For example, should the government be able to force offenders to accept treatment against their will? Although some states coerced inmates to take experimental drugs or submit to invasive medical procedures to supposedly cure them of their criminal tendencies, most states allowed offenders to choose whether they would participate in programs offered by the institutions. Offenders who opted out of the treatment programs, however, were denied parole. Consequently, offenders soon learned that participation in rehabilitation programs was necessary to secure early release and would go along with the therapies despite their personal objections.[12] Additionally, correctional personnel sometimes denied parole even after treatment was completed because they viewed the institution as being better for the individual than the outside world.[13]

Federal, state, and local policy makers also began to question the effectiveness of existing crime policy when crime rates began to escalate in the late 1960s. Federal statistics reveal that during 1960–1970, overall property crime rates increased by more than 200 percent. Burglary and larceny rates doubled and motor vehicle thefts jumped nearly 250 percent. Even more troubling, though, was the upsurge in violent crime. Within this same 10-year period, the rate of violent crime grew by 225 percent. The homicide rate rose from 5.1 to 7.9 per 100,000—an increase of 65 percent. Rates for forcible rape doubled from 9.6 to 18.7 per 100,000, and rates for aggravated assault nearly doubled, increasing from 86.1 to 164.8 per 100,000. Robbery rates almost tripled, increasing from 60.1 to 172.1 per 100,000.[14]

Congressional lawmakers responded to the rising crime rates by passing the Omnibus Crime Control and Safe Streets Act of 1968. This measure created a federal agency, the Law Enforcement Assistance Administration (LEAA), which was responsible for dispersing tens of millions of dollars of federal funds in the form of grants to help state and local governments fight crime.[15] Specifically, these grants were awarded to state and local agencies to facilitate activities related to the recruitment, training, and education of law enforcement personnel; for programs to help police apprehend criminal suspects; for programs that were designed to rehabilitate offenders; for the development of research and information systems; and for the scholarly evaluation of new and existing programs.[16] However, after seeing no decline in crime rates—in fact, crime rates continued to increase to record-high levels—Congress quietly ended the LEAA and its ambitious crime-reduction program just 12 years after its inception.[17]

Interestingly, studies funded by these federal grants found that rehabilitation programs were largely ineffective in their mission. The most famous of these was an analysis of rehabilitation research by Robert Martinson. The original purpose of his study was to assess which of the many rehabilitation strategies was most successful in reducing crime; however, after the analysis was complete, Martinson determined that nearly all failed to lower rates of reoffending.[18] His widely-reported conclusion was that "with few and isolated exceptions, the rehabilitative efforts that have been reported so far have had no appreciable effect on recidivism."[19]

In particular, Martinson found very little evidence to support the premise that in-prison educational programs and vocational training gave offenders the skills they needed to lead productive lives. He also discredited the assumption that individual counseling helped inmates to stay law-abiding after they were released from prison. Group counseling was also seen as a failure, as were attempts to modify prison environments to make them less coercive and more rehabilitation-friendly. Similarly, offenders subjected to medical treatment, including psychiatric drug therapies, did not show measurable improvement after being returned to the community.[20]

Martinson did point out, however, that the news was not all bad. His findings revealed that although rehabilitation programs were not likely to make offenders better, they were also not likely to make them worse. Additionally, he found one area of research that suggested that offenders who were placed on probation and given close supervision were less likely to commit additional crimes. However, Martinson noted that this success was almost certainly due to a deterrent effect. Offenders placed in these types of probation programs probably refrained from committing additional offenses because they feared being discovered by their probation officer—not because they had been reformed.[21]

Despite objections to his findings by other researchers within the criminal justice community, Martinson's conclusion, quickly summed up by the phrase "nothing works," became the impetus for nationwide prison reform. Lawmakers, concerned about rising crime and the costs associated with expensive treatment programs, quickly shelved plans to expand rehabilitation efforts within the prison system. Instead, they began to reexamine the potential benefits of more traditional correctional approaches.

Criticism over the effectiveness of rehabilitative programs also coincided with growing opposition to indeterminate sentencing systems. Although a few states had adopted indeterminate sentencing solely as a prison management tool, offering parole in exchange for good behavior, most used indeterminate sentencing in conjunction with their rehabilitation philosophies. Because indeterminate sentencing allows offenders to serve open-ended sentences, subject perhaps only to legislatively imposed minimum or maximum limits, correctional authorities could design an individualized rehabilitation program that fit the needs of the offender; some offenders would require more treatment whereas others would require less. In most indeterminate systems, offenders would be denied parole and remain incarcerated until their rehabilitation program had been satisfactorily completed. While this parole requirement was not originally intended to make indeterminate sentences longer or more severe, statistics show that sentences did become longer over time. For example, after California embraced a system of rehabilitation and indeterminate sentencing in the early 1960s, median prison terms in general increased by 50 percent. Furthermore, from 1959 to 1969, the number of inmates in California per 100,000 residents more than doubled, and prison officials scrambled to find room for the additional inmates.[22]

Concern about the arbitrariness or randomness of punishment associated with indeterminate sentencing also surfaced during the late 1960s and early 1970s. Observers pointed out that because indeterminate sentencing allowed for individualized sentences, some offenders received unusually long sentences whereas others escaped with little or no punishment. For example, a study found that only 27 percent of armed robbers convicted in Los Angeles County in 1970 were sentenced to prison. The remaining 73 percent received no prison sentence at all, even though a substantial number in this group were repeat offenders. In contrast, many first-time offenders convicted of indecent exposure—an offense considered to be much less serious than armed robbery—were sentenced to life in prison.[23] Gross sentencing disparities like these left the impression that indeterminate sentencing systems treated offenders unjustly. Furthermore, sentences that were perceived as either too lenient or too severe led some to believe that indeterminate sentencing was also disproportionate to the crime and thus was unfair.

Under indeterminate sentencing, disparate sentences were possible because most states gave judges large amounts of discretion over the determination of individual sentences. Discretion is often considered a necessary component of any system of governance because it prevents decision making from becoming unduly mechanical or rigid;[24] however, unfettered discretion is not usually viewed in a positive light. When government actors have sole responsibility for decision making and checks on **that** authority are few and far between, decisions may become arbitrary or capricious over time.[25] In the case of indeterminate sentencing, judges were mostly free to choose a sentence they thought appropriate; the only restraints placed on them were cases in which state legislatures identified a minimum or maximum prison term (or both) for a given offense.[26] Everything else was left to the judge's own determination of what would be an appropriate sentence in a given case or for an identified offender. This led to situations wherein similarly situated offenders (similar crime plus similar criminal history) were sentenced differently.

Judges and scholars who regularly studied the indeterminate system also pointed out that unconstrained judicial discretion allows judges to act upon their biases or prejudices under the guise of individualized sentencing. Different outcomes for white and black offenders are justified under the rehabilitative scheme.[27] For example, judges might treat white offenders more favorably because they appear to have a more stable social support network or access to greater financial assets. Judges might also view minority offenders, who often come from lower socioeconomic backgrounds, less favorably because they have fewer assets—both social and financial—to draw upon. The result is that white offenders are more likely to receive a shorter sentence (or no sentence at all), whereas black offenders typically receive longer sentences. Their crimes might be the same, or at least similar in terms of their severity, but their rehabilitation prospects would be judged differently because of factors beyond their control.[28]

LET THE REFORMS BEGIN!

By the early 1970s, the public had become convinced that the nation's penal system needed a major overhaul. Studies had called into question the effectiveness of expensive rehabilitation programs, inmates had begun to balk over coercive rehabilitative programs and techniques, and judicial discretion was deemed to be out of control. Furthermore, escalating crime and high recidivism rates convinced many that offenders were being treated too leniently. In short, the general consensus was that the system needed to be revised.

As a bipartisan coalition in favor of reform emerged, lawmakers began to debate various ways to fix the broken system. Liberals wanted to reduce discretion to eliminate discrimination in the sentencing process while conservatives wanted to reduce discretion to make sentences tougher. In the end, all

50 states and the federal government moved away from a purely indeterminate sentencing system toward one that featured more determinate sentences. However, because each system operates independently, the policies that were enacted varied across jurisdictions.

As can be seen in Table 1.1, the types of comprehensive reforms adopted by the states can be sorted into two separate categories. The reform most commonly referred to as determinate sentencing refers to a system wherein

Table 1.1
Summary of Sentencing Reforms, 1974–1994

Criminal History Score			
	Name	**Reform**	**Purpose**
Comprehensive Reforms	Determinate sentencing	Criminal sentences are fixed and determined in advance. Sentence length is based primarily on severity of the offense. Sentences may be fixed by the legislature or a sentencing commission.	Reduce judicial discretion and increase uniformity in sentencing. Improve predictability of sentences, thus enhancing deterrent effect. For some jurisdictions, sentences are increased to incapacitate certain kinds of offenders. For others, sentences are reduced to make the sentence proportionate to the offense.
Specific Reforms	Mandatory sentencing	Specific penalties are imposed upon conviction of certain offenses. Sentences may be added to the regular sentence and can be dramatic in their severity.	Impose tougher sentences on offenders who have committed target offenses. Use criminal penalties to maximize deterrent and incapacitation effect.
	Plea-bargaining restrictions	Prosecutors are required to fully charge offender. Reducing the severity of the charge and/or sentence in exchange for a guilty plea is restricted or prohibited.	Minimize prosecutorial discretion; impose tougher sentences on offenders who may have been sentenced lightly in the past.
	Parole restrictions	Requires parole boards to follow guidelines when making parole decisions; minimum sentence lengths for certain types of offenses are determined in advance.	Minimize discretion of parole board; promote uniformity of sentencing and longer sentences for certain types of offenders.

penalties for offenses are fixed or determined in advance. The overall goal of determinate sentencing is to eliminate sentencing disparity by reducing the amount of discretion within the system. This means that individual judges have much less influence over the sentencing decision and parole boards are stripped of their authority to grant discretionary release. Sentences may be fixed by the state legislature or determined in advance by a sentencing commission.

States also modified their penal codes to incorporate specific mandatory penalties for certain offenses. Mandatory sentencing laws differ from regular determinate sentencing measures in that they attempt to eliminate *all* forms of discretion from the sentencing process.[29] Judges typically have no discretion to alter the penalty, parole boards have no authority to release offenders early, and prosecutors are often required to charge offenders with a qualifying offense if sufficient evidence is available. Mandatory penalties, implemented as sentence enhancements, are also used to increase the overall sentence length for certain types of crimes.

Although all states had begun to move away from a purely indeterminate-based system by the early 1980s, a majority of states still followed some policies implemented under their old systems.[30] Yet, even those states that continued to use some indeterminate-based statutes pursued specific reforms designed to address particular problems or concerns. For example, some states chose to place restrictions on the plea-bargaining process, because it was believed that setting parameters around plea bargaining would curb some of the sentencing disparity found in the indeterminate system. It would also likely result in sentence increases for offenders who might otherwise have been treated too leniently. In addition, some states chose to reform the parole process, either by establishing parole guidelines or by setting minimum parole eligibility dates. Both of these reforms reduced or restructured the discretion exercised by the parole boards to increase the certainty involved in the sentencing and parole processes.[31]

DETERMINATE SENTENCING

Although determinate sentencing is a label broad enough to encompass many different types of fixed-sentencing systems, it is most often used to describe a specific reform strategy adopted by the states to reduce discretion and promote uniformity in sentencing. As originally conceived, determinate sentencing was to be a type of reform wherein "[d]iscretionary parole release was abolished and, with the exception of reductions for good time, prison terms were definite and known at the time of sentencing."[32] These changes meant that sentences would be based primarily on the offense—not the rehabilitative needs of the

offender—and that the traditional systems of parole would be virtually eliminated. No longer would the parole board have the authority to decide which
offenders would remain in prison and which ones were eligible for release; prisoners would be free to go once their terms were completed.[33]

Maine was the first state to adopt a determinate sentencing system, in
1975, and within the next few years more than a dozen other states followed
suit.[34] By 1981, 15 states reported having a sentencing structure that was best
characterized as determinate. As would be expected, each of the states adapted
the determinate sentencing idea to meet its unique political needs.[35] Yet, in
spite of these differences, the policies were similar enough that they can be
described as falling within three general categories: presumptive sentencing,
discretionary determinate sentencing, and guideline sentencing.

The first category, presumptive sentencing, describes a system wherein the
legislature identifies a normal or presumptive sentence that the judge is expected to apply. Judges no longer have the flexibility or freedom to impose
a sentence of their own making. Instead, the legislature assumes the responsibility for deciding which offenses shall be punished by imprisonment and
how long offenders will serve in prison. Nonetheless, the sentencing judge re-
tains a limited amount of discretion even within the presumptive sentencing
framework. If the defendant is convicted of conduct that involves mitigating
circumstances or is less severe than what is typically expected for an offense
of that type, the judge is authorized to impose a lesser or low-end penalty
identified by the legislature. But the pendulum swings the other way, too. If
the trial court judge determines instead that the offense represents behavior
that is aggravated in nature or more severe than what is common for that type
of crime, the judge may select a high-end penalty that is also identified by
the legislature. If neither mitigating nor aggravating circumstances are present, then the presumptive (or average) sentence that is identified should be
applied.[36]

Prior to 1976, California was considered to have one of the most extreme
versions of indeterminate sentencing.[37] Individualized sentences were handed
out by the trial court judge based only on the rehabilitation needs of the
offender; the nature or severity of the offense was usually considered to be
of little significance. Sentencing parameters for many felony offenses ranged
from six months to life in prison, which gave judges almost unlimited discretion to select the initial minimum term. This meant that as long as the judges'
decisions conformed to the minimum and maximum terms as set by the state,
the sentence would be considered lawful.

During this time, parole boards also had unfettered discretion to determine when offenders had been sufficiently rehabilitated to be released back
into society. The state also required offenders to undergo lengthy periods of

parole supervision to verify that the rehabilitation process was indeed complete.[38] Not surprisingly, when criticisms began to surface about abuses of discretion under indeterminate sentencing, California was among the states that received the majority of complaints. However, it was not until the American Friends Service Committee documented the disparities and injustices of the California system in its influential 1971 report *Struggle for Justice* that the scope of the problem was fully revealed.[39]

When California lawmakers began debating changes to the state's indeterminate sentencing law in the mid-1970s, they relied heavily upon the recommendations of the American Friends Service Committee and other notable criminal justice scholars.[40] Both liberals and conservative policy makers agreed that the state should adopt a determinate sentencing system; however, they disagreed about how long sentences should be. Liberals, for instance, wanted shorter sentences and endorsed prison terms only for the most serious offenders. Conversely, conservatives felt that the proposed sentences were too short and did not adequately consider the nature of the offender's prior record.[41]

The final version, which passed in 1976 under the title Uniform Determinate Sentencing Law, attempted to satisfy all interested parties. Both liberals and conservatives agreed that the system should limit the amount of discretion exercised by judges and parole boards. Under the new law, the sentencing judge could still make the final determination as to whether a person should be sent to prison or placed on probation, but the term of imprisonment was narrowly constructed so as to limit the sentence to three predetermined terms: a low term, a presumptive middle term, and an upper term. The lower term would be reserved for cases involving mitigating circumstances and the upper term for cases involving aggravating circumstances. For example, an offender convicted of assault with a deadly weapon could receive two, three, or four years in prison. The presumptive or normal sentence would be three years in prison; however, if mitigating circumstances were present, then the sentence of two years might be appropriate. Conversely, if aggravating circumstances were present, then the judge could sentence the offender to the maximum penalty of four years.[42] Any judge who deviated from the presumptive middle term would be required to provide justification for the deviation.[43]

The bill also tried to strike a balance between the two ideological positions with regard to the toughness of the sentences. Conservatives in California, for example, wanted to eliminate rehabilitation as a state-sponsored sentencing goal for the correctional system. Accordingly, the Uniform Determinate Sentencing Law includes the following preamble: "The sole purpose of sentencing is punishment and the goals of the sentencing system should be the elimination of sentencing disparity and the promotion of sentence uniformity."[44] Liberals, on the other hand, were more concerned about the length of criminal sentences; they thought that sentences under the indeterminate sentencing system were too long. Therefore, they insisted that the new sentences be short in duration and roughly proportionate to one another. The legislature complied, and criminal offenses were divided into four broad categories, each with a range of penalties that were deemed appropriately proportional to the offenses. The most severe of the categories (Category A) included offenses such as second-degree murder and violent rape. The corresponding penalty included a prison sentence of five, six, or seven years in state prison. The least severe of the categories (Category D) included offenses such as second-degree burglary and auto theft. Penalties for these offenses included a low term of 16 months in state prison to a presumptive term of two years. The upper term brought three years in state prison.[45]

Despite the initial compromise between the two political ideologies, California's presumptive sentencing system was almost immediately amended to stiffen criminal penalties. Conservatives felt that the punishment associated with these four categories was too lenient and that the traditional goals of deterrence and retribution would not be realized by short prison sentences. Public opinion supported their argument as crime rates continued to rise. As a result, changes in 1977 and 1978 increased the middle and upper terms of criminal sentences and also added additional categories of offenses to bring the total number to 10.[46] The range of penalties for second-degree robbery, for example, increased from 2, 3, or 4 years in prison to 2, 3, or 5 years and the sentencing for options of second-degree murder increased from 5, 6, or 7 years in prison to 5, 7, or 11 years.[47]

The second type of determinate sentencing has been labeled discretionary determinate. Though the phrase appears to be oxymoronic, it describes a system wherein the judge is required to select a fixed and determinate sentence within a broad range of possible options. The legislature identifies a range of penalties—which broadens in scope with the increasing severity of the offense—and the judge must select a specific sentence within the preestablished parameters.[48] For example, the Indiana legislature identified the sentence range for Class A felonies (which is the state's most severe classification) to begin with a minimum of 40 years in prison and end with a maximum of 80 years in prison. Thus, the judge has considerable discretion over the selection of the sentence; however, the sentence must be fixed or close-ended, such as 52 years instead of 50 years to life. Moreover, the parole board will not have the authority to keep the inmate incarcerated once the term of imprisonment expires. Initially five states (Tennessee, Missouri, Colorado, Illinois, and Indiana) enacted this type of determinate sentencing, but in the end it proved not to be as popular as the other versions of determinate sentencing.[49] Early analysis of Indiana's discretionary determinate system revealed that sentencing disparity was still a problem in that the discretion in other parts of the system had not been sufficiently constrained.[50]

The third version of determinate sentencing has been labeled guidelines sentencing because the sentencing process is directed by formulas or guidelines. It is based on the recommendations made by federal judge Marvin Frankel in his book *Criminal Sentences: Law without Order.* Judge Frankel explained that judges struggle with sentencing decisions because there are no objective criteria to guide the decision-making process; sentences are instead based on subjective assessments.[51] For example, one judge may believe that the crime or burglary deserves two years in prison, whereas another may believe it deserves five years in prison. Without some sort of standard by which judges can gauge the severity of the crime or the deservedness of the offense, criminal sentences will naturally be disparate and arbitrary.

To remedy this problem, Judge Frankel suggested that administrative agencies formulate sentencing guidelines to direct the sentencing process. Believing that an impartial agency would be better suited for the task than a politically driven legislature, policy makers in Minnesota, Pennsylvania, and Washington initially favored Frankel's recommendation. Early successes in these states resulted in other states—and the federal government—adopting some variation of a guidelines system. By 1994, 22 states and the federal government used a form of guideline sentencing.[52]

Although states modified Judge Frankel's recommendation to suit their own needs, some common elements are found in each of the guidelines. First, all of the states adopting a guideline system have declared that the purpose of the system is to promote uniformity of sentences and to eliminate sentencing disparity. To ensure that this shared goal is met, most states adopting a guideline system have established independent sentencing commissions typically composed of criminal justice professionals (e.g., judges, prosecutors, defense attorneys, corrections officers) and members of the public. In a few states, legislators serve on the commissions as well.[53] These commissions are responsible for establishing recommended or presumptive sentences for judges to use in the sentencing process. In 15 states, the sentence recommendations are required, not optional.[54] Judges who depart from the presumptive sentence and sentence offenders against guideline recommendations are usually required to justify their decisions in writing. Some states also require appellate courts to review the appropriateness and constitutionality of nonguideline sentences.

In most states, presumptive sentences are based on a combination of two primary factors: current conduct and criminal history. The commissions typically use gridlike structures that place the severity of the current offense along one axis and the number of prior offenses along the other. Judges simply follow the two axes until they meet; the sentence that is in the corresponding square is the presumptive sentence for that defendant. For example, using the grid in Table 1.2, the Minnesota guidelines stipulate that a first-time offender (criminal history score = 0) who is convicted of aggravated robbery (severity level = VII) shall be sentenced to 24 months in state prison. Although the presumptive sentence is fixed at 24 months, the judge has a limited amount of discretion to alter the sentence: he can sentence to 23 months (in the event of mitigating circumstances) or 25 months (in the event of aggravating circumstances). Any other sentence is considered a departure and must be justified, in writing, by circumstances that are "substantial and compelling."[55] Despite the presumptive nature of the sentencing recommendations, most guideline states allow for some form of parole release, although the discretion of the parole board is often guided by the sentencing commission, too.[56]

Minnesota was the first state to adopt sentencing guidelines, and its system is often heralded as the model for other states to follow. Enacted in 1978, the newly established Minnesota Commission considered sentence uniformity its most important sentencing goal. A secondary goal, however, was to implement sentences that were prescriptive rather than descriptive.[57] This meant that the commission started its work afresh, without considering any of the status quo sentences that had been previously used in the old system. Using a just deserts rationale, the commission reserved incarceration for violent offenders and property offenders with multiple prior convictions. Sentence lengths were proportionate to one another, and the severity of the sentence increased as the severity of the crime increased. Judges were given the discretion to choose probation for the less serious offenders below the in/out line (see Table 1.2); however, if they decided to sentence an offender to prison, they were required to do so according to the presumptive guidelines.[58] To keep sentences uniform, judges were strongly discouraged from departing from the guidelines, and any deviation from the presumptive sentence was subject to appellate review.[59]

The federal government also implemented a guidelines system in 1984. The Sentencing Reform Act (SRA) called for the establishment of the United States Sentencing Commission, which would be responsible for developing and implementing federal sentencing guidelines. The goal of the SRA is threefold: increase the certainty of punishment; eliminate unwarranted disparity; and fulfill the purpose of sentencing, which is to promote just punishment, deterrence, incapacitation, and rehabilitation. The commission also wanted to make sentences more proportional to the offenses; therefore, it developed guidelines that linked the length of the sentence to the seriousness of the current crime. The offender's criminal past, while considered as one factor in the sentencing decision, does not play as large a role in the federal system as it does in some of the state systems. Additionally, judges are allowed to depart

Table 1.2
Minnesota Sentencing Guidelines Grid: Presumptive Sentence Length (in Months)

Severity Levels of Conviction Offense		0	1	2	3	4	5	6 or more
Unauthorized use of motor vehicle Possession of marijuana	I	12*	12*	12*	13	15	17	19 *18–20*
Theft-related crimes ($250–$2,500) Aggravated forgery ($250–$2,500)	II	12*	12*	13	15	17	19	21 *20–22*
Theft crimes ($250–$2,500)	III	12*	13	15	17	19 *18–20*	22 *21–23*	25 *24–26*
Nonresidential burglary Theft crimes (over $2,500)	IV	12*	15	18	21	25 *24–26*	32 *30–34*	41 *37–45*
Residential burglary Simple robbery	V	18	23	27	30 *29–31*	38 *36–40*	46 *43–49*	54 *50–58*
Criminal sexual conduct, 2nd deg. Intrafamilial sexual abuse, 2nd deg.	VI	21	26	30	34 *33–34*	44 *42–46*	54 *50–58*	65 *60–70*
Aggravated robbery	VII	24 *23–25*	32 *30–34*	41 *38–44*	49 *45–53*	65 *60–70*	81 *75–87*	97 *90–104*
Criminal sexual conduct, 1st deg Assault, 1st degree	VIII	43 *41–45*	54 *50–58*	65 *60–70*	76 *71–81*	95 *89–101*	113 *106–120*	132 *24–140*
Murder, 3rd degree	IX	105 *102–108*	119 *116–122*	127 *124–130*	149 *143–155*	176 *168–184*	205 *195–215*	230 *218–242*
Murder, 2nd degree	X	120 *116–124*	140 *133–147*	162 *153–171*	203 *192–214*	243 *231–255*	284 *270–298*	324 *309–339*

Note: First degree murder is excluded from the guidelines by law and continues to have a mandatory life sentence. Italicized numbers within the grid denote the range within which a judge may sentence. Offenders with nonimprisonment felony sentences are subject to jail time according to law. The dark heavy line is the dispositional line; above the line (i.e., within the shaded area) indicates possible probationary sentences (OUT); under the line indicates sentences of incarceration (IN). For offenders who fall within the shaded categories, the judge has the discretion to sentence up to a year in jail. Other non-jail sanctions can be imposed as conditions of probation.

Source: Michael Tonry, *Sentencing Reform Impacts* (Washington, D.C.: National Institute of Justice, U.S. Department of Justice, Office of Communication and Research Utilization, 1987), 50.

* one year and one day.

from the guidelines, but only under appropriate mitigating or aggravating circumstances. The judge's decision to impose an alternate sentence is also subject to review by the federal appellate courts.[60]

MANDATORY SENTENCING

At the time that state legislators were debating how to make sentences more uniform and more consistent, members of the public were also expressing concern that sentences were not harsh enough. Crime continued to rise unabated, and many blamed the high crime rate on lenient judges who appeared to be more concerned about the well-being of the offenders than the safety of the public. New studies suggested that crime rates would decrease if more felons were incarcerated. Scholars attributed this finding to the deterrent and incapacitation effects of harsher punishment. Deterrence could be achieved if sentences were made more severe in that this would increase the cost of crime to the perpetrator. Moreover, mandatory prison sentences would also produce an incapacitation effect because offenders would be unable to harm members of the community if they were safely locked up inside prison cells.

Although the various determinate sentencing reforms enacted in the mid-1970s had done much to make sentences more uniform and more certain, the priority of lawmakers at the time these reforms were debated was to curb excess discretion, not to make sentences harsher. However, as crime rates continued to rise and public opinion called for tougher sentences, lawmakers also began to consider various ways to make sentences more severe.[61] Mandatory penalties, also known as mandatory minimums, quickly became the preferred solution. By 1983, nearly all states had adopted at least one mandatory sentencing law.[62]

Although each state enacted different policies designed to meet its own specific needs, these policies usually consisted of three components. First, lawmakers enacted reforms that removed the possibility of probation for certain types of crimes. Prison would be the prescribed punishment for these offenses instead. Second, policy makers identified a minimum prison term that would need to be served before the prisoner could be released on parole. This would ensure that offenders could not escape the more severe punishment. Third, legislators often eliminated prosecutorial and judicial discretion in order to keep prosecutors from plea bargaining down to lesser sentences and to prevent judges from imposing shorter or less severe sentences.

The quick adoption of mandatory minimum sentences surprised many since state and federal lawmakers had repudiated mandatory sentences just a decade before. In 1967, for example, the New York Bartlett Commission recommended that mandatory sentences be eliminated for most felonies because judges could not modify the sentences to meet the individual needs of the offenders; a one-sentence-fits-all approach was inappropriate in a system that tailored sentences for the purpose of rehabilitation.[63] In 1970, Congress removed mandatory drug penalties from the federal penal code, citing similar reasons. Lawmakers objected to the inability of the trial court judge to reduce the sentence in the case of mitigating circumstances, or to impose an alternate sanction, such as probation. Furthermore, legislators cited research findings suggesting that prosecutors were less likely to press charges and juries were less likely to convict when mandatory minimum sentences seemed disproportionate to the offense.[64]

Despite their previous reservations, lawmakers became enamored of mandatory sentencing once again as the rehabilitation-based system gave way to one that favored deterrence- and incapacitation-based philosophies. Some criminal justice scholars have commented that mandatory sentencing grew rapidly in the 1970s and 1980s because lawmakers of both political parties realized the political benefit of responding to crimes of particular public concern. Legislators who endorsed tougher sentencing laws were often rewarded with reelection, whereas so-called soft-on-crime legislators who objected to such measures became fearful of defeat.[65] Some observers lamented that this political pressure led legislators to enact mandatory penalties based on the crime-of-the-month, which would undo some of the progress made in sentencing uniformity under the determinate sentencing systems.[66]

Although all mandatory minimum sentencing laws use additional punishment as a way of deterring and incapacitating would-be offenders, not all mandatory policies involve sentences of extreme length. Deterrence philosophy operates on the premise that the sentence need not be overly harsh to be effective; it simply needs to be severe enough to detract from the attractiveness of the crime. Therefore, some states chose to implement mandatory sentences that were more moderate in length.[67] In response to its rising violent crime rates, Massachusetts, for example, adopted a policy in 1974 that imposed a mandatory one-year jail term for any offender convicted of carrying a firearm. The law was widely publicized, and prosecutors were reportedly enthusiastic about the measure. Although the number of persons actually receiving the sentence was small, statistics reveal that assaults with a gun decreased from 31 incidents per 100,000 people to 25 incidents per 100,000—a decline of nearly 20 percent.[68]

In 1977, Michigan also tried to deter gun violence by enacting a mandatory minimum sentencing policy. Advertised under the slogan "One with a Gun Will Get You Two," the Michigan Gun Law imposed a mandatory two-year enhancement on the sentence of any person convicted of using a gun during the commission of a felony. The law also included restraints on judicial discretion to maximize its impact; judges could not shorten or suspend the sentence, nor could offenders be paroled until the two-year enhancement had been served.[69] Although the statute did not specifically prohibit the practice of plea bargaining, the county prosecutor of Wayne County, which includes Detroit, stated publicly that the prosecutors in his office would be prohibited from plea bargaining with eligible offenders and would fully prosecute all offenders who were subject to the law.[70] Nonetheless, researchers found that not all of the criminal justice actors agreed with the Wayne County prosecutor. In fact, they discovered that within six months of the law's implementation, judges and other county prosecutors neutralized the sentence enhancement by a variety of methods, including altering the underlying charge, reducing the base sentence, or dismissing the gun charge altogether.[71]

In some states, legislators opted to enact lengthier mandatory minimums for particular crimes. New York, for example, was one of the first states to adopt stiff mandatory sentences for drug crimes. Dubbed the Rockefeller drug laws after Nelson Rockefeller, the New York governor who approved the legislation, the 1973 reform sought to reduce drug crimes by deterring potential users and incapacitating repeat offenders. Those who were caught in possession of two ounces of heroin for personal use faced a minimum sentence of 15 years to life in prison. Offenders caught with one ounce of heroin intended for sale were given a minimum sentence of 25 years to life in prison. Repeat users of other narcotics also faced stiff penalties (1–8.5 years minimum), and even marijuana possession was targeted for increased penalties.[72]

Despite high hopes, subsequent research revealed that New York's drug laws may have lowered heroin usage only slightly. Furthermore, police officers were largely resistant to the measure, and there were no appreciable increases in arrest rates after the laws went into effect. The average sentence length of drug users did increase as intended, but the gain was accompanied by a number of substantial side effects. Because prosecutors were prohibited from plea bargaining, trial rates increased, which placed considerable pressure on the state's courtroom resources. In addition, offenders tried to overturn their convictions or at least delay the sentencing for as long as possible. Consequently, the record number of motions at trial and appeals after trial nearly doubled the average time from arrest to sentencing from 173 days in 1973 to 340 days in 1976.[73]

Mandatory minimum sentencing policies were also used to target repeat offenders for additional punishment. Although the attention given to the recent Three Strikes movement suggests that this is a new strategy, states have traditionally imposed harsher penalties for offenders who continue to commit crime. Under the rationale that more crimes should equal more time, some states required very lengthy prison sentences to deter would-be offenders. Some chose to impose mandatory sentences upon conviction of the second offense, whereas others waited until an offender had committed three or four crimes before requiring a harsher sentence. States have also varied with regard to the kinds of offenses that would be considered (e.g., whether only felonies would count) and also whether older offenses would be counted or excluded.[74]

Furthermore, research developments on the magnitude of crimes committed by repeat offenders convinced many that mandatory sentencing could be used as a crime-fighting tool.[75] Research studies concluded that chronic offenders often commit crimes at a high rate—sometimes more than 20 per year. Identifying these offenders and isolating them from the rest of society would reduce crime by as much as 200 percent to500 percent.[76] However, the success of any selection incapacitation policy rests solely on the ability of judges to accurately predict who is a high-rate offender and who is not. If a high-rate offender who has a tendency to commit numerous crimes is incapacitated by a lengthy prison sentence, then the crime reduction results of that policy will be great.[77] If, on the other hand, a low-rate offender is incarcerated by mistake, then the incapacitation effects will likely be minimal and the offender will have been incarcerated in vain.

To help judges predict which offenders were at risk for recidivism, researchers devised mathematical models to identify factors that were linked to criminal behavior. Early models considered juvenile delinquency and recent drug use to be significant predictors of recidivism,[78] but later models concluded that length of criminal history and early onset of criminal behavior were more important predictors.[79] Despite the promise of these models, selective incapacitation sentencing policies were never fully adopted. Researchers concluded that even with sophisticated analyses, accurately predicting who would and would not become a chronic offender would be a near-impossible task, especially because any error in prediction would have devastating ethical consequences. Offenders who were falsely predicted to be chronic recidivists would be needlessly incarcerated for long periods, and true chronic offenders who were falsely labeled as safe for release would be returned to the community, where they could continue to prey on members of society.[80]

Moreover, proponents of the just deserts model of sentencing objected to selective incapacitation because under such a policy sentences are based on what an offender *might* do instead of being sentenced according to what he *deserves*.[81] Additionally, lengthy prison sentences based on a predictive formula would likely encounter constitutional challenges under claims of cruel and unusual punishment.[82] But most importantly, many scholars and policy makers objected to selective incapacitation because it would increase the discretionary authority of judges and prosecutors in the area of sentencing. If sentences were altered to maximize utilitarian goals, criminal justice personnel would once more have the responsibility of crafting individualized sentences based on potential recidivism risk—and this particular feature of the theory was deemed unacceptable by all. By the time the Three Strikes movement emerged in 1993, many states had enacted laws that featured enhanced incarceration for repeat offenders, yet none had implemented mandatory sentencing policies that based incarceration decisions entirely on predictions of offender recidivism.

RESTRICTIONS ON PLEA BARGAINING AND PAROLE DISCRETION

For the most part, states used comprehensive reforms, such as determinate sentencing and mandatory sentencing laws, to fix flaws in their old sentencing systems. The three goals of these reforms—reduce sentencing discretion, make sentences more uniform, and punish offenders more harshly—were largely realized within these major initiatives. However, additional reforms were often needed to curb excess discretion in two additional areas: plea bargaining and parole.

Plea bargaining describes the discretionary practice of the prosecutor to grant some form of concession to the defendant in exchange for his admission of guilt. This exchange between prosecutor and defendant can come about in three different ways. First, the prosecutor can engage in charge bargaining, wherein the charge is reduced in exchange for a guilty plea. Second, the prosecutor can initiate count bargaining, which takes place when the number of charges pending against the defendant is reduced in exchange for a guilty plea. Third, the prosecutor can participate in sentence bargaining, which occurs when she recommends to the judge that a defendant be sentenced more leniently because he has demonstrated a great potential for rehabilitation through his confession of guilt and cooperation with authorities.

Although plea bargaining became routine by the late 1960s and received the U.S. Supreme Court's approval in 1971, lawmakers expressed concerns about the legitimacy of the practice.[83] First, researchers found that defendants are often at a disadvantage in the negotiation process because prosecutors routinely inflate the charges against them to better their bargaining positions. For example, an offender who stole an inexpensive watch from a department store might be initially charged with commercial burglary—a more serious offense—instead of shoplifting. While the charges against the defendant are usually reduced as part of the bargaining process, the initial inflation can place much pressure on the defendant to negotiate.[84] Second, the public often perceives plea bargaining as a process that helps a defendant "get away with murder." When crime rates began to increase in the 1970s, the public became critical of any practice that made sentences more lenient. Specifically, public opinion polls revealed strong opposition to plea bargaining because of the belief that the process gives defendants a way to escape the punishment that they deserve. The public also had poor opinions of prosecutors who plea bargained because of the assumption that they negotiate with defendants only because they are lazy and unwilling to take their cases to trial. Consequently, when lawmakers started revising the criminal sentencing systems, they also targeted the plea-bargaining process for additional reforms.

Traditional sentence bargaining largely ended when states adopted their determinate sentencing reforms. Presumptive sentencing and sentencing guidelines eliminated the discretion of the prosecutor and the judge to reduce sentences, which removed the traditional incentive for defendants to plead guilty to their charges. However, after the move to determinate sentencing was completed, prosecutors were able to plea bargain with defendants by lowering the severity of the charges pending against them. Since the severity of the sentence is largely determined by the severity of the charge, pleading guilty to a lesser offense would result in a less severe sentence.

Legislators were also able to reduce prosecutorial discretion by requiring mandatory sentences for certain crimes. For example, the Rockefeller drug laws in New York imposed specific limitations on plea bargaining. Other mandatory sentencing policies, such as the Massachusetts and Michigan gun laws, placed limitations on plea bargaining as well. However, scholars observed that prosecutors were often able to skirt mandatory sentencing laws to facilitate the plea-bargaining process. They could do this by charging an alternate offense that was not covered under the sentencing law or by dropping the charge altogether.[85] In Massachusetts, for example, if prosecutors wanted to avoid the one-year sentence for carrying a gun, they could charge the offender with gun possession—which was not subject to the one-year penalty—or refuse to prosecute the gun charge altogether. Unless mandatory sentencing laws specifically require prosecutors to charge all eligible offenders, charge bargaining will allow them to bypass the sentencing requirement and permit them to continue with business as usual.

Concerned that prosecutorial discretion might undermine their sentencing reform efforts, many states passed laws that set parameters around the plea-bargaining process. But, given that nearly 90 percent of all criminal cases end in a negotiated plea, state lawmakers were hesitant to ban plea bargaining altogether.[86] Only Alaska implemented a complete ban on plea bargaining, under orders from the state attorney general in 1975.[87] Other states were afraid that a total ban on plea bargaining would lead to more defendants insisting on jury trials and that demand would overwhelm the entire judicial system. Instead, more populous states adopted partial reforms, such as limiting the types of crimes that could be plea bargained and placing conditions on the way that plea bargaining could be conducted.

Many states also implemented reforms that addressed excessive parole board discretion. In the era of indeterminate sentencing, parole commissions or boards, which were made up of mostly appointed officials, largely operated without any preestablished standards or procedures. Their job was to decide when a particular offender had been rehabilitated to a point that warranted release. States offered parole boards no objective criteria upon which they were to base their decision; therefore, parole board members often relied on subjective factors in the decision-making process. Consequently, many states chose to restrict the amount of discretion available to the parole board. Missouri, for example, implemented a parole guidelines system that promoted uniform decision making. Structured like a sentencing guideline system, parole decisions were to be based on objective factors, including severity of offense, offender characteristics, and aggravating and mitigating considerations.[88] Additionally, over half the states also implemented policies that restricted inmates' eligibility for parole. Between 1971 and 1981, 27 states reduced parole eligibility for offenders; 8 states implemented policies that eliminated parole for certain offenders; 14 states made no adjustments to their parole criteria; and only 4 states enacted policies that relaxed eligibility requirements.[89]

Other states chose to adopt reforms that regulated good-time accrual. Restrictions of this sort were favored because they helped to make the sentences more uniform and more predictable. In addition, limiting the amount of good-time credit could also make the sentence more severe. Although most states implemented changes to their good-time policies at the same time they were completing the move to determinate sentencing, some chose to adopt changes separately. Kansas, for example, altered its good-time law so that offenders with sentences over three years would have limited possibilities to earn good-time credit.[90] Other states, such as Arkansas, tied the rate of good-time accrual to the severity of the offense so that more serious offenders earn less good time credit than less serious offenders.[91] Many of the states altered their good-time requirements again, however, when the federal government enacted the truth-in-sentencing program in 1994. This initiative authorized the distribution of federal funds for prison construction if states required violent offenders to serve at least 85 percent of their sentences. By 1999, 27 states and the District of Columbia had made the requisite change.[92]

SUMMARY

By the early 1990s, all states and the federal government had implemented some form of sentencing reform. The previous indeterminate system that was based on the premise of rehabilitation had been abandoned, and in its place was a system of determinate and mandatory sentencing that sought to deter, incapacitate, and fairly punish offenders. Judges were stripped of their unlimited discretion, prosecutors encountered restrictions on their plea-bargaining powers for the first time, and parole boards were completely remade to abolish excess discretion. Legislators expressed concern over uniformity in sentencing and authorized research studies to ensure that similar offenders were being treated the same.

Although much had been accomplished during this brief period, legislators would not be given much time to rest before beginning the next round of reforms. Soon, rising crime rates and frustration with inadequacies of the criminal justice system would create additional public demand for law makers to do something about crime. Ultimately, this public pressure would become the main impetus for the future Three Strikes movement.

NOTES

1. Andrew Von Hirsch, *Doing Justice: The Choice of Punishments* (New York: Hill and Wang, 1976).

2. Marvin E. Wolfgang, Robert M. Figlio, and Thorsten Sellin, *Delinquency in a Birth Cohort*, Studies in Crime and Justice (Chicago: University of Chicago Press, 1972), 86–105.

3. Roscoe Pound, *Criminal Justice in America,* Da Capo paperback, the Colver Lectures, 1924 (New York: Da Capo Press, reprinted 1975).

4. David J. Rothman, "For the Good of All: The Progressive Tradition in Prison Reform," in *History and Crime: Implications for Criminal Justice Policy,* ed. James A. Inciardi and Charles E. Faupel (Beverly Hills, Calif.: Sage, 1980), 271–84. See also Francis A. Allen, "Criminal Justice, Legal Values and the Rehabilitative Ideal," *Journal of Criminal Law, Criminology, and Police Science* 50 (1959), 226–32.

5. Allen, "Criminal Justice," 226–32.

6. Edward Lindsey, "Historical Sketch of the Indeterminate Sentence and Parole System," *Journal of Criminal Law, Criminology, and Police Science* 16 (1925), 9–69.

7. Ibid., 21–40; Rothman, "For the Good of All," 271–84.

8. Lindsey, "Historical Sketch," 39.

9. Ibid., 9–69.

10. Ibid., 9–69.

11. Ibid., 69.

12. American Friends Service (AFS) Committee, *Struggle for Justice* (New York: Hill and Wang, 1971), 88.

13. Allen, "Criminal Justice," 230–32.

14. Bureau of Justice Statistics Crime and Justice Data Online, http://www.ojp.usdoj.gov/bjs/.

15. Law Enforcement Assistance Administration, *Two Hundred Years of American Criminal Justice: An LEAA Bicentennial Study* (Washington, D.C.: U.S. Department of Justice, Law Enforcement Assistance Administration, 1976).

16. Ted Gest, *Crime & Politics: Big Government's Erratic Campaign for Law and Order* (New York: Oxford University Press, 2001), 17–39.

17. Ibid., 17–39.

18. Robert Martinson, "What Works? Questions and Answers about Prison Reform," *The Public Interest* 35 (1974), 22–54.

19. Ibid., 24.

20. Ibid., 22–54.

21. Ibid., 22–54.

22. AFS Committee, *Struggle for Justice*, 91–92.

23. Twentieth Century Fund Task Force on Criminal Sentencing, *Fair and Certain Punishment* (New York: McGraw Hill, 1976), 4.

24. Kenneth Culp Davis, *Discretionary Justice: A Preliminary Inquiry* (Baton Rouge: Louisiana State University Press, 1969).

25. Samuel Walker, *Taming the System: The Control of Discretion in Criminal Justice 1950–1990* (New York: Oxford University Press, 1993).

26. Richard G. Singer, *Just Deserts: Sentencing Based on Equality and Desert* (Cambridge, Mass.: Ballinger, 1979).

27. James Q. Wilson, *Thinking about Crime* (New York: Basic Books, 1975), 170–177.

28. Marvin E. Frankel, *Criminal Sentences: Law without Order* (New York: Hill and Wang, 1972).

29. Michael Kannensohn, *A National Survey of Parole-Related Legislation Enacted during the 1979 Legislative Session* (Washington, D.C.: U.S. Department of Justice, Bureau of Justice Statistics, 1979).

30. Sandra Shane-DuBow, Alice P. Brown, and Erik Olsen, *Sentencing Reform in the United States: History, Content, and Effect* (Washington, D.C.: U.S. Department of Justice, National Institute of Justice, Office of Development, Testing, and Dissemination, 1985).

31. Kannensohn, *National Survey.*

32. Pamala Griset, *Determinate Sentencing: The Promise and the Reality of Retributive Justice* (Albany: State University of New York Press, 1991), 40.

33. Jonathan D. Casper, David Brereton, and David Neal, *The Implementation of the California Determinate Sentencing Law* (Washington, D.C.: U.S. Department of Justice, National Institute of Justice, Office of Research Programs, 1982).

34. Griset, *Determinate Sentencing,* 40.

35. Shane-DuBow et al., *Sentencing Reform,* 12.

36. Kannensohn, *National Survey,* 5–6.

37. Shane-DuBow et al., *Sentencing Reform,* 33.

38. Sheldon L. Messinger and Phillip E. Johnson, "California's Determinate Sentencing Statute: History and Issues," in *Determinate Sentencing: Reform or Regression?* Proceedings of the Special Conference on Determinate Sentencing, June 2–3, 1977, Boalt Hall School of Law, University of California, Berkeley (Washington, D.C.: National Institute of Law Enforcement and Criminal Justice, Law Enforcement Assistance Administration, 1978), 13–58.

39. Shane-DuBow et al., *Sentencing Reform*, 7–8

40. Shane-DuBow et al., *Sentencing Reform*, 7–12.

41. Griset, *Determinate Sentencing*, 47–60.

42. Messinger and Johnson, "California's Determinate Sentencing Statute," 30–31. For more information on California's Uniform Determinate Sentencing Law and its effects, see Casper, Brereton, and Neal, *The Implementation of the California Determinate Sentencing Law*.

43. Shane-DuBow et al., *Sentencing Reform*, 33–39.

44. Cal. Penal Code § 1170(a)(1).

45. Shane-DuBow et al., *Sentencing Reform*, 36.

46. Griset, *Determinate Sentencing*, 156–58.

47. Ibid., 156–158.

48. Kannensohn, *National Survey*, 6.

49. Ibid., 6.

50. Todd R. Clear, John D. Hewitt, and Robert M. Regoli, "Discretion and Determinate Sentence: Its Distribution, Control, and Effect on Time Served," *Crime & Delinquency* 25 (1978), 428–45.

51. Frankel, *Criminal Sentences*.

52. Richard S. Frase, "State Sentencing Guidelines: Still Going Strong," *Judicature* 78, no. 4 (1995), 173–79.

53. Ibid., 173–79.

54. Ibid., 173–79.

55. Michael Tonry, *Sentencing Reform Impacts* (Washington, D.C.: National Institute of Justice, U.S. Department of Justice, Office of Communication and Research Utilization, 1987), 48.

56. Frase, "State Sentencing Guidelines," 173–79.

57. Tonry, *Sentencing Reform Impacts*, 48.

58. Ibid., 48. The in/out line was used by the Minnesota Commission to visually demarcate on the guidelines grid the types of offenders who were ineligible or eligible for probation. Offenders in categories above the in/out line could be sentenced to probation, but those in categories below the line were required to serve time in prison.

59. For an examination of the effectiveness of the Minnesota guidelines at promoting sentencing uniformity, see Terance D. Miethe and Charles A. Moore, *Sentencing Guidelines: Their Effect in Minnesota* (Washington, D.C.: U.S. Department of Justice, Office of Justice Programs, National Institute of Justice, 1989); Terance D. Miethe and Charles A. Moore, "Socioeconomic Disparities under Determinate Sentencing Systems: A Comparison of Preguideline and Postguideline Practices in Minnesota," *Criminology* 23, no. 2 (1985), 337–63; Charles A. Moore and Terance D. Miethe, "Regulated and Unregulated Sentencing Decisions: An Analysis of First-Year Practices under Minnesota's Felony Sentencing Guidelines," *Law & Society Review* 20, no. 2 (1986), 253–77.

60. Paul J. Hofer, Charles Loeffler, Kevin Blackwell, and Patricia Valentino, *Fifteen Years of Guideline Sentencing: An Assessment of How Well the Federal Criminal Justice*

System Is Achieving the Goals of Sentencing Reform, November 2004 (Washington, D.C.: United States Sentencing Commission, 2004). Available online at http://www.ussc.gov/15_year/15year.htm.

61. Marvin Zalman, "Mandatory Sentencing Legislation: Myth and Reality," in *Implementing Criminal Justice Policies,* ed. Merry Morash, Sage Research Progress Series in Criminology (Beverly Hills, Calif.: Sage, 1982), 61–69.

62. Michael Tonry, "Mandatory Penalties," *Crime and Justice: A Review of Research* 16 (1992), 243–73.

63. Griset, *Determinate Sentencing.*

64. Tonry, "Mandatory Penalties," 246.

65. Ibid., 265.

66. Gary T. Lowenthal, "Mandatory Sentencing Laws: Undermining the Effectiveness of Determinate Sentencing Reform," *California Law Review* 81 (1993), 61–123. Because mandatory minimum sentences affected some crimes but left others untouched, the penal code could be skewed in such a way that some offenders—even violent ones—might still receive relatively lenient sentences. See Tonry, "Mandatory Penalties," 243–73.

67. Dale Parent, Terence Dunworth, Douglas McDonald, and William Rhondes, *Key Legislative Issues in Criminal Justice: Mandatory Sentencing* (Washington, D.C.: U.S. Department of Justice, Office of Justice Programs, National Institute of Justice, 1997).

68. Kenneth Carlson, *Mandatory Sentencing: The Experience of Two States* (Washington, D.C.: U.S. Department of Justice, National Institute of Justice, Office of Development, Testing, and Dissemination, 1982), 11.

69. Milton Heumann, Colin Loftin, and David McDowall, "Mandatory Sentencing and the Abolition of Plea Bargaining: The Michigan Felony Firearm Statute," *Law & Society Review* 13 (1979), 393–430.

70. Ibid., 393–430.

71. Ibid., 393–430.

72. Carlson, *Mandatory Sentencing,* 4–5.

73. Ibid., 7.

74. Joan Petersilia and Peter W. Greenwood, *Mandatory Prison Sentences: Their Projected Effects on Crime and Prison Populations* (Santa Monica, Calif.: RAND Corporation, 1977).

75. Joan Petersilia, Peter W. Greenwood, and Marvin Lavin, *Criminal Careers of Habitual Felons* (Washington, D.C.: U.S. Department of Justice, Law Enforcement Assistance Administration, National Institute of Law Enforcement and Criminal Justice, 1978).

76. Jacqueline Cohen, "The Incapacitative Effect of Imprisonment: A Critical Review of the Literature," in *Deterrence and Incapacitation: Estimating the Effects of Criminal Sanctions on Crime Rates,* ed. Alfred Blumstein, Jacqueline Cohen, and Daniel Nagin (Washington, D.C.: National Academy of Sciences, 1978), 188; See also Peter W. Greenwood and Allan F. Abrahamse, *Selective Incapacitation* (Santa Monica, Calif.: RAND Corporation, 1982).

77. Greenwood and Abrahamse, *Selective Incapacitation.*

78. Ibid.

79. Stephen D. Gottfredson and Don M. Gottfredson, "Accuracy of Prediction Models," in *Criminal Careers and "Career Criminals"* ed. Alfred Blumstein, Jacqueline Cohen, Jeffrey A. Roth, and Christy Visher, Panel on Research on Criminal Careers, Committee on Research on Law Enforcement and the Administration of Justice, Commission on Behavioral and Social Sciences and Education, National Research Council (Washington, D.C.: National Academy Press, 1986), 212–90.

80. Ibid., 212–90.

81. Von Hirsch, *Doing Justice.*

82. Tonry, *Sentencing Reform Impacts.*

83. *Santobello v. New York,* 404 U.S. 254 (1971).

84. Thomas Church, "Plea Bargaining, Concessions and the Courts: Analysis of a Quasi-Experiment," in *The Invisible Justice System: Discretion and the Law,* ed. Burton Atkins and Mark Pogrebin (Cincinnati: Anderson, 1978), 204–19; Donald Newman, "The Negotiated Plea Process," in *The Invisible Justice System: Discretion and the Law,* ed. Burton Atkins and Mark Pogrebin (Cincinnati: Anderson, 1978), 187–97.

85. For a more detailed discussion of the dangers of unlimited discretion, see Davis, *Discretionary Justice,* and Arthur Rosett, "Discretion, Severity, and Legality in Criminal Justice," *Southern California Law Review* 46 (1972), 12–50.

86. Robert Misner, "Recasting Prosecutorial Discretion," *Journal of Criminal Law & Criminology* 86, no. 3 (1996), 717–77.

87. Shane-DuBow et al., *Sentencing Reform,* 19–22.

88. Ibid., 173–76.

89. Ibid., Table 34, 296–98.

90. Ibid., 116–17.

91. Ibid., 30–31.

92. Paula M. Ditton, *Truth in Sentencing in State Prisons* (Washington, D.C.: U.S. Department of Justice, Office of Justice Programs, Bureau of Justice Statistics, 1999).

2

The Three Strikes Solution

After many states completed the dramatic move to determinate sentencing systems in the early 1980s, the nation's crime rates slowly began to decline, and policy makers breathed a sigh of relief. However, the respite did not last for long. In the early 1990s, crime began to climb once more and new government statistics revealed that repeat offenders had turned the criminal courts into a revolving-door system. Two-thirds of the offenders released on parole would turn around and almost immediately commit new crimes. Mounting public frustration over recidivism and soaring crime, coupled with intense media coverage surrounding a few high-profile crimes, combined to form the catalyst for the Three Strikes movement.

CRIME RATES ON THE RISE

Measuring the amount of crime that takes place in a given jurisdiction is an inherently difficult task. By nature, crimes are committed in secret so that the perpetrators can avoid detection. Consequently, calculations with regard to how much crime actually occurs are naturally prone to error. First, our awareness of crime is dependent on the willingness of individuals to report it; however, not all crimes are brought to the attention of police. Sometimes crimes, such as drug use, illegal gambling, and prostitution, involve consensual activities, and the so-called victims are not likely to report their involvement in these affairs. Crimes like these are usually discovered only through law enforcement undercover investigations and sting operations or reports filed by uninvolved third parties. Second, crimes may go unreported to police because victims are unwilling to file a complaint. Vulnerable parties, such as women, children, or the elderly, may not want to contact police to report a crime for fear of future retaliation by their attackers. For example, a wife may not call the police during an episode of domestic violence because she is worried about her husband's response once the police leave. Neighborhood residents might hesitate to report local gang activities out of fear that the gang might retaliate with violence. Other crimes may go unreported because victims or witnesses do not want the government to get involved. Illegal aliens, for instance, often hesitate to report crimes because they do not want the police asking too many questions about their residency status. Finally, crimes may not be reported because the victims are unable to communicate with authorities. Homicide victims, of course, cannot report the crimes committed against them, nor can most children who have been abducted by adults. Thus, crime statistics based on official information are assumed to be artificially low because of the unreported and undetected crime that occurs on a regular basis.

Even when crimes are reported to local police agencies, the record-keeping abilities of different jurisdictions may vary significantly. Some departments keep detailed records about reports filed, arrests made, and unresolved crimes, but some may not. Furthermore, criminal justice is a locally controlled operation, which means that the federal government has no authority over local police agencies. Therefore, when the federal government tries to collect data on crime, it must ask agencies for the requisite information and sort through incomplete or missing reports. Data collection is better now, though, due to the FBI's efforts at streamlining the process. Each year since 1929, the FBI has asked local agencies to submit information about major crimes committed in their jurisdictions. The information from the Uniform Crime Report (UCR) program is compiled and presented in an annual report. Although the federal government makes every effort to ensure the accuracy of the data, the information is still subject to the underreporting problems noted previously, given that even the best-kept records will reflect only the information that has been made known to police.[1]

In an attempt to address the underreporting problem, in 1973 the government began to administer a random survey to households, asking respondents to anonymously describe crimes that had been committed against them. The intent of the National Crime Victimization Survey (NCVS) is to help the government assess the crime rate without exposing fearful or concerned victims in the process. Although this instrument has helped authorities count previously undocumented crimes, it too is an imperfect measurement.[2] First, it records responses only from victims age 12 and older, which means that the input of younger victims is not included. Second, it fails to provoke responses from individuals who willingly participate in consensual crimes such as prostitution or drug-related offenses; these crimes are still underreported. Third, the survey asks participants to recall events over a six-month period, and this time lapse may allow a person's faulty memory to affect the accuracy of results. Last, the survey is administered to households, so individuals who are homeless or who move frequently because of economic instability—and who are often victimized at much higher rates than the general public—are often excluded from participation.

Despite the imperfect natures of these measurement instruments, criminal justice officials are able to combine information from the UCR and the NCVS to estimate the number of crimes committed each year and to analyze crime trends. In Figure 2.1, the merged data from the UCR and the NCVS produce four separate measurements of violent crime.[3] The first measurement, which is labeled UCR Arrests, counts only those crimes that resulted in arrests by local police agencies. The second measure, labeled UCR Reported, reflects those violent crimes that were reported to local police agencies but not necessarily cleared by an arrest. The third measure, NCVS Reported,

Figure 2.1
Four Measurements of Violent Crime in the United States

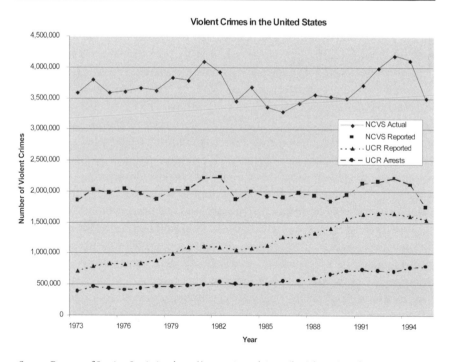

Source: Bureau of Justice Statistics, http://www.ojp.usdoj.gov/bjs/glance/cv2.htm.

reflects the number of self-identified violent crime victims who also reported crimes to the police. The final measurement, NCVS Actual, estimates the total number of violent crimes committed across the nation for that year using data from the NCVS and homicide data from the UCR.

A comparison of the various measures in Figure 2.1 reveals that the nation's violent crime rate dipped slightly in the late 1980s before escalating dramatically in the early 1990s. More violent crimes were reported to police during this period than ever before, and victimization rates beat the previous record high set in 1981. Between 1990 and 1993, the total number of violent crimes increased by nearly 20 percent, and in 1993 nearly 4.2 million forcible rapes, robberies, aggravated assaults, and homicides were committed across the nation—almost 600,000 more than had been committed in 1990.[4]

Although crime rates began to decline again in 1994, the public continued to believe that crime was a pressing social problem. A December 1993 Gallup opinion poll revealed that the public was worried about crime and frustrated with the government's inability to do something about the problem. For instance, 53 percent of Americans disagreed with the statement that police could protect them from violent crime, and more than one-third of the participants stated that it did not matter who was elected to office because the government was incapable of doing anything to fight crime. The public also thought that sentencing should be more punitive. Nearly three-fifths of Americans agreed that murderers should be sentenced to death, 73 percent indicated that juvenile offenders should be tried and sentenced as adults, and 66 percent supported tightening parole requirements for offenders serving time in prison. Furthermore, almost all of the respondents (86%) believed that the court system was too lenient on criminals.[5]

Public frustration with the criminal justice system was only exacerbated by a 1989 Bureau of Justice Statistics (BJS) report that revealed that repeat offenders were responsible for much of the nation's crime problem. By tracking the criminal careers of more than 108,000 inmates in 11 states, BJS researchers concluded that these felons committed an average of 12 crimes per person *before* being incarcerated and were quick to resume their criminal careers as soon as they were released on parole.[6] As noted in Table 2.1, the chances of an offender being rearrested, reconvicted, and resentenced to prison for a new violation were indeed quite high. These statistics led many to question the wisdom of new determinate sentencing policies based on the just deserts sentencing philosophy, which, in most cases, imposed short prison sentences on offenders. Even repeat offenders did not face lengthy sentences unless they committed a very violent felony. Consequently, a sizable percentage of Americans felt that it was once again time to reform the system.

Table 2.1
Rate of Recidivism by Repeat Offenders*

	Percentage of State Prisoners Released in 1983 Who Were		
	Rearrested	Reconvicted	Reincarcerated
6 months	25.0	11.3	8.4
1 year	39.3	23.1	18.6
2 years	54.5	38.3	32.8
3 years	62.5	46.8	41.4

*All percentages based on data regarding state prisoners released in 1983.
Source: Bureau of Justice Statistics, Recidivism of Prisoners Released in 1983, Table 2, 3.

THE BEGINNING OF THE THREE STRIKES MOVEMENT: WASHINGTON STATE

In March 1992, the state of Washington became the first state to officially propose a bill under the slogan "Three Strikes, You're Out." Members of the Washington crime victims' community held a press conference to introduce a ballot initiative that would have greatly enhanced prison sentences for repeat offenders. Specifically, the Three Strikes measure proposed a mandatory life sentence without parole for all offenders who were convicted of a third violent offense. It would have also required a life sentence for those who were convicted three times for dealing drugs to children. Early supporters of the law included several well-known Washington victims-rights advocates, including Helen Harlow, the mother of a young child who was raped, mutilated, and left for dead in 1989; Ida Ballasiotes, whose daughter, Diane, was abducted and murdered in 1988 by a repeat sex offender who had escaped from prison; and Terri Amrhein, who cofounded the Tennis Shoe Brigade victims' advocacy group with Harlow in 1989. All three women had previously been active in legislative efforts to strengthen penalties for sex offenders and felt that more still needed to be done to protect Washington communities from recidivist offenders. Although the group garnered modest media attention and had a fairly extensive network of supporters, they failed to collect enough signatures to qualify the initiative for the ballot.[7]

Career-criminal sentencing laws were not new to the Washington criminal justice system. In fact, the state had previously allowed judges to impose lengthy prison sentences on offenders who had committed three major felonies. However, this provision was eliminated in 1984 when the state adopted its sentencing guideline system that reduced judicial discretion and revised sentence lengths for felony offenders. Under the new system, lengthy prison sentences—even for repeat offenders—were discouraged because they contradicted the just deserts penal philosophy.[8]

The Washington victims-rights coalition introduced a similar Three Strikes initiative in January 1993. This version also required a life sentence without parole for violent offenders upon conviction of their third violent felony and would make more than 40 new crimes eligible for the enhanced punishment. Some of the offenses that could trigger the mandatory sentence included murder, arson, child molestation, rape, extortion, vehicular assault, and robbery.[9] It also would abolish good-time credit for first-degree murderers, require tougher sentences for juvenile offenders, and place restrictions on plea bargaining. Sponsors of the legislation said that they introduced the measure—known officially as Initiative 593—early in the year to collect the 182,000 signatures needed to qualify the proposal for the ballot. The initiative, however, appeared to be headed for defeat as supporters struggled to come up with the necessary funds to print and mail petition forms. Although supporters were optimistic that public frustration with crime would translate into success at the polls, there was concern that the initiative would never make it that far. However, efforts to qualify the initiative for the ballot received new life when the National Rifle Association pledged up to $100,000 to help with the signature-gathering process.[10] During May and June of 1993, nearly 400,000 petition forms were mailed across the state, which enabled supporters to collect more than double the required number of signatures.[11]

Once the initiative qualified for the ballot, debate over the merits of the law began in earnest. Supporters cited rising crime statistics and overly lenient sentences for sex offenders as justification for the Three Strikes initiative. Sponsors pointed out that under existing Washington law, a three-time child molester would receive a prison sentence of 9.5 years and a three-time adult rapist would receive a little more than 14 years. If the Three Strikes initiative passed, both types of offenders would be eligible for the mandatory sentence of life in prison without parole.[12] Additionally, supporters pointed to statistics released by the U.S. Department of Justice that indicated that career criminals admitted to committing between 187 and 287 crimes per year, and 10 percent of that group confessed to more than 600 crimes per year. Although not all recidivists would be targeted by the Washington initiative, supporters maintained that incarcerating just a fraction of these offenders would likely have a substantial impact on crime.[13]

Opponents argued that the proposed Three Strikes law would unfairly target less serious criminals, such as those convicted of second-degree burglary and second-degree assault. Under existing law at the time, three-time offenders sentenced for these types of offenses would serve only about 18 months in state prison. If sentenced under Initiative 593, these offenders would serve life in prison without parole and in the process incur a heavy tax burden for the state. Interestingly, a contradictory argument about the scope of the law was also used to oppose the initiative. Observers pointed out that the range of the proposed law was too narrow to substantially impact crime rates since only a small percentage of Washington's most notorious violent offenders would have been eligible had Three Strikes been in effect at the time they committed their crimes. Furthermore, opponents argued that habitual offender laws in other parts of the country had proved ineffective in reducing crime and had only produced larger inmate populations.[14]

The Washington Three Strikes initiative became national news in September 1993 when William J. Bennett, former Secretary of Education under President Reagan and former drug czar under President George H. W. Bush, published an editorial endorsing the measure in the *Seattle Times*. Bennett stated that the law was needed to help fight crime, to correct an overly lenient sentencing system, to combat the particular problem of recidivist crime, to help restore law and order to minority communities, and to reestablish the moral authority of the criminal law. He also argued that the annual cost to society of each unchecked career criminal—approximately $430,000—far exceeded the $25,000 cost of incarceration. Furthermore, Bennett argued that the government's constitutional responsibility to protect citizens against "all enemies, foreign and domestic" justified measures like the Three Strikes law.[15]

The political campaign for the adoption of Washington's Three Strikes law gained momentum as local politicians, community groups, law enforcement agencies, and newspaper editorial boards pledged their support.[16] Commentators observed that the law's slogan, "Three Strikes, You're Out" was "clear and simple," which made the proposal particularly appealing to the public.[17] A more significant factor, though, was the underlying public concern that prompted the measure in the first place. Despite its relatively small size, Washington had one of the highest crime rates in the nation, and people had grown weary of the constant battle against crime. Consequently, voters expressed their frustration on election day by passing one of the toughest sentencing laws in the nation. By a margin of three to one, the Three Strikes initiative was enacted into law.[18]

FUELING THE FIRE: THE MURDERS OF KIMBER REYNOLDS AND POLLY KLAAS

While Washington crime victims' advocacy groups were trying to rally support for their initial offering of "Three Strikes, You're Out," California lawmakers were being quietly lobbied to adopt a similar measure. Mike Reynolds, one of the authors of California's first Three Strikes proposal, was a wedding photographer, husband, and father before he became one of the state's leading crime victims' advocates. His daughter, Kimber, age 18, had just completed high school and planned to pursue a career in fashion design. Her future ended abruptly in June 1992 when she was shot in the head during an attempted purse snatching outside a restaurant in downtown Fresno. Her two assailants had lengthy criminal histories: Joe Davis was a repeat felon, who was later killed by police in a shootout, and Douglas David Walker was a drug addict who had been in and out of trouble with the law since he was 13 years old.[19] Reynolds' promise "to go after people like these dirtbags in a big way" prompted him to contact his home district legislators for help in strengthening sentencing laws for repeat offenders.[20] Assemblymen Bill Jones and Jim Costa introduced a measure, AB 971, informally titled "Three Strikes and You're Out," but the bill never made it out of the Committee on Public Safety. Reynolds then drafted a similar measure for adoption by the state's voters and used his modest personal savings to try to raise awareness of the issue and generate public support for the measure. However, by early December 1993, he had been unable to muster even a fraction of the nearly 400,000 signatures needed for qualification.[21]

The California Three Strikes law seemed destined for failure until the abduction and murder of 12-year-old Polly Klaas in late 1993 catapulted the problem of repeat offenders onto the national scene. On October 1, 1993, Polly was abducted from her bedroom at knifepoint while she and two friends were playing during a slumber party. Her mother slept nearby in another bedroom and was not aware of the abduction until it was too late. The quiet northern California town of Petaluma was instantly transformed into a community with a single purpose: to bring Polly back. Actress Winona Ryder, a Petaluma native, offered $200,000 for information leading to Polly's safe return. Within a week, Polly's photo and details of her abduction appeared in newspapers, on nationally syndicated shows such as *America's Most Wanted*, and on internet service provider Web sites across the country. Authorities estimated that approximately five million posters and flyers were mailed out across all 50 states and Canada.[22] Unfortunately, the volunteers' efforts were in vain. Polly's abductor, Richard Allen Davis, was picked up on parole violations and became the prime suspect after evidence was found linking him to the kidnapping. While in custody, Davis confessed to abducting and killing Polly and told authorities where they could find her. Based on this information, police searched a remote wooded area approximately 40 miles north of Petaluma and found Polly's body. The news of her murder was broadcast over the national media on December 5, 1993.[23]

The news of Polly's untimely death spawned expressions of collective anguish. Within two months' time, Polly Klaas had gone from an anonymous junior high school student in a small suburban town to a near-celebrity—"America's Child." Marc Klaas, Polly's father, reminded Americans that if it could happen to his family, then no one was safe from danger. Mike Reynolds, photographer turned crime advocate, agreed: "What these crimes have done is show people that you can do all the right things and it doesn't matter. You can lock your door, stay in the right neighborhoods. But when you come up against one of these creeps, the rules don't matter. They're hunting you."[24]

Polly's abductor, Richard Allen Davis, was a classic career criminal. He had a lengthy criminal history that began at age 12. As a juvenile offender, his first crimes were mainly property offenses, and as he moved into adulthood, he continued to commit burglaries and other property crimes. His first prison commitment in 1975 was for property offenses, but within weeks of his release in 1976, he kidnapped a woman and sexually assaulted her. After a suicide attempt in jail, he was transferred to a less-secure psychiatric facility, where he was able to escape. Before being recaptured, he committed a rash of new crimes, including burglary, assault, robbery, and kidnapping. His convictions for these offenses resulted in a six-year prison sentence, from which he was paroled in 1982.

In 1983, he was arrested—but never charged—for burglary, weapon possession, and contributing to the delinquency of a minor. Then, in 1984, he kidnapped a woman, forced her to withdraw $6,000 from her bank account, and assaulted her with his gun. For that event, he was sentenced to 16 years in prison. At that time offenders in California were allowed to shave off as much as 50 percent of their sentence with good-time credit, so Davis was granted parole in 1993 after serving approximately half his original sentence. Less than three months later, Davis abducted Polly Klaas, sexually assaulted her, and then strangled her to death.[25]

CALIFORNIA JOINS THE THREE STRIKES MOVEMENT

Within hours of the news that Polly's body had been discovered, feelings of grief turned to feelings of anger. Some directed their fury at her killer, but as more details emerged about Richard Allen Davis's lengthy criminal past, more expressed outrage over a criminal justice system that appeared to be broken. In fact, the news that Davis had been convicted twice before for kidnapping led many to call for immediate sentencing reform.[26] Mike Reynolds, who had been struggling to obtain signatures in support of his Three Strikes initiative, now found himself at the center of a political firestorm. On December 7, 1993, just two days after the news of Polly's death was broadcast to media outlets, Reynolds appeared at a press conference with California Attorney General Dan Lungren. Lungren not only personally endorsed the

Three Strikes initiative but also urged all Californians to support the measure by signing a Three Strikes petition. Soon afterward, Reynolds's Three Strikes headquarters was inundated with phone calls and letters from supporters. Within a matter of weeks, Reynolds had more than double the number of signatures needed to qualify the initiative for the November 1994 ballot.[27]

As signatures were being gathered to qualify Reynolds's Three Strikes initiative for the ballot, California lawmakers launched their own reform initiatives. Governor Pete Wilson reacted to the news of Polly's death by urging lawmakers to adopt a "one strike" rape law that would impose a mandatory lifetime sentence on anyone convicted of rape or child molestation. "It is incredible that we have permitted in this state the kind of statutes that allow someone as dangerous as this to repeatedly do great injury to children," Wilson said. "A fitting memorial for Polly Klaas is to see that she is the last child to suffer this."[28] Ironically, a law like this would not have helped to save Polly, as all of Davis's previous sex offenses had been dropped in plea bargaining negotiations. In the days after the news of Polly's death, Wilson also expressed general support for a Three Strikes law but declined to specifically endorse Reynolds's proposal.[29] A few days later, Wilson spoke at Polly's memorial service and again urged the legislature to take action against sex offenders and career criminals: "We must fight to put laws on the books to make sure career criminals become career inmates so that the tragedy that brings us here today will not be suffered by other families."[30]

By the time Wilson delivered his State of the State address in January, his reluctance to support the circulating Three Strikes proposal had disappeared. Much of Wilson's speech focused on issues related to crime, and he pressed legislators to pass a Three Strikes bill that would impose a lengthy sentence on three-time felons. The Klaas family attended the speech, and their presence served as a visible reminder that reform was needed to prevent further loss of life. Wilson also urged policy makers to adopt a "one strike" bill that would require a mandatory life sentence for certain violent offenders upon conviction of their first offense. He declared that "[f]or some vicious criminals, three strikes is two too many. For those who commit forcible rape, who molest a child or devastate a community through arson, the first offense should be the last."[31] Additionally, Wilson pledged to hire 500 new highway patrol officers and asked voters to support a $2 billion bond measure that would be used to construct new prisons.[32]

Early in the new year, Mike Reynolds expressed concern that a legislative version of Three Strikes might be less stringent than his proposed initiative version. Consequently, he warned lawmakers not to water down the language of the bill to appease Assembly Democrats.[33] He also told lawmakers that he intended to continue his efforts to qualify the initiative for the November ballot, which would, in effect, overwrite any legislative version that differed from the initiative language. Initially, it seemed as though Reynolds had nothing to fear since the original Three Strikes bill (AB 971) that had been previously proposed by Republican Assemblymen Jones and Costa in consultation with Reynolds was quickly resurrected.[34] By the end of February, however, a total of five Three Strike proposals were under consideration.[35]

The Jones measure, as well as the initiative version, proposed mandatory sentences for two groups of offenders: second strikers, defined as felons who had been convicted of at least one qualifying strike offense, and third strikers, who were three-time felons with at least two previous qualifying strike offenses. Second strikers would receive double the usual punishment, and third strikers would receive triple the usual punishment or a minimum sentence of 25 years to life, depending on which sentence was greater. In determining which offenses would count as prior strikes, AB 971 referenced other California penal codes that listed crimes already designated by the state as serious and/or violent offenses.[36] The list included a broad array of crimes, including, for example, homicide, rape, continuous sexual abuse of a child, kidnapping, arson, and robbery. The statutes also included less violent offenses, such as grand theft with a firearm and residential burglary. The broad list of eligible offenses raised some concern with lawmakers that the Three Strikes law cast too wide a net, covering burglars as well as murders, rapists, and kidnappers. For this reason, Marc and Joseph Klaas, Polly's father and grandfather, registered their objections to this Three Strikes bill on behalf of the Polly Klaas Foundation, arguing that AB 971 would ensnare the wrong type of criminal.[37]

More controversial, however, was the feature of the Jones bill and Reynolds initiative that allowed a second-strike or third-strike offender to be sentenced to the mandatory minimum sentence upon conviction of *any* felony offense. Thus, an offender with one prior strike who committed any other felony would be sentenced to double the usual sentence. An offender with two prior strikes would be sentenced to at least 25 years to life in prison upon conviction of any third felony offense. Since the last strike was not restricted to a serious and/or violent offense like the first strike(s), there was concern that the provision would allow lesser felonies, such as theft and drug possession, to trigger the mandatory minimum sentence.

An alternate bill, proposed by fellow Republican Richard Rainey, would have also imposed a minimum 25-year-to-life sentence upon repeat offenders. His proposal, however, stipulated that all three offenses had to be identified as serious and/or violent by the state to trigger the mandatory penalty—not just the first two. For instance, an offender who committed robbery and kidnapping for his first two offenses would have two strikes against him under both the Jones and Rainey proposals. If that offender then stole a car, he would be eligible for the 25-year-to-life sentence under the Jones proposal, but *not* under the Rainey proposal, since grand theft is not considered by the state to be a serious and/or violent offense. This change would mean that the scope of the Rainey bill would be much narrower than the Three Strike versions proposed by Jones and the initiative version circulated by Reynolds.[38]

By March 1994, the discussion over Three Strikes became a debate over which proposal was better. Governor Wilson urged the legislature to send him the Jones proposal because it was the toughest, even though it could potentially cost the state billions in prison-related costs. Mike Reynolds also urged the legislature to pass the Jones bill because it was nearly identical to the initiative proposal he was circulating for adoption in November. The California District Attorneys Association (CDAA), however, was concerned about the potential impact that a Three Strikes bill might have on the workload of the already-stressed criminal court system. Since three-strikers would likely insist on jury trials instead of voluntarily pleading guilty to charges that would result in 25-year-to-life minimum sentences, prosecutors favored the narrower Rainey bill because this proposal would result in fewer third strike defendants.[39] Although a number of amendments were proposed to make the Rainey bill tougher, it was unable to garner enough votes to win adoption. Instead, the legislature approved the Jones proposal under an urgency clause that allowed the legislation to take effect immediately upon approval. Governor Wilson signed the bill into law on March 7, 1994, warning career criminals to find a new occupation unless they wished to become "career inmates."[40] On the same day, Mike Reynolds delivered over 800,000 signatures—more than twice the number needed—to the Secretary of State to qualify his Three Strikes proposal for the November ballot. Reynolds, who supported the Three Strikes proposal that Wilson approved, expressed concern that the legislature might change its mind in the future and vote to relax the Three Strikes requirements with a simple majority vote.[41] In contrast, Reynolds's proposed Three Strikes initiative stipulated that it could be amended or repealed only by a majority of voters or by a two-thirds vote of the state legislature.

ROLE OF THE MEDIA, PUBLIC SUPPORT, AND PROPOSITION 184

Public support for Three Strikes among Californians started out strong and remained strong throughout much of 1994. In the weeks following the discovery of Polly Klaas's body, a national poll conducted by the *Los Angeles Times* found that a sizable majority (58%) of adults favored a Three Strikes measure no matter what the cost might be. Another 21 percent indicated that they would favor such a measure but would be mindful of the cost. Only 17 percent of those polled indicated that they would oppose a Three Strikes measure, and an additional 4 percent said that they had no opinion.[42] In California, registered voters were signing the Reynolds Three Strike petition at an unprecedented rate of 15,000 per day,[43] and public opinion polls taken in January by the Field Institute revealed that 84 percent of California registered voters indicated that they would vote for the Three Strikes initiative once it was on the ballot. This unusually high measure of support was consistent across political parties: 92 percent of registered Republicans and 78 percent of registered Democrats indicated support for the initiative.[44]

Public opinion is often shaped by personal life experiences, but it can also be influenced by the perceived experiences of others. In this regard, the media has a significant ability to shape public perception through the type of news stories that it chooses to cover. Statistics released in early 1994 revealed that crime rates had begun to decline, yet the media coverage of serious crime frequently gave the impression that crime was dramatically increasing. Sensational stories, especially those involving random acts committed by repeat felons, fueled the public's impression that crime was out of control. For instance, the murder of the father of basketball star Michael Jordan as he was napping in his car along a stretch of North Carolina highway received much media attention. Similarly, the murder of a German tourist, who was shot and killed in his rental car as he was leaving the Miami, Florida, airport was the subject of many news stories and media commentaries.[45] And, of course, the extensive national media coverage of the Polly Klaas abduction and murder convinced many that our system of justice was on the verge of collapsing. Although these stories may be important news events, the media often look for the most sensational crime story to report because it is likely to attract viewers and readers. The public, not aware that serious crime sells, may believe that the stories reported by the press are representative of those that occur on a regular basis.[46]

Furthermore, the amount of attention devoted to a serious crime news story can often influence how the public thinks about a problem or external event. If the news story is briefly described in a local paper or is buried in the back of a national newspaper, then the public may not pay much attention to it. However, researchers have found that if the story is prominently featured in a newspaper or television program, then public opinion will likely reflect a greater degree of concern.[47] In looking at the media's coverage of the Polly Klaas abduction case, the national print media ran in-depth front-page news stories on a regular basis, and the Klaas case was featured on many national news television programs. Even Polly's parents were surprised by the amount of media attention given to their daughter's story. When Polly's body was discovered, both parents decided to use the media coverage as an opportunity to press for sentencing reform, hoping that the national attention would at least help to channel public outrage over the crime in a productive direction.[48]

The Klaas case highlights how media coverage of a crime or criminal event can also affect the public's perception about the effectiveness of the criminal justice system. Stories of injustices, abuses of discretion, and overly lenient sentences are effective in convincing many that the criminal justice system is inept or more concerned with the rights of the suspects than with the rights of the victims. Furthermore, the media's emphasis on certain aspects of crime stories—such as the fact that a crime may have been committed by a repeat felon—can affect the way the public views a particular topic or concern.[49] Nearly all of the media reports about Richard Allen Davis, Polly's abductor and murderer, focused on his past criminal record; his status as a repeat felon and his prior convictions for kidnapping were well documented and served to call attention to the problem of recidivism. This, in turn, lent support to the California Three Strikes movement currently under way and spurred activists to pursue similar measures in other states and at the national level.

In the end, the extensive media coverage of the Polly Klaas case helped to galvanize public opinion in two specific ways. First, the public was now motivated to take matters into their own hands by introducing ballot initiatives that would put harsher sentencing measures before the voters. In California, the Three Strikes initiative qualified for the November 1994 ballot within a matter of weeks, and early in 1994, voters in Alaska, Florida, Kansas, Missouri, New Jersey, New York, North Carolina, Ohio, and South Carolina began efforts to adopt a Three Strikes initiative of their own. Second, the increased media coverage of the Klaas case and overwhelming public support for harsher sentences for repeat offenders created pressure on politicians to take immediate action. In California, lawmakers rushed to enact a statutory version of Three Strikes before a nearly identical measure could qualify for the ballot. In his State of the State address, New York Democratic governor Mario Cuomo urged legislators also to adopt a Three Strikes law that required life in prison without parole for repeat offenders: "Violence and crime have taken on a terrible urgency and we are determined to move quickly and decisively to protect our people ... In baseball, it's three strikes and you're out. Here, it's three strikes and you're in for life. Life imprisonment without parole."[50]

Because public support for Three Strikes laws was so high, politicians on both sides of the aisle supported tougher punishment for repeat felons. Furthermore, in many states, 1994 was an important election year, which served only to increase the pressure on lawmakers to do something about the crime problem. In California, Governor Pete Wilson, who faced a tough reelection battle in November, capitalized on the Three Strikes movement to showcase his law and order platform, but even his Democratic contender, Kathleen Brown, vowed support for Three Strikes in an attempt to convince voters that she was not "soft" on crime. At the federal level, congressional members from both parties embraced Three Strikes as a way of demonstrating to voters that they were serious about crime and justice issues.[51] President Clinton, who also faced faltering public opinion ratings, encouraged Congress in his January 1994 State of the Union address to pass his crime bill, which included a Three Strikes measure. He explained, "Those who commit crimes should be punished. And those who commit repeated, violent crimes should be told, 'when you commit a third violent crime, you will be put away and put away for good.'"[52]

Some politicians urged the adoption of even harsher measures. For example, in response to constituency pressure, Democratic governor of Georgia Zell Miller endorsed a "two strikes and you're out" measure that would impose a life sentence on offenders with two felony convictions. In other states, lawmakers considered a range of policy options designed to increase criminal penalties for gun users and other criminal populations.[53] However, the sudden attention given to criminal justice issues led to charges of grandstanding and political opportunism. Nationwide, Republicans, who have traditionally embraced tough penalties for offenders, became concerned that Democrats were on the verge of appropriating their issue.[54] In New York, for example, Republican lawmakers were wary of Governor Cuomo's sincerity with regard to his Three Strikes proposal. In California, Joseph Klaas, Polly's grandfather, accused Governor Wilson of using Polly's name for political purposes.[55]

In California, once the legislative version of Three Strikes was approved by the governor, attention focused on the passage of the initiative version of Three Strikes offered by Mike Reynolds. Early predictions indicated that the measure, recorded by the Secretary of State as Proposition 184, would win by a landslide. However, a number of influential reports later in the year eroded some of the support for the measure. In October 1994, shortly before Californians were to vote on Proposition 184, the RAND Corporation released a study that evaluated the costs and benefits of the new Three Strikes law. Based on sophisticated computer modeling and simulations, RAND predicted that if fully implemented, Three Strikes would cost the state between $4.5 and $6.5 billion more *per year* in prison-related expenses.[56] Since much of California's budget is tied up in required K–12 public education and health and welfare expenditures, researchers predicted that the additional costs would have to be covered by reductions in higher education and other government services. The alternative would be to pass along a substantial tax increase to California residents, which is a solution that they acknowledged to be politically untenable. Researchers did note, however, that California's crime rate would likely decrease substantially as a result of the new law. Without factoring in any deterrent effect, they estimated a 22 percent to 34 percent reduction in crime overall, with one-third of the reduction coming from decreases in murder, rape, and serious assaults. They also predicted the law would dramatically reduce the number of robberies, residential burglaries, and less serious assaults.[57]

Researchers at RAND stated that their purpose in conducting this cost-benefit analysis was to present voters with the information about the Three Strikes law before they voted on Proposition 184 in November 1994. Since the legislative version would be easier to alter than the initiative version, they speculated that if voters were not pleased with the predicted outcomes, then they could urge legislators to repeal AB 971 and replace it with a less comprehensive—and less costly—sentencing law. To facilitate that possible outcome, RAND also analyzed the impact of four additional reform possibilities: the Rainey bill, which had been proposed in January 1994 alongside AB 971; another measure that would incorporate only the doubled-sentence provision for two-strike defendants; a policy that would restrict the mandatory sentence of 25 years to life to violent felonies only; and a proposal that would eliminate good-time credits for all felony offenders but would not impose any additional punishment on repeat felons. In their analyses, the RAND researchers found that the actual Three Strikes law that had been enacted by the legislature and that would be before the voters as Proposition 184 offered the greatest potential crime reduction but also incurred the most cost. The least costly of the alternatives was the proposal that would impose a mandatory sentence on only those felons who committed three violent felonies, but the corresponding reduction in crime was not as great. Interestingly, the authors found that eliminating good-time credits for all felons would reduce about the same amount of crime but would cost 35 percent less than the official Three Strikes law. Of course, the underlying reason for the Three Strikes movement in the first place was to impose additional penalties on repeat offenders, so a policy that proposed to eliminate this important feature probably would not have been supported by the public even if it would have been more cost-effective in the long run.[58]

Although the RAND analysis and other reports released later in 1994 offered a negative prognosis about Three Strikes, California politicians and voters alike still seemed to overwhelmingly support Proposition 184 and the tough new Three Strikes law.[59] Some of the statistics offered by RAND were countered by other estimates in support of the law. For example, Governor Wilson's chief economist argued that even with the additional prison costs, Three Strikes law would *save* Californians nearly $23 billion in the long run because each inmate affected by the new law would no longer be able to commit new crimes.[60] In addition, Los Angeles County Sheriff Sherman Block publicly speculated just six months after the legislature enacted Three Strikes that the new law could be responsible for the noticeable reduction in crime in his jurisdiction.[61] Ultimately, Three Strikes critics were unable to convince Californians to vote no on Proposition 184. When voters went to the polls on November 8, 1994, the measure passed easily, by a margin of nearly three to one (72% in favor of Three Strikes, 28% opposed).

THREE STRIKES AT THE FEDERAL LEVEL

As voters in Washington and California were debating the merits of their respective Three Strikes bills, key congressional members began discussing ways that the federal government could join in the fight against crime. In 1993, the Democratic-controlled Congress had implemented a number of smaller anticrime measures, largely targeting treatment options for juvenile offenders and drug offenders and imposing additional federal penalties on gun users. But as the attention on Three Strikes began to intensify, congressional members from both parties thought it necessary to focus more attention on the problem of enforcement and sentencing. California Democratic Senator Dianne Feinstein, who spoke at Polly Klaas's memorial service, called for tougher sentencing laws for repeat felons. President Clinton also referenced the Polly Klaas case when he urged Congress to pass anticrime legislation in his January 1994 State of the Union address, which paved the way for other Democratic lawmakers to jump on the get-tough bandwagon. Soon afterward, Democratic and Republican lawmakers, who were previously on opposite ends of the punishment spectrum, spent much of 1994 quarrelling about which party was the toughest on crime.[62]

Despite the partisan wrangling, Congress passed a $30 billion comprehensive anticrime bill that combined prevention programs with punitive measures. HR 3355, which was titled the Violent Crime Control and Law Enforcement Act of 1994, was approved by President Clinton on September 13, 1994, just in time for the fall campaign season. The law authorized the expenditure of federal funds to help state and local law enforcement agencies hire an additional 100,000 police officers. It also provided funds to assist states with prison construction costs and authorized $7 billion to be spent on crime-prevention programs. Furthermore, the law banned ownership of certain types of semiautomatic weapons and extended the death penalty to more than 60 federal crimes.[63] More importantly for Three Strikes advocates, the federal legislation also imposed a mandatory sentencing requirement for repeat felons. Specifically, the law stipulated that any person who had been convicted of two or more serious violent felonies or one serious violent felony and one serious drug offense at either the state or federal level would be sentenced to life imprisonment upon conviction of any third serious violent federal offense. Congress defined serious violent felonies to include murder; voluntary manslaughter; assault with intent to commit murder; assault with intent to commit rape; aggravated sexual abuse; abusive sexual contact; kidnapping; aircraft piracy; robbery; carjacking; extortion; arson; firearms use; or attempt, conspiracy, or solicitation to commit any of these offenses. It also included all other violent crimes punishable by a maximum prison sentence of 10 years or more. Moreover, serious drug offenses were identified as those involving possession or importation of large quantities of controlled substances, such as heroin, cocaine, PCP, LSD, and methamphetamine. Drug offenses that were prosecuted at the state level would also be counted if they involved the same type of prohibited behavior.[64]

THREE STRIKES IN OTHER STATES

Shortly after Washington and California made national news with their adoption of Three Strikes policies, voters in other states began demanding Three Strikes laws in their jurisdictions. Many states already had a career criminal law on their books, yet the public's concern about crime prompted lawmakers to take additional action. Between 1993 and 1996, Three Strikes legislation was considered in 37 states and was successfully adopted in a total of 25 states.[65] Although all of these laws sought to impose lengthy prison sentences on repeat offenders to maximize the deterrent and incapacitation effect of imprisonment, the features of the individual laws varied widely. There were great differences with regard to what types of offenses would qualify, how many offenses were needed to trigger the sentencing enhancement, whether the sentence was mandatory or optional, how long a sentence the offender would be required to serve, and whether the offender would be eligible for release on parole.[66]

All Three Strikes-related laws targeted career criminals, but the crimes that were considered to be strikes for the purpose of enhanced sentencing often varied widely. Murder qualified as an eligible strike offense in all states, and other violent felonies such as rape, kidnapping, arson, and robbery were identified as eligible crimes in most jurisdictions. Yet, some states included crimes that the public might not condemn quite as strongly.[67] For example, Indiana, Louisiana, and California identified certain drug-related crimes as eligible strikes; Washington included treason; South Carolina included the offenses of embezzlement and bribery; and Florida included the crimes of lewd and indecent conduct, and escape. Furthermore, Maryland and Tennessee counted an offense as a strike only if the offender served time in prison for that offense.[68] The breadth of the eligible crime list also varied from state to state. New Mexico, for instance, identified only 5 crimes that would count as strikes, whereas Washington identified more than 50 separate crimes that would trigger the mandatory sentence.[69]

Even though the laws were often identified by the slogan "Three Strikes and You're Out," the states often differed with regard to how many prior strikes would have to be earned to trigger the mandatory minimum sentence. North Dakota and South Carolina, for instance, imposed a mandatory life sentence on offenders convicted of a second violent offense. Many states, including Arkansas, California, Connecticut, Georgia, Kansas, Montana, Pennsylvania, and Tennessee, created a two-tiered system of punishment for two- and three-strikers. Two-strikers would receive an enhanced sentence, but life sentences were reserved for three-strikers. A few states, such as Georgia, Louisiana, and Maryland, also identified special punishments for defendants who had four felony convictions.[70]

Most of the states also stipulated that Three Strikes sentences should be mandatory. Twenty states required judges to impose an enhanced sentence for offenders who met the relevant criteria, but four states allowed the court the discretion to decide if a lengthy sentence was justified. Connecticut, for instance, permitted a judge to sentence an offender to 40 years in prison upon conviction of a second violent offense and authorized a life sentence for a third violent offense, but did not make these sentencing recommendations mandatory. Additionally, Kansas authorized the judge to impose a double sentence upon conviction of any second violent felony and a triple sentence upon conviction of any third violent felony, but did not stipulate that these sentences were required. Arkansas and Nevada also made lengthy sentences optional—but not mandatory—for repeat offenders.[71]

In all states, the sentences identified for repeat offenders under the Three Strikes moniker were severe. Half the states stipulated that eligible offenders would be sentenced to life in prison without the possibility of parole. Laws in Georgia and South Carolina were the harshest, requiring a mandatory life sentence without the possibility of parole upon conviction of a second violent offense. The other states (Indiana, Louisiana, Maryland, Montana, New Jersey, North Carolina, Tennessee, Virginia, Washington, and Wisconsin) imposed a lifetime sentence upon conviction of a third eligible offense. Three states sentenced career criminals to life in prison with the possibility of parole, although offenders would have to serve a lengthy minimum term before applying for early release. In California, offenders would have to serve at least 25 years before becoming eligible for parole; in New Mexico, offenders would have to serve at least 30 years; and in Colorado, an offender could be eligible for parole after serving 40 years in prison.[72]

The adoption of Three Strikes legislation by nearly half the states suggested that offenders would now face much harsher consequences for their actions, but a few observers predicted that the new policies would not have a dramatic impact on crime or criminal sentencing. First, most states limited their Three Strikes law to violent offenses, which would have triggered lengthy sentences anyway. Only California adopted a law that would be applicable to a large number of offenders. Second, a review of preexisting legislation revealed that all states except Kansas already had adopted some form of sentence enhancement for career criminals. The new Three Strikes legislation may have changed the types of offenses that qualified for the additional punishment or expanded the definition of a career criminal, but in most cases, the law did not profoundly alter the way repeat offenders were sentenced by the system.

Despite these potential shortcomings, the Three Strikes movement did accomplish a number of specific objectives. First, it reassured voters in an election year that lawmakers were listening. The public's frustration and fears about rising crime rates, overlenient sentencing practices, and the threat of random violence to their families were deftly communicated to lawmakers. Consequently, policy makers from both political parties used Three Strikes and other anticrime legislation as a symbolic way of reassuring voters that their message was indeed received.[73] Second, Three Strikes represented another step in the trend to move sentencing authority away from judges and into the hands of elected politicians and, in some cases, the people themselves. For many voters, Three Strikes was used as a tool to counteract judges who were viewed as too soft on crime and more interested in protecting the rights of the accused than the rights of the victims. Mandatory penalties eliminated the discretion of these judges while sending a clear message to offenders about the consequences of committing crime. Furthermore, in most states, Three Strikes ended the long-standing practice of early release through the accumulation of good-time credits by imposing true lifetime sentences on dangerous repeat offenders. Citizens vowed that offenders like Richard Allen Davis, Polly Klaas's murderer, would never be released early again.[74]

SUMMARY

In the early 1990s, public frustration over rising crime rates, high rates of recidivism, and threats of randomized violence laid the foundation for the Three Strikes movement. After the abduction and murder of Polly Klaas, which captivated the attention of the American public, the desire to get even tougher on habitual offenders swept the county. From 1993 to 1996, nearly three-fourths of the states debated the merits of a Three Strikes policy, and half the states and the federal government ultimately adopted one.[75] This remarkable feat revealed the broad consensus among voters and policy makers for sentencing measures that enhanced the deterrence and incapacitation features of the penal system. Although the individual policies varied from jurisdiction to jurisdiction, the underlying sentiment was the same: People were tired of battling crime and would no longer tolerate lenient sentences for repeat offenders.

NOTES

1. Michael R. Rand and Callie M. Rennison, "True Crime Stories? Accounting for Differences in our National Crime Indicators," *Chance* 15, no. 1 (2002), 47–51.

2. Criminal justice officials estimate that as many as two-thirds of property offenses and half of all violent offenses are unreported to police.

3. Violent crime includes rape, robbery, aggravated assault, and homicide.

4. Bureau of Justice Statistics, http://www.ojp.usdoj.gov/bjs/glance/cv2.htm.

5. Leslie McAneny, "Americans Want Tougher Action on Crime," *St. Louis Post-Dispatch,* December 19, 1993. This poll was taken before the discovery of Polly Klaas's body on December 5, 2003.

6. Allen J. Beck and Bernard E. Shipley, *Recidivism of Prisoners Released in 1983* (Washington, D.C.: U.S. Department of Justice, Office of Justice Programs, Bureau of Justice Statistics, 1989).

7. Barbara A. Serrano, "Life Term Sought for Repeat Felons—Initiative Proposes '3 Strikes, You're Out,'" *Seattle Times,* March 25, 1992; Susan Gilmore, "Initiative Backers Try Again for Tough-Sentencing Plan," *Seattle Times,* January 7, 1993.

8. Gilmore, "Initiative Backers Try Again."

9. Peter Lewis, "'3 Strikes' Laws Have Struck Out Elsewhere—Other States See No Drop in Crime," *Seattle Times,* September 30, 1993.

10. David Schaefer, "NRA Backs 'Three Strikes' Initiative Campaign—Gun Lobby Puts Money, Time into Repeat-Criminal Crusade," *Seattle Times,* May 5, 1993.

11. Peter Lewis, "'Three Strikes' Initiative Gains Strength, Takes Aim at Felons—But Opponents Say Measure Will Be Drain on Taxpayers," *Seattle Times,* August 31, 1993.

12. Ibid.

13. Lewis, "'3 Strikes' Laws Have Struck Out."

14. Ibid; Peter Lewis, "I-593 Strikes Out on Death Row—Worse Killers Would Not Have Been Affected," *Seattle Times,* October 28, 1993.

15. William J. Bennett, "Yes on 593; Three Strikes and You're Out," *Seattle Times,* September 19, 1993.

16. Peter Lewis, "'Three Strikes You're Out': Three-Fourths Yes and It's In," *Seattle Times,* November 3, 1993.

17. Mindy Cameron, "Black-White Campaigns on Issues Bathed in Gray," *Seattle Times,* October 31, 1993.

18. Lewis, "'Three Strikes You're Out.'"

19. Michael Baker, "'Three Strikes' Convict Charged with Theft," *Fresno Bee,* December 13, 2003; Jane Gross, "Drive to Keep Repeat Felons in Prison Gains in California," *New York Times,* December 26, 1993.

20. Gross, "Drive to Keep Repeat Felons."

21. Ibid.

22. Linda Goldston, "Search for Missing Girl Called No Less than Petaluma Miracle; Effort to Find Kidnapped 12-Year-Old One of Largest Ever," *Houston Chronicle,* October 13, 1993.

23. Christine Spolar, "California Town Cries as Polly Klaas Is Found; Twice-Convicted Suspect Faces Murder, Kidnapping Charges in Abduction of 12-Year-Old," *Washington Post,* December 6, 1993.

24. Gross, "Drive to Keep Repeat Felons."

25. Oliver Starr Jr., "The Case of Richard Davis," *National Review,* May 30, 1994.

26. Richard Price, "Anger and Anguish Over Polly's Death: A Tragic End to California Kidnap Case," *USA Today,* December 6, 1993.

27. Gross, "Drive to Keep Repeat Felons"; Vlae Kershner and Carolyn Lochhead, "Politicians React with Calls for Stiffer Sentences: Wilson and Feinstein Join Cry for Less Leniency," *San Francisco Chronicle,* December 7, 1993.

28. Kershner and Lochhead, "Politicians React."

29. Ibid.

30. Susan Yoachum, "A Senseless Death, a Call to Action: Politicians at Polly's Memorial Urge Overhaul of Justice System," *San Francisco Chronicle,* December 10, 1993.

31. Robert B. Gunnison and Greg Lucas, "Wilson Pushes Crime, Economy in State of the State Address," *San Francisco Chronicle,* January 6, 1994.

32. Ibid.

33. Vlae Kershner and Greg Lucas, "'3 Strikes' Leader Warns Assembly: He Doesn't Want Ballot Measure Softened," *San Francisco Chronicle,* January 5, 1994.

34. This version of the law was nearly identical to the initiative version proposed by Reynolds, which meant that there would be no conflict between the bill and the ballot initiative if the initiative were to pass.

35. Vlae Kershner, "Governor Wants '3 Strikes' Plan That Is Toughest, Most Costly," *San Francisco Chronicle,* March 3, 1994.

36. Cal. Penal Code §§667.5(c), 1192.7(c), 1192.8.

37. Vlae Kershner, "Klaases Like Substitute 3 Strikes Bill: Polly's Kin Support Measure Excluding Nonviolent Felonies," *San Francisco Chronicle,* March 10, 1994.

38. The remaining Three Strike proposals introduced into the legislature differed on the types of qualifying offenses that would count as strikes, but none of them were seriously considered for adoption.

39. Kershner, "Governor Wants '3 Strikes' Plan."

40. Vlae Kershner and Greg Lucas, "'Three Strikes' Signed into California Law," *San Francisco Chronicle,* March 8, 1994.

41. Ibid.

42. John Balzar, "The Target: Repeat Offenders," *Los Angeles Times,* March 24, 1994.

43. Gross, "Drive to Keep Repeat Felons."

44. Vlae Kershner, "Poll Shows Commanding Lead for State's '3 Strikes' Initiative," *San Francisco Chronicle,* January 26, 1994.

45. Gross, "Drive to Keep Repeat Felons."

46. Julian V. Roberts, "Public Opinion, Crime, and Criminal Justice," *Crime and Justice: A Review of Research* 16 (1992), 99–180.

47. Ray Surette, "News from Nowhere, Policy to Follow," in *Three Strikes and You're Out: Vengeance as Public Policy*, ed. David Shichor and Dale K. Sechrest (Thousand Oaks, California: Sage Publications, 1996), 177–202.

48. Dan Freedman, "Polly's Dad Urges Clinton to Make America Safer," *Times-Picayune* (New Orleans), December 21, 1993; "An Open Letter from Polly Klaas' Mother," *St. Petersburg Times,* December 8, 1993.

49. Roberts, "Public Opinion."

50. Pierre Thomas, "Violent Crime Strikes a Chord Coast to Coast; '3-Time Loser' Laws Find Diverse Support," *Washington Post,* January 24, 1994.

51. Helen Dewar, "Republicans Are Racing to Collar Crime Issue Purloined by President," *Washington Post,* January 27, 1994.

52. William J. Clinton, "Address Before the Joint Session of the Congress on the State of the Union," January 25, 1994. Available online at http://www.gpoaccess.gov/sou/index.html.

53. Thomas, "Violent Crime Strikes a Chord Coast to Coast; '3-Time Loser' Laws Find Diverse Support."

54. Marshall Ingwerson, "GOP Is No Longer Bastion of Tough Talk on Crime," *Christian Science Monitor,* February 1, 1994.

55. Kershner, "Klaases Like Substitute 3 Strikes Bill."

56. RAND used California figures that estimated the prison operating costs at $20,800 per person and prison capital costs at $97,000 per inmate. See Peter Greenwood, C. Peter Rydell, Allan F. Abrahamse, Jonathan P. Caulkins, James Chiesa, Karyn E. Model, and Stephen P. Klein, *Three Strikes and You're Out: Estimated Benefits and Costs of California's New Mandatory-Sentencing Law* (Santa Monica, Calif.: RAND, 1994).

57. Ibid.

58. Ibid.

59. See also Center for Urban Analysis, Office of the County Executive, Santa Clara County, California, *Assessing the Impact of AB971 "Three Strikes, You're Out" on the Justice System in Santa Clara County, California* (Santa Clara, Calif.: Santa Clara County Board of Supervisors, 1994).

60. The governor's office calculated that the average crime costs society and the victim approximately $200,000, and that each inmate, before incarceration, is typically responsible for about 20 crimes per year.

61. Scott Armstrong, "Nation's Toughest Three-Strike Law Being Reassessed," *Christian Science Monitor,* August 30, 1994.

62. Dewar, "Republicans Are Racing."

63. Neil A. Lewis, "President Foresees Safer U.S.," *New York Times,* August 27, 1994.

64. Violent Crime Control and Law Enforcement Act of 1994, 103–322 (September 13, 2004).

65. Walter J. Dickey, *"Three Strikes" Five Years Later* (Washington, D.C.: Campaign for an Effective Crime Policy, 1998); Michael G. Turner and Jody L. Sundt, "'Three Strikes and You're Out' Legislation: A National Assessment," *Federal Probation* 59, no. 3 (1995).

66. John Clark, James Austin, and D. Alan Henry, *"Three Strikes and You're Out": A Review of State Legislation* (Washington, D.C.: U.S. Department of Justice, Office of Justice Programs, National Institute of Justice, 1997).

67. Turner and Sundt, "'Three Strikes and You're Out' Legislation."

68. Clark et al., *"Three Strikes and You're Out": A Review.*

69. Turner and Sundt, "'Three Strikes and You're Out' Legislation." Although the original Three Strikes legislation in Washington identified 51 crimes that would count as strikes, subsequent revisions to that legislation reduced the number of crimes eligible for enhanced punishment.

70. Clark et al., *"Three Strikes and You're Out": A Review.*

71. Ibid.

72. Ibid.

73. Ian Fisher, "Why '3-Strike' Sentencing Is a Solid Hit This Season," *New York Times,* January 25, 1994.

74. The impetus for the Three Strikes movement also brought about truth-in-sentencing legislation at the federal level, which promised federal funds for new prison construction to those states that required violent offenders to serve at least 85 percent of their sentences.

75. Alaska, the 25th state to enact a Three Strikes law, passed its legislation in 1996. See Dickey, *"Three Strikes" Five Years Later.*

3

The California Controversy

Of all the Three Strikes measures that were passed in the mid-1990s, the version adopted in California has received the most attention—and the most criticism. Some of the early interest could be attributed to the circumstances surrounding its initial adoption. The Polly Klaas kidnapping and murder case made for headline news across the country, and some of the nation's most prominent policy makers used the case to press for tougher sentencing measures. The attention could also be attributed to the fact that shortly after implementation, California set itself apart by using its broadly drawn law to incarcerate far more offenders than other states. In fact, within the first five years, California incarcerated more than 15 times as many people under its Three Strikes law than all of the other states combined.[1] Moreover, with California being the most populous state in the nation, the affairs of Californians are closely followed by observers in other states. In many cases, the political solutions adopted in California serve as a model for the rest of the nation to follow. For example, its wholehearted embrace of indeterminate sentencing in the early part of the twentieth century was subsequently replicated by many states across the country. Similarly, the state's 1976 decision to abandon indeterminate sentencing to adopt presumptive (determinate) sentencing also paved the way for other states to follow. This influence is deftly described by the political axiom "As California goes, so goes the nation." Thus, the state's Three Strikes law received more than its share of media attention and scrutiny as policy makers around the country questioned whether this policy might work for their states as well.

When legislators were debating the merits of the various Three Strikes proposals in spring 1994, there was little criticism about the version they ultimately adopted. It was generally favored among the various proposals because it was the broadest in scope and therefore the toughest. However, by the time voters were asked to ratify Three Strikes on the November 1994 ballot, concerns about the law's features had begun to surface. The RAND Corporation alarmed many with its predictions that because the law was so broad in its scope, the state would have to shoulder astronomically high costs to handle all the new Three Strikes inmates. Others predicted that the court system would soon collapse under the strain produced by numerous Three Strikes cases. Still others voiced concerns about the proportionality of the sentences and whether the law would be implemented fairly and consistently. In the weeks before the election, newspaper editorials urged voters to reject Proposition 184, the ballot initiative version of Three Strikes, so that lawmakers would be able to modify the law to make it a more workable alternative. Despite the numerous last-minute criticisms, voters overwhelmingly supported the law by a margin of nearly three to one.[2]

EXAMINING THE FEATURES OF THE CALIFORNIA THREE STRIKES LAW

The purpose of the Three Strikes law is "to ensure longer prison sentences and greater punishment for those who commit a felony and have been previously convicted of serious and/or violent felony offenses."[3] To accomplish that objective, the law identifies two groups of offenders that will receive enhanced sentences. The first group, two-strikers, consists of offenders who have one past conviction for a serious and/or violent crime. The second group, three-strikers, is made up of offenders who have two or more such convictions in their criminal histories. Two-strikers receive double the usual sentence upon conviction of any subsequent felony offense. Three-strikers receive an indeterminate sentence of life imprisonment once convicted of any subsequent felony. Three-strikers are eligible for parole but must serve a minimum term that is the greater of (a) three times the usual sentence, (b) a minimum term of 25 years, or (c) another term stipulated by other sentencing statutes (e.g., life without parole or death).

Almost all three-strikers are sentenced under the greatest minimum term of 25 years to life. Although a tripled sentence might appear to be greater, for most felony offenses even a tripled sentence will fall far short of the 25-year minimum threshold. For example, the presumptive baseline sentence for residential burglary is 4 years in prison. A tripled sentence for a third-strike offender would produce a sentence of only 12 years in prison, which is less than 50 percent of the required minimum term of 25 years. Even an offender who committed an aggravated forcible rape for his third strike would receive a tripled sentence equaling 24 years, which is still less than the required minimum of 25 years to life.[4]

The law also references other sections of the penal code that limit the amount of work-time (a variation of good-time) credits that a strike offender can earn. At the time the law was enacted, two-strikers could earn only a 20 percent maximum reduction for work-time credit, which was substantially less than the 50 percent that other inmates could earn.[5] Later changes consistent with the truth-in-sentencing program initiated by the federal government reduced the maximum amount of work-time credit to 15 percent for two-strikers who committed a violent crime.[6] Three-strikers are prohibited from earning any work-time reduction at all, according the state penal code and the California Supreme Court.[7] In the 2001 case *In re Cervera,* the court declared that the intent of the language of the Three Strikes law precluded a three-striker from reducing his sentence below the 25-year minimum threshold. Thus, three-strikers who receive the indeterminate life sentence must serve the full 25 years before they are eligible for parole.

The law also enhances the punishment for three-strikers by stipulating that the mandatory life sentences be served consecutively, not concurrently. Specifically, the law states that anyone sentenced to the mandatory life term must first complete any outstanding prison sentences before beginning the Three Strikes sentence. In other words, the defendant may not fold other outstanding prison terms into the minimum 25-years-to-life Three Strikes sentence. Instead, the offender must finish serving the old sentences first before he can begin serving his new life sentence. Additionally, any offender who is sentenced to multiple life sentences must also serve them consecutively. Once he has completed the first 25-year-to-life sentence and meets the qualification for parole, he is then to begin serving the second 25-year-to-life sentence. The statute will not allow the offender to serve the sentences simultaneously. For instance, if a person with two strikes is released on parole and in the course of a month burglarizes four different homes, he would be facing four separate Three Strike sentences, each carrying a minimum penalty of 25 years to life. If he is convicted of all four burglaries, then the sentencing judge would be required to impose the four sentences consecutively. The total amount of time that the offender would be required to serve is 100 years to life.

Although a scenario like this one does highlight the significance of the Three Strikes sentence, the most important feature of the California Three Strikes law is not the severity of the sentencing provisions—because many other states have sentences that are more severe—but the breadth of the strike zone. To be eligible for the Three Strikes sentence, the offender's previous offenses must be designated as serious and/or violent according to the lists of offenses found in Cal. Penal Code §§667.5(c), 1192.7(c), and 1192.8.[8] Cal. Penal Code §1192.7(c), the most comprehensive of the lists, identifies more than 40 offenses that qualify as either serious or violent. Most of the crimes involve some form of violence, harm, or trespass against persons; however, two offenses, residential burglary and the sale of illegal drugs to a minor, do not involve physical harm to the victim. Eligible offenses, identified in Table 3.1, currently include murder, voluntary manslaughter, rape, robbery, kidnapping, assault with a deadly weapon or causing great bodily injury, and arson. Any changes to this list can greatly impact the number of strike offenders; adding crimes to this list consequently increases the number of potential strike offenders. Reducing or narrowing the list of offenses would correspondingly decrease the number of offenders who would qualify under the law.

To qualify for the enhanced Three Strike sentences, offenders must have been previously convicted of one or more offenses included on the serious and/or violent felony list. Two-strikers must have one conviction from the list; three-strikers at least two. The last-strike offense—Strike 2 for two-strikers and Strike 3 for three-strikers—need not come from the serious and/or violent felony list; *any* felony offense will suffice to trigger the mandatory sentence. This last-strike provision widens the strike zone to include less serious felony offenses, such as grand theft, involuntary manslaughter, weapon possession, drug possession, and commercial burglary. Other comparatively less serious crimes, such as driving under the influence of alcohol or drugs, or shoplifting, may also count for the third strike if the offender already has one or more previous convictions for that offense in his record.

The authors of the Three Strikes law drew an intentionally wide strike zone to capture a greater percentage of repeat offenders.[9] Recidivism studies, like the one released in 1983 by the Bureau of Justice Statistics, reveal that more than two-thirds of prison inmates continue to violate the law after being released on parole. Furthermore, studies have also shown that many offenders increase the severity of their offending behavior over time. Therefore, a good portion of repeat offenders will commit violent offenses if given the opportunity. Instead of waiting for the offender to commit a third violent offense and causing grave harm to another victim, the authors of the Three Strikes law believed that it would be better for the state to incapacitate the offender at the first sign that he had resumed his criminal career.

A comparison in Table 3.2 of the prison sentences for two- and three-strike offenders under the previous law and under the Three Strikes law shows that punishment for repeat offenders is much more severe under the new law. Consistent with the philosophy of deterrence and incapacitation, the new sentences are much longer. For example, the third-strike offender in example 1, who was convicted of receiving stolen property, which is a nonserious and

Table 3.1
Offenses Classified as Serious, Violent, or Both

The following list contains representative offenses identified by the State of California as being serious, violent, or both, under Cal. Penal Code § 1192.7(c). Prior convictions for offenses included on this list count as strikes under the Three Strikes law.

Homicide
- Murder, attempted murder, or voluntary manslaughter

Sexual Assault
- Rape
- Sodomy or oral copulation by force, violence, duress, menace, threat of great bodily injury, or fear
- Sexual penetration where the act is accomplished against the victim's will by force, violence, duress, menace, or fear of immediate and unlawful bodily injury on the victim or another person
- Lewd or lascivious act on a child under the age of 14 years
- Continuous sexual abuse of a child
- Commission of rape or sexual penetration in concert with another person

Assault
- Assault with intent to commit rape, sodomy, oral copulation, mayhem, or robbery
- Assault with a deadly weapon or instrument on a peace officer or firefighter
- Assault that causes great bodily injury
- Assault with a deadly weapon, firearm, machine gun, assault weapon, or semiautomatic firearm
- Assault with a deadly weapon against a public transit employee, custodial officer, or school employee
- Assault with a deadly weapon by an inmate or by a life prisoner on a noninmate

Other Felonies
- Mayhem
- Arson
- Robbery or bank robbery
- Kidnapping
- Residential burglary
- Carjacking
- Grand theft involving a firearm
- Holding a hostage by a person confined in state prison
- Exploding a destructive device or any explosive with intent to injure or murder
- Throwing acid or flammable substances
- Discharge of a firearm at an inhabited dwelling, vehicle, or aircraft; shooting from a vehicle
- Intimidation of victims or witnesses; criminal threats
- Selling, furnishing, administering, giving, or offering to sell to any minor heroin, cocaine, phencyclidine (PCP), or any methamphetamine-related drug
- Any felony offense committed for the benefit of, at the direction of, or in association with any criminal street gang, with specific intent to promote, further, or assist in any criminal conduct by gang members

nonviolent offense, received a 23-year sentence increase under the new law. Even the third-strike offender convicted of robbery for the offense received a substantial enhancement under the Three Strikes law compared to what he would have received under the prior law.

California's Three Strikes law is also considered to be broad because it allows juvenile offenses to count as strikes. Juvenile offenders, 16 years of age and older, may accumulate strikes for offenses that are charged against them in the juvenile justice system. However, the list of eligible strike offenses is narrower for juveniles. Adult strikes must come from the list of serious and/ or violent felonies identified by Cal. Penal Code §§667.5(c), 1192.7(c), and 1192.8, yet the California Supreme Court has stipulated that only offenses identified in Welfare and Institutions Code §707(b) may be counted as strikes for juvenile offenders.[10] Although most of the offenses included on this list are similar to the ones found on the adult list, residential (first-degree) burglary, which counts as a strike for adults, is excluded from the juvenile list. Thus, as long as the underage offender is charged and convicted of the crime in juvenile court, residential burglary cannot count as a strike on his criminal history record. However, if the state charges a juvenile offender as an adult, then he is eligible to earn strikes for all offenses found on the list that applies to adults.

Table 3.2
Examples of Prison Sentences (Prior Law versus Three Strikes Law)

Offender Type	Crimes Committed		Time to Serve in Prison[*]	
	New Offense	Prior Offense[**]	Prior Law	Three Strikes Law
First-striker	Residential burglary	None	2 years	2 years
Second-striker	Residential burglary	Residential burglary	4.5 years	10.4 years
Third-striker (Example 1)	Receiving stolen property	Assault on peace officer Residential burglary	2 years	25 years to life
Third-striker (Example 2)	Robbery	Residential burglary Robbery	7 years	25 years to life

[*] Assumes the offender received typical prison sentence for the new offense, received sentence enhancements for prior offenses, and earned maximum credits from participation in work or education programs.
[**] Assumes prior offense resulted in a prison sentence.
Source: Brown, Brian and Greg Jolivette. *A Primer: Three Strikes. The Impact after More than a Decade.* Sacramento, California: Legislative Analyst's Office, 2005, Figure 2, 8.

To ensure that the mandatory sentences are imposed as intended, the California Three Strikes law includes several restrictions on areas of discretion typically exercised by judges and prosecutors. First, judges are prohibited from sentencing a strike offender to probation; they must sentence all eligible offenders to prison. This provision is designed to prevent judges from skirting the mandatory sentencing requirement by imposing an alternate sentence—such as probation—instead. If an offender is eligible for the mandatory sentence, then the judge must impose it. Second, judges must impose all sentences consecutively, as discussed earlier. Thus, a two-striker must receive doubled sentences for all convictions, and a three-striker is to be sentenced to multiple consecutive 25-year-to-life sentences if he is convicted of more than one third strike.

Third, judges are prohibited from aging out any eligible strike offenses, which means that the offender's entire criminal history is to be considered at the time of sentencing, not just his recent activity. Under other sentencing policies, judges are permitted to exclude from consideration offenses that are relatively old (e.g., 20 years or more). The rationale behind this decision is that older behavior is not necessarily indicative of current or future behavior, and thus it may be excluded as irrelevant to the present sentencing decision. The Three Strikes law specifically requires the judge to consider *all* previous strike offenses, no matter how long ago they may have occurred. Three-strike defendants could have earned their first two strikes in the early 1970s, more than 20 years before the adoption of the law, but the law states that once an eligible strike has been earned it may be considered for the purposes of enhanced sentencing for the rest of the offender's life. Opponents of the aging-out philosophy argue that past behavior—no matter how long ago it may have occurred—informs current and present behavior and therefore should be considered in the present sentencing decision.

The Three Strikes law also places limitations on the charging discretion of state prosecutors. Under a system of determinate or mandatory sentencing, the charging decision of the prosecutor is significant because criminal penalties are linked to the offenses that are charged. Therefore, the prosecutor's decision to charge, or not to charge, a suspect with the targeted offense determines whether the mandatory sentence will be applied. Previous experience in other states has shown that prosecutors sometimes help offenders avoid the mandatory penalty by charging alternate offenses or by reducing the level of the charge (e.g., from a felony to a misdemeanor) to avoid the mandatory penalty.[11] They may do this to encourage the offender to cooperate with ongoing investigations, to facilitate the plea-bargaining process, or because they feel that the mandatory penalty would be unjust for that particular offender.[12] Even when used to further legitimate purposes, prosecutorial discretion has the potential to undermine the effectiveness of any mandatory sentencing law. A study commissioned by the state of Arizona revealed that because of prosecutors' charging decisions, only 10 percent of offenders eligible for mandatory sentencing enhancements actually received them. Furthermore, 26 percent of offenders who should have received mandatory life sentences received probation instead.[13] The United States Sentencing Commission found this type of behavior at the federal level as well. Over 40 percent of federal offenders who should have received mandatory penalties received less stringent penalties instead, and 35 percent of offenders charged with trafficking large quantities of illegal narcotics failed to receive the mandatory minimum sentence as required by law.[14]

To prevent this from happening in California, the Three Strikes law includes language that requires prosecutors to charge all eligible offenders with the mandatory sentencing enhancement. Procedurally, it is the responsibility of the prosecutor to alert the court about any offenses in the offender's criminal history that could qualify as strikes. The jury (or judge, if a defendant foregoes a jury trial) is responsible for verifying that the offender's prior offenses qualify as serious and/or violent felonies as required by law. The mandatory sentence cannot be applied until these two requirements are met: the prosecutor must include the Three Strikes allegation in the criminal complaint against the defendant, and the jury (or judge) must verify that the prior offenses qualify as eligible strikes. Although normally the prosecutor would have discretion to decide whether an enhancement is charged, the language of the law makes it clear that prosecutors are to "plead and prove all known prior felony convictions."[15] Furthermore, the law prohibits prosecutors from engaging in any plea bargaining with two- or three-strike offenders. Prosecutors retain the ability to decide what level the current offenses should be charged, such as whether to charge a person with first- or second-degree robbery, but they do not have the authority to dismiss or otherwise ignore an offender's past convictions to secure a guilty plea.

Despite the many restrictions against the use of discretion by judges and prosecutors, the law does contain language that allows them to sidestep the Three Strikes sentencing requirement in certain circumstances. First, both judges and prosecutors may dismiss consideration of prior offenses if there is insufficient evidence to prove their characterization as strikes. To assess whether prior convictions qualify as strikes under Cal. Penal Code §1192.7(c), prosecutors must present evidence to the jury (or judge) that supports the allegation that the offender has committed one or more offenses that match the crimes designated as serious and/or violent felonies. If the jury (or judge) decides that the evidence is sufficient to warrant that declaration, then the prior convictions are accepted as strikes. If, however, there is insufficient evidence to support their characterization as strikes, as might be the case with very old or out-of-state convictions that lack complete records, the law gives prosecutors the option of asking the court to dismiss consideration of those offenses as strike offenses. This prevents a prosecutor from having to go through the motions of trying to prove that an old conviction is truly a strike when there is insufficient evidence to support such a finding. The judges also have the ability to dismiss a prior offense from consideration if there is insufficient evidence to support the allegation. If, for example, a prosecutor discovers that a suspected Three Strikes offender has a previous conviction for burglary but cannot ascertain that it qualifies as residential burglary (which is the only type of burglary that may be counted as a strike), he or she may petition the court to remove the offense from consideration. If the judge approves, the offense will be dismissed from consideration and cannot be counted as a strike.

Second, the language of the Three Strikes law also allows prosecutors to petition the court to dismiss one or more prior strikes "in the furtherance of justice." This means that after a Three Strikes allegation has been charged against a defendant, the prosecutor may ask the court to dismiss consideration of one or more strike offenses present in the defendant's record. If the judge grants the prosecutor's motion, then a three-strike offender facing a 25-year-to-life sentence would avoid the mandatory minimum sentence. For instance, a three-striker who had one prior conviction dismissed in the furtherance of justice would be sentenced as a two-striker, and a two-striker who had his prior strike dismissed in the furtherance of justice would escape the enhanced sentencing provision altogether. Although the phrase "in the furtherance of justice" is not defined explicitly in the statute, subsequent judicial interpretation has indicated that discretion may be used for offenders who fall outside the "spirit of the law" and for whom a lengthy mandatory sentence would be unjust.[16]

Judges may also dismiss prior strikes in the furtherance of justice, but the authorization to do so is not found in the language of the Three Strikes law. Instead, the authority for this use of discretion originates with the California Supreme Court in the 1996 case *People v. Superior Court (Romero).*[17] In this case, the California high court declared that the state's separation of powers doctrine assumes that prosecutors, as representatives of the executive branch of government, and judges, as representatives of the judicial branch, have equal authority under the law. The state may impose restrictions on judicial discretion, but the law must include specific language to that effect. Since the Three Strikes law does not prohibit judges from dismissing a prior strike in the furtherance of justice, the separation of powers doctrine assumes that they have the same authority as prosecutors. In its opinion, the court also extended the use of discretion retroactively to cases that were sentenced before the June

1996 ruling. This gave judges who were unaware that they had discretion under the law the opportunity to resentence Three Strike defendants in accordance with the *Romero* ruling.

CONCERNS ABOUT CALIFORNIA'S THREE STRIKES LAW

Although the California Three Strikes law enjoyed a great deal of support when it was enacted in 1994, it has since encountered much criticism. Objections to the law can be divided into two general categories: arguments that are related to mandatory sentencing laws in general, and criticisms about the specific features of California's law. Critics of mandatory sentencing laws in general argue that mandatory sentences are inherently unjust because judges are incapable of altering sentences in response to individual circumstances. They contend that sometimes the unique characteristics of the case—or the offender—may warrant differential treatment, yet judges are prevented from taking these factors into consideration. These arguments have recently found favor with U.S. Supreme Court Justices Stephen G. Breyer and Anthony Kennedy, who have publicly spoken against the use of mandatory minimum sentences at the federal level. In fact, in his 2003 address to the American Bar Association, Justice Kennedy encouraged Congress to repeal all mandatory sentencing laws because they often produce unfair results.[18]

Some scholars have also registered objections to mandatory penalties, arguing that they are inherently flawed. They note that although mandatory sentencing laws are successful in constraining judicial discretion, the corresponding increase in prosecutorial discretion can still lead to sentences that are arbitrarily applied. Additionally, they point out that mandatory sentencing laws often interfere with the determinate sentencing goals advanced by the legislature because they usually impose lengthy sentences that are out of sync with the rest of the proportionally based determinate sentences. Finally, scholars still disagree among themselves as to whether mandatory sentencing laws are effective in reducing crime. Research studies have failed to discern a clear relationship between deterrence and incapacitation policies and lower crime rates. Thus, scholars argue that legislatures that adopt such policies under the belief that they will work to reduce crime may be disappointed with the results.[19]

Concerns about the specific features of California's Three Strikes law focus on two main areas. First, critics point out that the breadth of California's strike zone, which is much larger than that of other states, has produced a variety of problems: the law ensnares the wrong type of offender; the law applies to too many offenders, which increases the costs of the law; and the law leads to sentences that are unjust. Second, Three Strikes opponents argue that the varied implementation of the law has produced unjust results. Specifically, the different prosecutorial policies among the state's 58 counties means that an offender in one county may receive the mandatory minimum sentence while a similar offender in another county may escape the severe sentence.

Concern #1: The California Strike Zone May Be Too Big

In California, the size of the strike zone is the source of many objections because the dimensions of the strike zone determines how many offenders will strike out. If the strike zone is narrow, then only a few offenders will be affected. For example, when residents of Washington were debating whether to adopt the Three Strikes law in 1993, the state Sentencing Commission estimated that only 70–75 offenders would be sentenced under the law each year.[20] However, when the strike zone is wide, many offenders—potentially thousands—will strike out. This, in turn, influences other parts of the criminal justice system and increases the costs associated with implementation.

The first dispute over the size of California's strike zone was raised as the legislature debated which version of Three Strikes to adopt. The original version, AB 971, authored by Assemblymen Jones and Costa in conjunction with Mike Reynolds, stipulated that only prior offenses that qualified as serious and/or violent felonies in accordance with Cal. Penal Code §§667.5(c), 1192.7(c), and 1992.8 could count as strikes. The comprehensive list from Cal. Penal Code §1192.7(c), which is presented in Table 3.1, includes mostly offenses against persons. However, two offenses, residential burglary and the sale of narcotics to minors, do not involve any direct harm to others. Consequently, some felt that this list was inappropriately broad for a Three Strikes law because an offender could be sentenced to the mandatory minimum sentence of 25 years to life having never committed a violent crime. It would be possible for an offender to commit two residential burglaries for strikes 1 and 2 and another nonserious or nonviolent offense for strike 3 and be sentenced to life in prison.

This was the objection publicly voiced by Marc and Joseph Klaas, Polly Klaas's father and grandfather, on behalf of the Polly Klaas Foundation. They specifically objected to the inclusion of residential burglary as an eligible strike offense and argued that the law should count only violent crimes as strikes. They also urged legislators to adopt a Three Strikes version that targeted only violent offenders like Richard Allen Davis, who was responsible for Polly's death.[21] However, the inclusion of residential burglary was done intentionally. In fact, when the various Three Strikes proposals were being debated, Governor Wilson specifically asked for residential burglary to be included as an eligible strike. His argument was that residential burglary was similar to robbery; the only difference between the two crimes is that residents are not home when the offense takes place.[22] Others have pointed out that the definition of residential burglary is not limited to a scenario wherein a person enters a residence for the purpose of theft. Rather, residential burglary is defined in the state's penal code as the entry into a home for the purpose of committing *any* felony offense, such as assault, robbery, or rape. As such, the courts have long recognized that the potential for violence makes burglary a dangerous offense.[23]

Another dispute over the size of the strike zone focuses on the nature of the triggering offense—strike 2 for two-strikers and strike 3 for three-strikers—that generates the mandatory sentence. In many states, the triggering offense is of the same quality as the other strike offenses. For example, the law in Kansas, which includes a two- and three-strike tier system as in California, stipulates that all strikes must involve crimes against persons. However, in California, *any* felony offense committed as the last strike can force the mandatory sentence; the first strike(s) must be serious and/or violent felonies but not the last one. This means that the strike zone is wide enough for the last offense to include less-serious felony offenses, such as commercial burglary, grand theft, weapon possession, and drug possession. It even allows "wobbler" offenses, which are crimes that can be treated as either felonies or misdemeanors, to serve as triggering offenses. For instance, in California, petty theft is a misdemeanor offense; however, if an offender has a previous theft conviction on his record, then the charge becomes a wobbler—"petty theft with a prior"—and is treated as a presumptive felony.[24]

Does the Broad Strike Zone Capture the Wrong Type of Offender?

Soon after the law was implemented, cases involving relatively minor third strikes served as examples for those who thought the strike zone was drawn too broadly. These cases also illustrated the practical realities of the tough sentencing law for both offenders and members of the public. Shortly after the law was enacted, a San Francisco juror broke out in tears when she realized that the defendant was facing a third strike for robbing a security guard and trying to take his car. As a result, the case ended in a mistrial.[25] In perhaps the most notorious of California's Three Strikes cases, the infamous "pizza thief," Jerry Dewayne Williams, was sentenced to 25 years to life in March 1995 for stealing a slice of pizza from a group of children on the Redondo Beach pier. Since the theft was accomplished through intimidation and fear, prosecutors originally charged Williams with robbery. Still, because the underlying behavior for this triggering offense was relatively minor, it was used by Three Strikes critics as a primary example of the flaws associated with drawing a strike zone too broadly.[26] Critics point out that Williams's sentence was not an anomaly. Reports of Three Strikes defendants receiving life sentences for felony petty thefts, of such items as a pair of blue jeans, a six-pack of beer, and a cell phone, invoked additional criticism of the law, even among its previous supporters.[27] In objecting to petty crimes counting as third strikes, Marc Klaas, Polly's father, stated, "I've had my car broken into and my radio stolen and I've had my daughter murdered, and I know the difference."[28]

Although critics use the Williams example and others like it to argue that California's broad strike zone captures the wrong type of offender, supporters of the Three Strikes law assert that the law was functioning exactly as it was intended. They argue that cases like Williams's only confirm the premise that repeat offenders pose a particular danger to others because they refuse to conform to the dictates of lawful society. They also point out that Williams was sentenced to 25 years to life not because he stole a piece of pizza from a group of children but because he exhibited consistent predatory and violent behavior. At six-foot-five and 225 pounds, Williams had an intimidating posture and a threatening demeanor. Furthermore, by age 27, he had accumulated an extensive criminal record.[29] At the time of his Three Strikes sentencing, Williams had been arrested 13 times and convicted of five felony offenses, including robbery, attempted robbery, drug possession, and joyriding. A prosecutor involved with the Williams case dismissed the argument that the sentence was inappropriate by declaring, "If the foremost purpose of [the justice system] is to protect society, then Jerry Dewayne Williams is a person we need protection from. He is a repeat offender. He has not learned. He has not repented."[30]

Furthermore, supporters of Three Strikes dispute the argument that the law ensnares minor, undeserving offenders. Rather, they argue that *all* offenders sentenced under the law have been convicted of at least one serious and/or violent felony and, if given the opportunity, will likely commit such a crime again. Additionally, they point out that the law allows police, prosecutors, and judges to intervene early enough to save lives instead of waiting for that violent offender to victimize another person. Not surprisingly, family members of crime victims are among the law's strongest supporters. They note that by the time an offender gets caught for his crime, he has likely committed numerous offenses that escaped detection and punishment. Therefore, any punishment that is administered has been earned, even if the triggering offense happens to be a nonviolent offense.[31]

Researchers have had some difficulty trying to assess the true character of strike offenders sentenced under the law. State agencies are often unable to provide information on the criminal history of each strike offender, which prevents analysts from describing the specific characteristics of the various

offenders. Nonetheless, the California Department of Corrections and Rehabilitation (CDCR) provides quarterly reports indicating the number of total
two- and three-strike offenders currently incarcerated in the state prison system and the type of offense that triggered the mandatory sentence. The summary report of second- third-strike offenders in correctional institutions as of
December 31, 2001, which is presented in Table 3.3, reveals that 45 percent
of all 7,072 three-strikers and 33 percent of all 34,656 two-strikers had a triggering offense that involved a crime against a person. Furthermore, 30 percent
of all two- and three-strikers received their enhanced sentences for property
crimes. Petty theft with a prior, one of the felony offenses that has generated some of the most heated debate about the law, triggered the enhanced
sentence for 331—less than 5 percent—of three-strikers and 2,061—about
6 percent—of two-strikers. Far more two-strikers were sentenced under the
law for drug crimes (28% as compared to 17% for three-strikers), yet about
the same number of offenders from each group were convicted and sentenced
for miscellaneous felony offenses, such as arson, possession of a weapon, and
escape from a correctional institution.[32]

Statistics from December 31, 2005, almost 12 years after the Three Strikes
law was enacted, revealed that the total number of two-strikers, who serve
much shorter sentences, had decreased in the intervening years, but the overall number of three-strikers, who serve much longer sentences, had increased.
Although the combined number of offenders was less than the totals from
2001, the triggering offense distributions were relatively similar to those in
the December 31, 2001, report. More two-strikers and just slightly fewer
three-strikers had been incarcerated for crimes against persons. Property-based
crimes were responsible for fewer two-strikers, but slightly more three-strikers,
and fewer two-strikers, received an enhanced sentence for drug offenses. The
much-maligned "petty theft with a prior" offense accounted for far fewer two-
strikers (1,562, or 4.7%) and 30 more three-strikers (361, or 4.6%). Miscellaneous felonies, such as arson and illegal possession of a weapon, constituted
roughly 10 percent of all two- and three-strike convictions.[33]

Does the Broad Strike Zone Produce Unjust Sentences?

Few would argue that a triple murderer or serial rapist is undeserving of
a lengthy Three Strikes sentence, but offenders who have committed property-based offenses or who have never harmed others are often seen as undeserving of a life sentence. Even defendants who commit serious crimes are
often viewed as undeserving of a life sentence. For example, Kevin Weber,
who had been convicted of two residential burglaries, was apprehended after
burglarizing a restaurant at night. His total gain from the burglary was four
cookies, which had been shoved in his pockets. His sentence under the Three

Table 3.3
Distribution of Triggering Offenses for Strike Offenders

Offense Type	December 31, 2001		December 31, 2005	
	Two-striker	Three-striker	Two-striker	Three-striker
Total number of offenses	34,656	7,072	32,951	7,813
Number of crimes against persons (and %)	11,368 (33)*	3,192 (45)	12,548 (38)	3,419 (44)
Number of crimes against property (and %)	10,547 (30)	2,125 (30)	9,338 (28)	2,399 (31)
Number of crimes involving drugs (and %)	9,769 (28)	1,198 (17)	7,835 (24)	1,292 (17)
Number of miscellaneous felonies (and %)	2,972 (9)	557 (8)	3,230 (10)	703 (9)

* Figures may not add up to 100% because of rounding.
** Comparisons using earlier data are unreliable because of modifications made to the Department of Corrections database in 2001.
Source: Data Analysis Unit, Estimates and Statistical Analysis Section, Offender Information Services Branch, California Department of Corrections.

Strikes law (plus an additional one-year enhancement) was 26 years to life. In another case, a three-striker was caught stealing a power tool from a garage, which in California is considered residential burglary—a serious offense— and sentenced to 25 years to life in prison. His prior strike convictions were also residential burglaries, one of which dated back to the late 1970s.[34]

Opponents of the law argue that sentences for repeat offenders should have some proportional relationship between the sentence and the crime. Otherwise, the sentences become unfair or unjust. Proportionality, which is at the heart of the just deserts sentencing philosophy, is also a standard for constitutionality. Previous rulings by the U.S. Supreme Court have stipulated that the Eighth Amendment prohibition against cruel and unusual sentences requires some form of proportionality, although it has struggled to find a specific rule through which proportionate sentences may be distinguished from disproportionate sentences. Nonetheless, it has established the precedent that a sentence is unconstitutional when it is "grossly disproportionate" to the crime. Consequently, California defendants facing lengthy 25-year-to-life sentences have also raised constitutional challenges to the law, alleging that their sentences, too, were grossly disproportionate to their offenses.

In 2003, two defendants sentenced under the California Three Strikes law for minor felony convictions claimed that their sentences were cruel and unusual punishment. The offenders in *Lockyer v. Andrade* (2003) and

Ewing v. California (2003) maintained that the mandatory life sentences that were imposed for minor theft offenses were grossly disproportionate to their crimes, and thus were unconstitutional.[35] In *Andrade,* the defendant was sentenced to two consecutive 25-year-to-life prison sentences for two separate shoplifting incidents for merchandise that had a combined value of less than $185. Under California law, theft of property valued less than $400 is typically treated as a misdemeanor offense. However, because Andrade's criminal record included several theft offenses, he was charged with felony theft and sentenced to two consecutive Three Strikes sentences. *Ewing* involved a similar scenario, although the value of his stolen merchandise qualified as felony grand theft under the California Penal Code. Despite the fact that the felonies were comparatively minor, the U.S. Supreme Court upheld the constitutionality of the Three Strikes sentences and rejected the argument that they were grossly disproportionate to the crimes.[36]

Supporters of the law contend that the judicious use of discretion by prosecutors and judges prevents defendants from being sentenced unjustly. The ability of judges and prosecutors to dismiss a prior strike in the furtherance of justice independent of one another means that there are two opportunities for the fairness of a sentence to be reviewed: first, when the prosecutor reviews the appropriateness of the case for discretionary review prior to sentencing, and second, when the judge has the opportunity to review the appropriateness of the sentence prior to imposing it. Research has found that prosecutors and judges use this discretion most often when a defendant has committed a low-level felony and does not present a safety threat to the public; however, when the offender presents a significant danger to the community, the full sentence is applied. This ability to shield undeserving offenders from unjust sentences has persuaded many elected county prosecutors to change their position on the law. Many district attorneys, including Paul Pfingst of San Diego County and James P. Fox of San Mateo County, publicly opposed the Three Strikes proposal in 1994 out of concern that prosecutors and judges would be forced to charge and sentence offenders who were not necessarily deserving of the mandatory minimum sentence.[37] Yet, after seeing how the use of discretion can shield those offenders who are undeserving offenders of the minimum sentence, most prosecutors now enthusiastically support the law. In fact, when California voters were asked to narrow the strike zone in November 2004, all 58 county district attorneys publicly opposed the measure.

The use of discretion does not mean that all offenders who have committed a less-serious current offense will escape the minimum sentence. In many cases, prosecutors and judges will fully prosecute and sentence such offenders because they feel that the offenders are dangerous and pose an imminent risk to the community. For example, in their 10-year retrospective, the California District Attorneys Association identified several three-strikers who were fully prosecuted and sentenced despite the fact that their third strike was not a serious or violent felony. One of the most famous cases is that of Kenneth Parnell, who had committed numerous violent crimes against children, including kidnapping and sexual assault. In January 2003, at age 70, Parnell was arrested for attempting to buy a five-year-old boy so that he could sexually assault him. His plan was thwarted by an undercover sting operation, and his third-strike convictions for solicitation to commit kidnapping, attempting to buy a person, and attempted child stealing gave him a 25-year-to-life sentence. Prosecutors noted that even though these most recent offenses were considered to be nonserious crimes, the sentence imposed in this case was just.[38]

Concern #2: Three Strikes May Be Unevenly Applied

In matters involving plea bargaining and sentencing of offenders, research has revealed that prosecutors and judges often work together to establish acceptable ranges of punishment for common offenses. The establishment of these penalty ranges, often referred to as the going rates, facilitates the plea-bargaining process because the sentences for most offenders are informally decided in advance. For example, in one jurisdiction, everyone might agree that the going rate for robbery is three to four years in prison. Therefore, when plea-bargaining, both the prosecutor and the defense attorney would negotiate with this understanding in mind. In another jurisdiction, the prosecutor and judge might agree that a one- to two-year sentence for robbery is appropriate. These norms not only reduce the uncertainty about the outcome of the case, but also allow the plea-bargaining process to be completed quickly.[39]

Restrictive sentencing laws, including ones that impose mandatory penalties, threaten the established system by requiring sentences for certain crimes that are likely to be inconsistent with the previously established going rate. As a result, plea-bargaining negotiations become less predictable and charging and sentencing outcomes become less certain—at least until a new going rate is established. Previous studies of mandatory sentencing laws have revealed that prosecutors and judges often respond to mandatory sentences by either avoiding them, as was the case with the Massachusetts and Michigan gun laws, or adapting to them by establishing new going rates. Although the new going rates may be higher than the previous ones, since completely avoiding the tougher sentencing policies may be impossible, research has also shown that prosecutors and judges try to keep the new rates close to the old rates. The result is that the corresponding sentences are not as severe as what the legislature or the voters intended them to be.[40]

When the Three Strikes law was implemented in California, much of pros-ecutors' and judges' traditional discretion was eliminated. Prosecutors were instructed to file Three Strikes charges against every eligible offender and were prohibited from plea bargaining in all Three Strikes cases. Judges could no longer sentence strike offenders to probation, nor could they impose sen-tences concurrently as they had in the past. Furthermore, judges could not reduce offenders' sentences, even if there were compelling mitigating circum-stances. Interviews with prosecutors, defense attorneys, and judges—mem-bers of the "courtroom workgroup"—confirmed that all of these changes disrupted the preestablished norms. Even by 1996, two years after the law's enactment, the courtroom workgroup reported higher levels of uncertainty in predicting case outcomes and less efficient negotiations.[41]

Still, prosecutors and judges found ways to adapt the law to fit individual circumstances. In some cases, prosecutors would use their charging discretion to charge a strike offender with a misdemeanor instead of a felony to avoid triggering the mandatory sentence. Similarly, judges could sentence defen-dants convicted of wobbler offenses to misdemeanor sentences to avoid the Three Strikes sentence. However, prosecutors and judges found greater adap-tive potential in the exercise of discretion that allows them to dismiss prior strikes in the furtherance of justice. Their ability to temporarily overlook prior strike convictions to shield undeserving offenders from the full effects of the law has become the primary way in which prosecutors and judges cre-ate flexibility in an otherwise inflexible law.

Shortly after the law was implemented, prosecutors were hesitant to use their discretion to dismiss prior strikes because they were concerned about public backlash. In California, chief prosecutors in each county are elected by residents of the county, so district attorneys frequently monitor public opinion on crime and justice issues to make sure that they are operating within public expectations. Because Three Strikes was so popular among voters, prosecutors opted to fully enforce the law in all cases. However, by 1995, prosecutors in the more liberal counties began using their discretion to dismiss prior strikes out of concern that voters might not welcome full enforcement, especially in cases where a three-striker had been charged with a relatively low-level felony. The district attorney in San Francisco, for example, speculated that juries in his county would refuse to convict defendants of drug and theft crimes if they found out that the defendant was facing a Three Strikes sentence. Rather than risking jury nullification in these cases, he began to use his discretion to dismiss prior strikes. Soon, the unofficial policy in San Francisco was that Three Strikes would be enforced only against offenders charged with a vio-lent crime. For everyone else, the district attorney would use his discretion to dismiss a prior strike to avoid the mandatory sentence.[42]

This type of adaptive strategy soon raised concerns, though, about the consistency and fairness of application. District attorneys in the more conservative counties in the southern and inland areas were still pressing for full enforcement against all eligible Three Strikes offenders, but prosecutors in more liberal jurisdictions, such as San Francisco and Alameda counties in the north, were using their discretionary authority to selectively impose the law.[43] Researchers studying the courtroom workgroup in 1996 found that it was difficult to predict when prosecutors might exercise discretion, especially if a three-strikes case involved a nonserious felony. Inconsistent practices across county lines meant that no one, including the defendant, could accurately predict when the full sentence might be applied.[44] Conceivably, this difference in prosecutorial strategies meant that a three-strike offender charged with drug possession in San Francisco might be sentenced instead as a two-striker and receive a four-year prison sentence, whereas another three-strike offender charged with drug possession in San Diego would be fully prosecuted and sentenced to 25 years to life.[45] The crime would be the same, the criminal background might also be the same, but because of the prosecutor's use of discretion, the sentences would be vastly different. This problem was magnified when the California Supreme Court extended the use of discretion to judges. Now, the implementation of the law could vary from courtroom to courtroom within the same jurisdiction.

Supporters of Three Strikes countered, however, with evidence suggesting that many of these fears are unfounded. Although they concede that in the early days of implementation there were major differences between counties with regard to how discretion was used, they maintain that by late 1996, prosecutors all over the state had become more comfortable with their ability to petition the court to dismiss prior strikes. This was due in part to a ruling by the California Court of Appeal that confirmed that the law allowed prosecutors to use a substantial amount of discretion in Three Strikes cases.[46] Prosecutors also had come to realize that the public was supportive of discretionary measures that shielded less deserving offenders from the full effects of the law.

By 1998, district attorneys in the state's most populous counties, which produced the most Three Strikes candidates, had implemented internal policies, usually in the form of written guidelines, to help constrain the use of discretion by deputy prosecutors. Most of these policies specified the conditions under which discretion could and could not be used. For example, all of these policies required deputy prosecutors to first consider the severity of the current charge before petitioning the court to dismiss prior strikes. In most counties, a defendant who had been charged with a serious and/or violent felony would be ineligible for discretionary leniency. Conversely, defendants who had been charged with nonserious felony offenses would be considered prime candidates for this type of discretion. Furthermore, a three-striker who had both of his strike offenses originate from a single criminal incident (e.g., a single robbery with multiple victims that resulted in multiple strike convictions) would be a good candidate for discretionary leniency. However, deputy prosecutors were also instructed to examine the offender's entire criminal history as well. Any offender with multiple violent offenses or who had a record of weapon use would be an inappropriate candidate for this use of discretion, as such offenders presented an ongoing public safety threat.[47]

Supporters also argued that the enforcement of internal policies has produced consistent decision making within and across the individual counties. Without some form of oversight, compliance with the law is difficult to maintain. Some counties, like Riverside County in southern California, require deputy prosecutors to attend frequent trainings on Three Strikes to ensure that they fully understand the policy and to address any problems with the policy that may arise. Additionally, almost all urban counties require deputy prosecutors to seek approval from a supervisor before petitioning the court to dismiss a prior strike. Only Los Angeles County, under the direction of District Attorney Steve Cooley, has dropped the supervisory requirement. Although Cooley has retained an internal policy that stipulates what type of cases do and do not qualify for discretionary leniency, deputy prosecutors now have the ability to decide on their own whether an offender's prior strikes should be dismissed. Nonetheless, deviance from the norm is discouraged and prosecutors largely adhere to the policy requirements.[48]

Although there is no state policy on when discretion should and should not be used, the California District Attorneys Association has concluded that district attorneys agree on the most basic premise of the law: dangerous offenders need to be incapacitated. They also agree, for the most part, as to what qualifies an offender for the dangerous rating. Current strikes that involve serious and/or violent felonies are almost always fully prosecuted; only in extreme circumstances might a second- or third-striker escape full punishment for a serious and/or violent felony. Second, strike offenders who have committed less-serious felonies are likely to receive discretionary leniency, but only if their record does not contain a history of violence or weapon use.[49]

Judges' use of discretion is less visible in many ways because it happens on a case-by-case basis. Thus, little is known about how judges exercise their use of discretion in strike cases. Judges, unlike prosecutors, do have more accountability to the system because their decisions may be appealed to a higher court. The appellate courts have on occasion intervened when a judge was perceived as being too lenient. For example, in *People v. Gatson* (1999), a California Court of Appeals ruled that the judge's decision to dismiss a prior strike for a 17-year-old two-strike candidate constituted an unlawful use of discretion. This offender's history (despite his age) identified him as an appropriate candidate for the mandatory doubled sentence.[50] Additionally, the California Supreme Court ruled in *People v. Williams* (1998) that judges must not use their discretion to dismiss prior strikes "in the furtherance of justice" if the past and present record of the offender fell within the "spirit of the law." Thus, offenders with lengthy records or who pose a public safety and recidivism risk fit the profile of offender that the law was intended for; therefore, the court ruled that judges may not use their discretion to dismiss prior strikes for these offenders.[51]

SUMMARY

The California Three Strikes law has generated a great deal of interest from criminal justice professionals, scholars, the media, and policy makers. Its benefits and its problems have been widely publicized and heavily debated. Since the law was implemented in 1994, there have been numerous attempts to reduce its scope and more strictly govern its application. Yet, Californians still support the law and have rejected attempts to change it. However, this support may fade if the concerns identified in this chapter prove valid. Whether the state can continue to shoulder a law that incarcerates 40,000 offenders for long periods remains to be seen. Prison budgets have declined in recent years, but if crime begins to escalate again, financial costs may prove to be the law's undoing. Furthermore, how the state responds to concerns about implementation, fairness, and the effectiveness of long-term punishment will likely determine whether the public will continue to support the law. If it does not, then repeal or substantial reform is only an election away.

NOTES

1. Dickey, *"Three Strikes" Five Years Later.* Dickey presents tallies of Three Strikes inmates through 1998. Twenty-two states reported a combined total of approximately 2,400 offenders sentenced under the newly enacted Three Strikes law. In comparison, California sentenced 40,511 under its Three Strikes law.

2. The initiative version of Three Strikes, which the California courts have declared to be functionally identical, is codified in Cal. Penal Code §1170.12. Although the initiative version technically supersedes the original statute enacted by the legislature, prosecutors and judges typically use the legislative version (Cal. Penal Code §667(b)-(i)) when applying or referencing the Three Strikes law.

3. Cal. Penal Code §667(b)-(i).

4. Under Cal. Penal Code §261(a)(2), the sentence for forcible rape is three, six, or eight years. Six years is the presumptive sentence; three years may be imposed if

there are mitigating circumstances, and eight years may be imposed if there are aggravating circumstances.

5. Cal. Penal Code §2931(b).

6. Cal. Penal Code §2933.1(a).

7. Cal. Penal Code §667(c)(5), *In re Cervera,* 24 Cal.4th 1073 (2001).

8. These lists are not static and can be modified at any time by the legislature or by the people through the initiative process.

9. James A. Ardaiz, "California's Three Strikes Law: History, Expectations, Consequences," *McGeorge Law Review* 32, no. 1 (2000), 1–36.

10. *People v. Garcia,* 21 Cal. 4th 1 (1999).

11. Carlson, *Mandatory Sentencing.*

12. Lowenthal, "Mandatory Sentencing Laws"; Tonry, "Mandatory Penalties."

13. Lowenthal, "Mandatory Sentencing Laws."

14. United States Sentencing Commission, *The Federal Sentencing Guidelines: A Report on the Operation of the Guidelines System and Short-Term Impacts on Disparity in Sentencing, Use of Incarceration, and Prosecutorial Discretion and Plea Bargaining* (Washington, D.C.: United States Sentencing Commission, 1991).

15. Cal. Penal Code §667(g).

16. *People v. Williams,* 17 Cal. 4th 148 (1998).

17. *People v. Superior Court (Romero),* 13 Cal. 4th 497 (1996).

18. Martin Finucane, "Breyer Criticizes Mandatory Minimum Sentences," washingtonpost.com, September 22, 2003; "Supreme Court Justice: Prison Terms Too Long," USAToday.com, August 10, 2003.

19. Zalman, "Mandatory Sentencing Legislation: Myth and Reality."

20. Lewis, "'Three Strikes You're Out.'"

21. Kershner, "Klaases Like Substitute 3 Strikes Bill."

22. Ibid.

23. Ardaiz, "California's Three Strikes Law."

24. Cal. Penal Code §484 defines petty theft, a misdemeanor offense, as theft of property valued at less than $400. In 1977, Cal. Penal Code §666 was amended to allow petty theft with a prior theft offense to trigger a felony sentence for the convicted offender. For more information on the history of petty theft, see Marc Babus, Joseph Perkovich, and Vincent Schiraldi, *Big Time for Petty Crime: The Story of Petty Theft Offenders in California* (San Francisco: Center on Juvenile and Criminal Justice, 1995).

25. Tony Perry and Maura Dolan, "Two Counties at Opposite Poles of '3 Strikes,'" *Los Angeles Times,* June 24, 1996.

26. Greg Krikorian, "Judge Slashes Life Sentence in Pizza Theft Case," *Los Angeles Times,* January 29, 1997. A judge later reduced Williams's sentence to four years in prison after the California Supreme Court gave judges discretion to dismiss prior strike convictions "in the furtherance of justice" in 1996.

27. Joe Domanick, "Dumb Kid, Petty Crimes: A Life Term?" *Los Angeles Times,* July 24, 1998; Greg Krikorian, Ann O'Neill, Miles Corwin, Edward J. Boyer, and Alan Abrahamson, "Front-Line Fights Over 3 Strikes," *Los Angeles Times,* July 1, 1996; Perry and Dolan, "Two Counties at Opposite Poles."

28. Domanick, "Dumb Kid, Petty Crimes."

29. Jim Morrissey, "Nobody Gets Life Just for Stealing a Pizza," *Los Angeles Times,* August 29, 1996.

30. Krikorian, "Judge Slashes Life Sentence."

31. Stephanie Simon, "Backers of Three Strikes Unflinchingly Defend Law," *Los Angeles Times,* July 3, 1996.

32. California Department of Corrections, "Second and Third Strikers in the Institution Population, December 31, 2001" (Data Analysis Unit, Estimates and Statistical Analysis Section, Offender Information Services Branch, California Department of Corrections, 2001).

33. California Department of Corrections and Rehabilitation, "Second and Third Strikers in the Adult Institution Population, December 31, 2005" (Data Analysis Unit, Estimates and Statistical Analysis Section, Offender Information Services Branch, California Department of Corrections and Rehabilitation, 2005).

34. Michael Vitiello, "Three Strikes: Can We Return to Rationality?" *Journal of Criminal Law and Criminology* 87, no. 2 (1997), 395–481.

35. *Ewing v. California,* 538 U.S. 11 (2003); *Lockyer v. Andrade,* 538 U.S. 63 (2003).

36. These cases and the constitutional challenges to Three Strikes are discussed at length in chapter 4.

37. Perry and Dolan, "Two Counties at Opposite Poles"; California District Attorneys Association (CDAA), *Prosecutors' Perspective on California's Three Strikes Law: A 10-Year Retrospective* (Sacramento, Calif.: California District Attorneys Association, 2004).

38. CDAA, *Prosecutors' Perspective.*

39. James Eisenstein, Roy B. Fleming, and Peter F. Nardulli, *The Contours of Justice: Communities and Their Courts* (Lanham, Md.: University Press of America, 1999); Peter F. Nardulli, James Eisenstein, and Roy B. Fleming, *The Tenor of Justice: Criminal Courts and the Guilty Plea Process* (Urbana: University of Chicago Press, 1988).

40. Malcolm M. Feeley and Sam Kamin, "The Effect of 'Three Strikes and You're Out' on the Courts: Looking Back to See the Future," in *Three Strikes and You're Out: Vengeance as Public Policy,* ed. David Shichor and Dale K. Sechrest (Thousand Oaks, Calif.: Sage, 1996), 135–54.

41. John Harris and Paul Jesilow, "It's Not the Old Ball Game: Three Strikes and the Courtroom Workgroup," *Justice Quarterly* 17, no. 1 (2000), 186–203.

42. Perry and Dolan, "Two Counties at Opposite Poles."

43. Ibid.

44. Harris and Jesilow, "It's Not the Old Ball Game."

45. The presumptive sentence for possession of a controlled substance under Cal. Health & Safety Code § 11350(a) is two years. A two-strike sentence for this offense would result in a double sentence of four years.

46. *People v. Kilborn,* 41 Cal. App. 4th 1325 (1996).

47. Jennifer E. Walsh, "Dismissing Strikes 'In the Furtherance of Justice': An Analysis of Prosecutorial and Judicial Discretion Under the California Three-Strikes Law" (Ph.D. Dissertation, Claremont Graduate University, 2000).

48. Jennifer E. Walsh, *Tough for Whom? How Prosecutors and Judges Use Their Discretion to Promote Justice Under the California Three-Strikes Law* (Claremont, Calif.: The Henry Salvatori Center, Claremont McKenna College, 2004).

49. CDAA, *Prosecutors' Perspective.*

50. *People v. Gatson,* 74 Cal. App. 4th 310 (1999).

51. *People v. Williams.*

4

Constitutional Challenges to Three Strikes and You're Out

Three Strikes laws were enacted with the understanding that repeat offenders would no longer be sentenced under the status quo system but would face longer, more severe punishments for continued bad behavior. Proponents reasoned that offenders who remained incorrigible presented a continued public safety threat and that the only way to keep them from reoffending would be to remove them from society for a long time. Deterrence advocates presumed that if felons were threatened with extended sentences upon reoffending, then they would stop their unlawful behavior. Some have also argued that recidivists deserved lengthy punishments because their continued lawlessness demonstrated their lack of remorse and their unwillingness to conform to the requirements of the law. Although Three Strikes laws have been popular with a majority of the public, they have been quite unpopular with offenders who have been subject to their provisions. Consequently, there have been a number of constitutional challenges by offenders who have claimed that habitual offender provisions violated their constitutional rights.

DOUBLE JEOPARDY CLAIMS

Shortly after Three Strikes laws were implemented, opponents challenged the validity of the laws on constitutional grounds. Specifically, they argued that enhanced sentences violated the Constitution's Fifth Amendment double jeopardy clause because offenders' prior crimes subjected them to longer punishments. The double jeopardy clause, which states that no person "shall be subject for the same offence to be twice put in jeopardy of life or limb," prohibits the government from retrying a person once a case has been settled. The clause has also been interpreted as prohibiting multiple punishments for the same crime.[1] In *Price v. Georgia* (1970), the U.S. Supreme Court stated that the double jeopardy provision also prevented a person from being threatened with multiple punishments.[2]

The Court has also stated clearly that habitual offender laws do not impose additional punishment for older offenses. As early as 1948, the Court explained in *Gryger v. Burke* that recidivist offenders are not placed in a new position of jeopardy, nor are they given additional punishment for past offenses.[3] Rather, they face greater punishment for the current offense because the government views the new crime as more severe because of its repetitive nature. Furthermore, the Court has held in *Williams v. Oklahoma* (1959) that details involved in the offender's crime—as well as past convictions—may be considered as aggravating or mitigating factors by the sentencing court.[4]

Since that time, the U.S. Supreme Court has allowed the courts to consider all past behavior—even behavior not resulting in a conviction—when imposing sentences for current crimes. In *Witte v. United States* (1995), the offender was convicted of marijuana possession with intent to distribute. In calculating how much prison time should be imposed, the judge also considered Witte's involvement in a conspiracy to import and distribute cocaine even though he had not yet been charged with that crime. When Witte was subsequently prosecuted and convicted for the cocaine-related offenses, he claimed that he had been subjected to double jeopardy because this conduct had already been used against him in the sentencing of the marijuana case. The Supreme Court rejected Witte's double jeopardy claim, using the *Williams* case to explain that a court may consider evidence of related criminal conduct in the sentencing of one crime without disqualifying it from use in the prosecution of another.

Although the Supreme Court has previously rejected claims that habitual offender sentencing laws violate the Constitution's double jeopardy provision, the Court recently considered a double jeopardy challenge to the California Three Strikes law. The case *Monge v. California* (1998) involved an offender who had been charged with a second strike and was subject to double the usual punishment.[5] His prior offense, assault with a deadly weapon, could qualify as a strike if it could be determined that he personally used the weapon or inflicted great bodily injury on the victim. The California Three Strikes law requires the prosecutor to prove these necessary elements to a judge or jury beyond a reasonable doubt before the strike can be counted against the defendant. In this particular case, the prosecution introduced evidence showing the court that the offender had been sentenced to prison for assault with a deadly weapon, but he did not introduce evidence that proved that the offender had inflicted great bodily injury or had personally used the weapon. The trial court imposed the enhanced sentence anyway, but Monge appealed, arguing that the strike offense had not been proven according to the requirements of the law.

The California Court of Appeal agreed with Monge that the evidence presented was insufficient to trigger the Three Strikes enhancement. Furthermore, the state court told prosecutors that they could not order a new sentencing hearing to present the necessary evidence because doing so would constitute double jeopardy. On appeal, the California Supreme Court reversed the ruling, stating that the U.S. Supreme Court had barred sentencing retrials only in capital cases.

In a 5–4 decision, the U.S. Supreme Court upheld the California Supreme Court ruling, stating that the double jeopardy clause of the Fifth Amendment does not prohibit prosecutors from resubmitting evidence in the sentencing hearing of a noncapital case. Justice O'Connor, writing for the majority, stated that a recidivist enhancement does not constitute an element of the current offense. Therefore, the offender may be retried on the sentencing enhancement because doing so does not subject the offender to a second prosecution on the offense itself. Moreover, the Court stated that "sentencing decisions favorable to the defendant … cannot generally be analogized to an acquittal."[6] Last, the Court reasoned that because the sentencing hearing fulfilled a legislative safeguard—not a constitutional one—the double jeopardy protection did not extend to this particular stage of the process.

Given the Court's unwavering refusal to extend double jeopardy protection to sentencing enhancements, it is unlikely that Three Strikes opponents will be successful in overturning the laws on Fifth Amendment grounds. Habitual offender statutes, regardless of their particular configuration, have been consistently upheld by both state and federal courts. Even if the U.S. Supreme Court undergoes substantial personnel changes in the future, it is unlikely to significantly alter its view of double jeopardy protection.

CRUEL AND UNUSUAL PUNISHMENT

Three Strikes laws have also been challenged on the grounds that lengthy mandatory sentences violate the Eighth Amendment's prohibition against cruel and unusual punishment. While the U.S. Supreme Court has rejected similar claims in the past, its most recent decisions have left open the possibility that sentences like those imposed under Three Strikes might be considered unconstitutional in the future. Therefore, a careful examination of the issues surrounding Eighth Amendment jurisprudence is necessary to understand the possible constitutional implications for Three Strikes sentences.

As with most constitutional issues, the U.S. Supreme Court's interpretation of the Eighth Amendment prohibition against cruel and unusual punishment is predominantly guided by historical and legal considerations. However, historical information on the background on this particular passage is scarce. Congressional records documenting the debate over the Bill of Rights include little information about the origin of the prohibition and other writings fail to reveal the specific reason for its inclusion. Although they cannot be certain, constitutional scholars believe that since the phrase was taken directly from the English Declaration of Rights of 1688, the prohibition against cruel and unusual punishment was likely prompted by a general distrust of those in political power and a concern over a repeat of past abuses perpetrated by the British monarchy.

The Supreme Court recounts much of this history in the landmark case *Weems v. United States* (1910).[7] *Weems* is important to an understanding of the Eighth Amendment because it was the first case in which the Court declared a sentence to be unconstitutionally severe. Additionally, the *Weems* decision identified a "proportionality principle" that the Court has cited repeatedly in subsequent Eighth Amendment challenges. Furthermore, *Weems* is the first to articulate the idea that public opinion about what is constitutionally cruel and unusual may change over time. As a result, the Supreme Court's consideration of the death penalty, lifetime imprisonment for drug offenders, and Three Strikes prison terms have all been influenced by this case (see Table 4.1).

WEEMS V. UNITED STATES (1910)

Weems was a public official with the federal Bureau of Coast Guard and Transportation at a United States government base on the Philippine Islands. His primary responsibility was to disperse funds and to keep accounts of public expenditures. However, while employed by the federal government, Weems falsely recorded that two lighthouse employees had been paid their earned wages when, in fact, they had not. Weems was convicted of intentionally falsifying a public record—a statute found in the Philippine Code—and was sentenced under the law to 15 years of *cadena temporal,* a form of imprisonment that requires the individual to perform "hard and painful labor" while shackled at the ankle and wrist. The statute also prohibited Weems from receiving any external contact or support from family or friends during his period of imprisonment. Furthermore, upon release from prison, he was to be subjected to additional punishment "accessories." Specifically, this meant that he could not participate in any civic or political activities, such as voting or running for political office. Furthermore, he lost his retirement benefits and was prohibited from holding any type of government job. He

Table 4.1
Summary of U.S. Supreme Court Cases Examining Constitutionality
of Lengthy Prison Sentences

U.S. Supreme Court Case	Offender Status	Offense	Sentence Received	Ruling of the Court
Weems v. United States (1910)	First-time offender	Falsifying a public document	15 years of hard labor + lifetime restriction and supervision	Sentence violates the Eighth Amendment. The imprisonment and punishment that follows is cruel and its character is unusual.
Rummel v. Estelle (1980)	Repeat offender	Theft of $120.75 by false pretenses	Life in prison with parole	Mandatory life sentence does not constitute cruel and unusual punishment under the Eighth Amendment.
Solem v. Helm (1983)	Repeat offender	Passed $100 no-account check	Life in prison without parole	Eighth Amendment forbids a lifetime sentence without parole for a seventh nonviolent felony.
Harmelin v. Michigan (1991)	First-time offender	Possession of 672 grams of cocaine	Life in prison without parole	Mandatory term of life in prison without possibility of parole is not cruel and unusual punishment
Ewing v. California (2003)	Repeat offender	Theft of golf clubs valued at $1,200	25 years to life in prison	Sentence is not grossly disproportionate and does not violate the Eighth Amendment prohibition on cruel and unusual punishment.

was also to be supervised by public authorities for the remainder of his life, seeking permission, for example, whenever he wished to move residences.

The statute under which Weems was convicted required a minimum sentence of 12 years plus one day of *cadena temporal* for a single instance of falsifying a public record and a maximum sentence of 20 years of *cadena temporal* for falsifying all public records. Because Weems was convicted of two false entries, the judge sentenced Weems to the minimum sentence of 12 years and a day for the first entry and an additional 3 years for the second entry.

Since he was convicted and sentenced under Philippine law, Weems first appealed his sentence to the Philippine Supreme Court. After he was denied relief, he then petitioned the U.S. Supreme Court for review. Although his request identified a number of complaints, his last argument—that his sentence was cruel and unusual in violation of the Eighth Amendment—was the one that the Court chose to review. In doing so, the Court focused not on Weems's individual sentence of 15 years, but on the statute itself, questioning whether the minimum sentence was constitutional for the crime of falsifying a public document.

In exploring Weems's claim, Justice McKenna, writing the majority opinion for the Court, readily acknowledged that the Court was traveling in uncharted territory. The Court's previous encounters with Eighth Amendment claims had been brief. In *Pervear v. Massachusetts* (1866), the Court declared that a $50 fine and three months' imprisonment and hard labor was not cruel and unusual punishment for the crime of illegally storing and selling liquor without a license.[8] The Court stated in *Wilkerson v. Utah* (1878) that the state's capital punishment statute sanctioning execution by firing squad, hanging, or beheading to be constitutional.[9] Other cases entertained by the Court presenting Eighth Amendment challenges were either dismissed outright or resolved on the basis of other issues.

The Court's decision in *Weems* reiterated that the common interpretation of the Eighth Amendment prohibition precluded the government from committing acts of barbarism and torture. Disemboweling, quartering, burning alive, and other forms of execution involving extreme pain and terror were prohibited. The Court, however, was not willing to declare that sentences were unconstitutional only when they involved "torture or a lingering death." Instead, the Court indicated that the Eighth Amendment prohibition could extend to other types of punishment.

By declaring Weems's sentence to be cruel and unusual, the Court established a precedent for the treatment of noncapital sentences. Specifically, the Court identified three principles by which criminal sentences should be reviewed. First, the sentence ought to be proportional to the offense in both type as well as degree. Though not stated explicitly in the Eighth Amendment, the Court reasoned that this was a precept found in fundamental law and had been accepted as a component of the American justice system. Dissenting justices in the case *O'Neil v. Vermont* (1892) had earlier posited that the Eighth Amendment prohibition applied to "all punishments which, by their excessive length or severity, are greatly disproportioned to the offenses charged."[10] In the *Weems* case, this belief is reiterated by the Court: "[We] believe that it is a precept of justice that punishment for crime should be graduated and proportioned to the offense."[11]

Second, the Court reasoned that constitutional standards ought to evolve to keep up with contemporary standards; what is accepted today may not be tolerated in the future.

Legislation, both statutory and constitutional, is enacted, it is true, from an experience of evils, but its general language should not, therefore, be necessarily confined to the form that evil had theretofore taken. Time works changes, brings into existence new conditions and purposes. Therefore a principle, to be vital, must be capable of wider application than the mischief which gave it birth. This is peculiarly true of constitutions. They are not ephemeral enactments, designed to meet passing occasions. They are, to use the words of Chief Justice Marshall, "designed to approach immortality as nearly as human institutions can approach it." ... In the application of a constitution, therefore, our contemplation cannot be only of what has been, but of what may be.[12]

While acknowledging that a sentence could be found to be disproportionately severe in length so as to violate the prohibition against cruel and unusual punishment, the Court chose to declare the law under which Weems was sentenced to be unconstitutional because of the degree and the kind of punishment it authorized. The length of the punishment was judged to be "cruel in its excess of imprisonment and that which accompanies and follows imprisonment," and the type of punishment was found to be foreign to the American justice system: "[I]t is unusual in its character."[13]

In this decision, the Court also declared that it was the responsibility of the judicial branch to review the constitutionality of criminal sentences. It affirmed that the legislature had the prerogative to identify crimes and set the corresponding penalties; it also confirmed that the judiciary was normally subordinate in this process. However, the Court declared that when excesses were present, the judiciary had a legal duty to ensure that constitutional standards were met.

Subsequent Eighth Amendment challenges added to the logic begun in *Weems*. In the case *Trop v. Dulles* (1958), the Court reasoned that "the basic concept underlying the Eighth Amendment is nothing less than the dignity of man. While the State has the power to punish, the Amendment stands to assure that this power be exercised within the limits of civilized standards."[14] Furthermore, the meaning of the Eighth Amendment prohibition changes according to the "evolving standards of decency that mark the progress of a maturing society," and it is the responsibility of the judiciary to determine what the amendment currently means.[15]

Later, the Court would cite changing societal standards as justification for placing limitations on the use of capital punishment. *Furman v. Georgia* (1972) resulted in a temporary ban on all executions, as the Court declared the administration of the death penalty to be fatally flawed when measured against contemporary standards of justice.[16] Four years later, the Court restored the use of the death penalty under limited circumstances and used the reasoning found in *Weems* and *Trop v. Dulles* to establish criteria for determining when punishment "excesses" occur. First, the Court declared that punishment could not involve the "unnecessary and wanton infliction of pain"; if it did, then it would be considered cruel and unusual. The Court applied this criterion in the case *Hudson v. McMillan* (1992) when it ruled that prisoners could not be subjected to excessive physical force.[17] Second, the Court stated that punishment could not be grossly disproportionate to the severity of the crime. This was used to justify the decision in *Coker v. Georgia* (1977) when the Court declared the death penalty to be disproportionate to the crime of raping an adult woman.[18] It also stated in *Enmund v. Florida* (1982) that a person could not be executed for committing a robbery.[19] Neither crime was judged to be severe enough to warrant execution.

The Court has also applied the grossly disproportionate criterion in cases involving lengthy terms of imprisonment. Three cases in particular, *Rummel v. Estelle* (1980), *Solem v. Helm* (1983), and *Harmelin v. Michigan* (1991), have asked the Court to rule on the constitutionality of lengthy prison sentences. Despite trying to provide an objective, uniform answer for when a prison sentence may be excessive, the Court's trio of responses has created much confusion over how long a sentence can be. Later on, the Court would acknowledge this lack of clarity when it entertained arguments regarding the California Three Strikes law.

RUMMEL V. ESTELLE (1980)

In the first of its contemporary rulings on constitutional proportionality, the U.S. Supreme Court tackled the issue of whether a prison sentence could be considered cruel and unusual in violation of the Eighth Amendment to the U.S. Constitution. In *Rummel v. Estelle* (1980), the Court was asked to consider whether Rummel's allegation that he had been subjected to an excessive punishment for a trivial offense was similar enough to the situation presented in *Weems* so as to support a finding of cruel and unusual punishment.[20] In this case, however, the Court rejected the comparison. Unlike Weems, Rummel was a two-time felon who had previously committed crimes of credit card theft and passing a forged check. Although the total dollar amount of the thefts was low—the combined amount was less than $110—each of the crimes was considered to be a felony punishable by a substantial prison term. Rummel's most recent offense was the crime of obtaining $120.75 by false pretenses, which was normally punished by a prison sentence of 2 to 10 years.

Since he had previously been convicted and sentenced to prison for two prior felonies, Texas sentenced him under its recidivist offender law to a mandatory sentence of life imprisonment with the possibility of parole.

Rummel appealed his sentence, first to the federal district court in West Texas, and then later to the Fifth Circuit Court of Appeals, arguing that his lifetime sentence for a third nonviolent felony was grossly disproportionate to the offense. When an en banc hearing of the circuit court rejected his claim, he filed a final habeas corpus appeal with the U.S. Supreme Court. In his petition, Rummel asked the Court to strike down his lifetime sentence, arguing that it was grossly disproportionate to his offenses. The Court disagreed, stating in a 5–4 opinion that his sentence did not violate the Eighth Amendment's prohibition against cruel and unusual punishment.

In his brief to the Court, Rummel did not dispute the constitutionality of mandatory lifetime sentences but contended that they be reserved for offenders who had committed violent crimes. However, the Court noted that the presence or absence of violence was not a reliable indicator of the severity of the crime; white-collar criminals could commit grave offenses that jeopardized the well-being of many without being considered violent. The Court also stated that the responsibility for determining the appropriate length of a prison sentence belonged to the legislature, not the judiciary.

The Court also declined Rummel's invitation to adopt an interjurisdictional approach to determining when sentences might be excessive. Although Rummel offered evidence that Texas's sentencing law was harsher than that of most states, the Court was not impressed by the comparison. Noting that the distinctions between the states were slight rather than extreme, the Court also stated that the presence or absence of recidivist enhancements, the different parole structures of each state, and the availability of discretion by prosecutors or judges within the judicial system would make direct comparison difficult.

Finally, the Court validated the use of recidivist sentences to accomplish the sentencing goals of deterrence and incapacitation. Noting that Texas was not obligated to treat Rummel the same for his third offense as it had for his first offense, the Court stated that "Texas was entitled to place upon Rummel the onus of one who is simply unable to bring his conduct within the social norms prescribed by the criminal law of the State."[21]

The dissent disputed the notion that a "term of years" sentence was largely immune from constitutional excessiveness, arguing instead that the proportionality principle should be applied to prison sentences as well as capital sentences. Citing examples in English common law, the dissent expressed its belief that proportionality should apply not only to the severity of the sentence but also to the length of the sentence. It also rejected the argument of the majority that utilitarian benefit was enough to justify lifetime sentences for repeat offenders. In explaining its position that deservedness is a requisite component of the proportionality analysis, the dissenting justices argued that "[a] statute that levied a mandatory life sentence for overtime parking might well deter vehicular lawlessness, but it would offend our felt sense of justice."[22]

The dissenting justices were in favor of adopting an objective standard, such as the interjurisdictional comparison proposed by Rummel, and this argument was later to be embraced by a majority of the Supreme Court justices in the case *Solem v. Helm* (1983).[23] In identifying the factors that would make up such a determination, the dissenting justices suggested that federal judges look at the severity of the crime, the sentences imposed for the same crime in other jurisdictions, and the sentences imposed for other crimes within the same jurisdiction. After applying this rule to *Rummel,* the dissenting justices concluded that his sentence was grossly disproportionate to his offenses, and thus violated the Eighth Amendment's prohibition on cruel and unusual punishment.

The *Rummel* decision, despite its attempt to quell constitutional attacks on prison sentences with a firm decision, would not remain law for long. In 1983, just three years after *Rummel,* Justice Blackmun changed positions and sided with the dissenting justices from *Rummel* to rule in favor of the proportionality principle in the follow-up case *Solem v. Helm.* Justice Sandra Day O'Connor, who had replaced Justice Potter Stewart, sided with the former *Rummel* majority in its dissent in *Solem v. Helm.*

SOLEM V. HELM (1983)

In 1983, the U.S. Supreme Court ruled that a prison sentence could be considered cruel and unusual punishment if it violated the proportionality principle inherent in the Eighth Amendment to the United States Constitution. The Court ruled in the case *Solem v. Helm* that a lifetime sentence for a nonviolent recidivist offender without possibility of parole was unconstitutional. Helm was a recidivist offender who had committed six nonviolent felonies, including third-degree burglary, obtaining money under false pretenses, grand larceny, and driving while intoxicated. For his last offense, Helm passed a no-account check (one drawn from a nonexistent bank account) worth $100, which is a felony crime in South Dakota. For this offense, a typical offender would be sentenced to five years' imprisonment and a $5,000 fine. However, because of Helm's extensive record, South Dakota elevated his offense to a Category 1 felony and sentenced him to life in prison without parole.

Helm appealed to the South Dakota Supreme Court, arguing that the sentence constituted cruel and unusual punishment in violation of the Eighth

Amendment to the U.S. Constitution. The state high court affirmed his sentence and the district court denied his writ for habeas corpus. Helm appealed once more to the U.S. Circuit Court of Appeals for the Eighth Circuit, and this time the court agreed with him. In its decision, the circuit court noted that the facts of Helm differed substantially from the facts of the controlling precedent, *Rummel v. Estelle.* Specifically, Rummel's record contained more serious crimes, and although he was also sentenced to life in prison, he would have been eligible for parole after approximately 12 years.

The U.S. Supreme Court upheld the circuit court's decision, declaring Helm's sentence to be disproportionate to his offense in violation of the Eighth Amendment. Previous Supreme Court cases had identified a constitutional principle of proportionality, but these prior instances largely involved incidents of corporal or capital punishment. In this case, the Court established a new precedent wherein a prison term could be ruled cruel and unusual because of its length, not because of the treatment that the prisoner received during the course of his incarceration.

Perhaps anticipating the difficulty of determining an excessive sentence from a nonexcessive sentence, the Court established a three-pronged objective test to aid judges in their assessment of proportionality. First, judges were to evaluate the seriousness of the offense, considering both the severity of the offender's conduct and the harshness of the punishment. Second, courts were to compare the offender's sentence with other sentences within the jurisdiction. The sentence may be excessively long if more serious offenders serve the same amount of time as—or even less time than—the offender in question. Third, judges were to look at sentences in other jurisdictions to determine if the sentence is disproportionate.

Applying these criteria to Helm's case, the Court noted that his offense of passing a no-account check was not trivial, but neither was it serious. It did not involve violence or threats of violence, nor did it result in a great financial loss for the victim. Additionally, his prior offenses, which qualified him for the sentence enhancement under the recidivist offender law, were also relatively minor. In evaluating the sentence, the Court observed that Helm received the harshest punishment—life in prison without parole—offered by the state.

In comparing Helm's sentence with other lifetime sentences imposed in South Dakota, the Court found that only first-time offenders convicted of murder, kidnapping, treason, first-degree manslaughter, and first-degree arson could be sentenced to the maximum penalty. While acknowledging that his recidivist status prevented a direct comparison with these offenders, it also noted that for a second- or third-time felon to receive a lifetime sentence, he would have had to have been convicted of such serious felonies as attempted murder, placing an explosive device on an aircraft, and first-degree rape. Comparing Helm's record with others within the state of South Dakota led the Court to declare that Helm had received the same sentence as those who had been convicted of far more serious crimes.

Last, in comparing Helm's sentence with sentences of similar offenders in other jurisdictions, the Court noted that he could have been sentenced to life in prison for this offense in only one other state—Nevada. But even Nevada's statute merely authorized the possibility of a lifetime sentence without parole. In fact, the Court could not document that Nevada had ever sentenced any defendant under this particular provision. Thus, the Court concluded that Helm's sentence was likely harsher than sentences in any other state in the nation. Concluding that Helm received the maximum sentence for minor conduct, and that this sentence was harsher than what was given to more serious offenders in the state of South Dakota, and harsher than what was being imposed on similar offenders in other states, the Court ruled that his sentence was "significantly disproportionate" to his crime and thus violated the Eight Amendment prohibition on cruel and unusual punishment.

HARMELIN V. MICHIGAN (1991)

When the crack epidemic began to sweep the nation in the mid-1980s, the state of Michigan responded quickly by imposing stiff penalties on drug users. Specifically, the state imposed a mandatory life sentence without the possibility of parole upon first-time offenders found to be in possession of a substantial quantity of controlled substances. This policy resulted in a life sentence for the defendant in *Harmelin v. Michigan* (1991) who was a first-time offender convicted of possessing 672 grams of cocaine.[24] On appeal, Harmelin attacked the Michigan sentencing statute on two constitutional grounds. First, he argued that the sentence was "significantly disproportionate" to his offense in violation of the Eighth Amendment. Second, he contended that mandatory sentences in general were unconstitutional because they fail to consider the individualized circumstances of the offense and the offender. The Michigan Court of Appeals denied Harmelin's claim and the Michigan Supreme Court subsequently refused to hear the appeal, but the U.S. Supreme Court agreed to review the case.

Since the *Solem* decision in 1983, the Court had undergone substantial personnel changes. Now, seven years later, the reconfigured Court upheld Haremlin's sentence in a fractured 5–4 decision. Newly appointed Justice Scalia announced the decision of the Court, although a majority of justices agreed to only part IV of his opinion. Justice Kennedy, also a new appointee, offered a substantial concurring opinion that was joined by Justices O'Connor and Souter.

Citing the apparent contradiction between the Court's decisions in *Rummel* and in *Solem,* Justice Scalia declared that the Court had erred in its decision in *Solem,* concluding that "the Eighth Amendment contains no proportionality guarantee."[25] Scalia argued that the prohibition of cruel and unusual punishment was originally understood to prohibit certain methods of punishment, such as drawing and quartering, burning, beheading, and disemboweling. Scalia also noted that at the time that the Federal Constitution was being drafted, a number of states had already incorporated a proportionality principle explicitly into their State Constitutions. Because early Americans chose not to use explicit language to that effect in the drafting of the Eighth Amendment, the omission appeared to be purposeful, not accidental.

Furthermore, Scalia argued that *Solem*'s objective tests were impossible to administer. The gravity of the offense is often difficult to determine, as there is no objective standard by which we can measure gravity. This prevents the courts from engaging in parts I and II of the *Solem* test, which requires judges first to assess the severity of the offense in light of the sentence and then to compare the sentence with other offenses within the same jurisdiction. Scalia concedes that while the third prong of the *Solem* test—comparison of sentences across jurisdictions for the same offense—can be easily accommodated, it has no bearing on Eighth Amendment standards. Just because one sentence is more severe than a sentence in another jurisdiction does not render the more severe sentence unconstitutional.

Finally, Scalia argued in part IV—the section that a majority of justices agreed upon—that mandatory sentences were not unconstitutional. Scalia noted on behalf of the Court that "severe, mandatory penalties may be cruel, but they are not unusual in the constitutional sense, having been employed in various forms throughout our Nation's history."[26] He acknowledged that the Court had previously required individualized consideration with regard to the imposition of capital sentences. However, maintaining that "death is different" with regard to degree and also with regard to kind, Scalia refused to extend the individualized consideration requirement to noncapital sentences.

Only Chief Justice Rehnquist agreed with Justice Scalia's clear pronouncement that *Solem* was wrongly decided. Justices Kennedy, O'Connor, and Souter voted to uphold Harmelin's sentence and joined Justices Scalia and Rehnquist in rejecting Harmelin's request to ban mandatory sentences but refused to join them in reversing *Solem.*

In his concurring opinion, which was joined by Justices O'Connor and Souter, Justice Kennedy articulated his preference for upholding the "narrow proportionality principle" found throughout the Court's Eighth Amendment jurisprudence. Believing that the apparent contradictions found between

Rummel and *Solem* could be reconciled, Kennedy identified four principles that could be used to guide judges in future cases. First, Kennedy stated that the assessment of a prison term is primarily a legislative judgment and that judges should not attempt to second-guess the wisdom of the legislators. Second, Kennedy acknowledged the different sentencing philosophies (e.g., deterrence, rehabilitation, retribution) to be equally valid and declared that the Eighth Amendment does not require states to adopt one at the expense of another. Third, Kennedy explained that our federal system with independent states will necessarily produce differences with regard to criminal sentencing. Reinforcing a premise found in *Rummel,* he noted, too, that just because one state punishes a crime more harshly than the others does not mean that the punishment violates the Constitution. The lack of clear objective standards by which sentences can be judged means that decisions declaring a term-of-years sentence to be unconstitutional ought to be rare. The fourth principle, Kennedy asserted, offers a summation of his view. "The Eighth Amendment does not require strict proportionality between crime and sentence. Rather, it forbids only extreme sentences that are 'grossly disproportionate' to the crime."[27]

Applying these four principles to the facts of *Harmelin* led Kennedy, O'Connor, and Souter to agree with Scalia and Rehnquist that Harmelin's sentence was not unconstitutionally severe. Kennedy also noted that when the gravity of the offense is severe enough to justify the sentence, which corresponds to the first prong of the *Solem* test, the remaining two tests, comparing the sentence to others within the jurisdiction and comparing like offenders across jurisdictions, are no longer necessary.

Although Kennedy's restatement of the proportionality principle failed to capture the support of a majority of justices, it was followed closely by lower court judges across the nation. Known as the rule of *Harmelin,* it allowed courts to preserve the rudiments of a proportionality principle with a constitutional analysis that was more conservative than the one identified in *Solem.* Nonetheless, the question over whether *Solem* remained valid law created sufficient confusion in the lower courts to justify the Court's revisitation of the matter 13 years later.

CHALLENGES TO THE CALIFORNIA THREE STRIKES LAW

In 2002, the U.S. Supreme Court heard arguments on two cases involving the California Three Strikes law. Although the cases were similar in fact and circumstance, each presented the Court with a separate legal question. *Lockyer v. Andrade* (2003)[28] asked the Court to rule whether the Ninth Circuit Court of Appeals violated the provisions of the Anti-Terrorism and Effective Death

Penalty Act of 1996 (AEDPA) when it agreed to hear Andrade's claim.[29] *Ewing v. California* (2003) asked the Court to rule whether a Three Strikes sentence of 25 years to life for the crime of stealing golf clubs violated the Eighth Amendment's prohibition against cruel and unusual punishment.[30] In spring 2002, the Court agreed to hear the two cases together. Oral arguments were scheduled for the following election day: Tuesday, November 5, 2002.

LOCKYER V. ANDRADE (2003)

A year after California voters ratified Three Strikes, Leandro Andrade was arrested on two separate occasions for shoplifting. In the first instance, he stole videotapes worth $84.70 from a Kmart store in Ontario, California. For the second offense, just two weeks later, he stole more videotapes from another Kmart store in Montclair, California. These tapes were worth $64.84. Andrade told prosecutors that he intended to sell the videotapes to obtain money for heroin.

In both cases, Andrade was charged with the aggravated offense of petty theft with a prior under Cal. Penal Code §§484(a), 486, 666. Under California law, Andrade's theft was considered worse than a typical petty theft because he had one or more previous theft convictions on his record. Petty theft with a prior is treated as a felony offense, punishable by a maximum of one year in county or state prison. However, because Andrade had a prior record that made him eligible for an extended sentence under the California Three Strikes law, he was sentenced to two consecutive 25-year-to-life sentences—one for each theft offense.

Andrade's prior offenses included a misdemeanor drug possession and misdemeanor theft in 1981, for which he was granted participation in a drug diversion program and sentenced to six days in jail and 12 months of probation for the theft offense. In 1982, Andrade was indicted on 10 counts of first-degree residential burglary. He pled guilty to three counts and was sentenced to 120 months in prison. After his release from prison, he was convicted on federal charges of transportation of marijuana and was sentenced to 8 years in federal prison. In 1990, he was convicted of a misdemeanor petty theft charge and was sentenced to 180 days in jail. Later that same year, Andrade was again convicted of transporting marijuana in federal court and was sentenced to federal prison for 5.9 years. In 1991, Andrade escaped from federal prison but was returned to serve out the remainder of his term. He was granted parole in February 1993.

Upon conviction of his two petty theft offenses in 1995, he was sentenced in spring 1996 to two consecutive counts of 25 years to life. Andrade's three residential burglary convictions are considered eligible as strikes under the

California law because they are considered to be serious offenses under Cal. Penal Code §1192.7(c). Each of the petty theft convictions triggered its own 25-year-to-life sentence, but because the court is required to sentence each offense consecutively, the cumulative sentence was 50 years to life in prison.

Andrade filed a habeas corpus petition with the California Court of Appeal, arguing that his sentence violated the Eight Amendment prohibition against cruel and unusual punishment. The California Court of Appeal rejected his claim and the California Supreme Court declined to review the case. The federal district court refused to grant Andrade's habeas corpus petition; however, the United States Court of Appeals for the Ninth Circuit granted his petition under the provisions of the federal Antiterrorism and Effective Death Penalty Act of 1996 (AEDPA) and reversed the California Court of Appeal's ruling.

The AEDPA was enacted to streamline the appeals process for offenders seeking case review by the federal courts. The act prohibits federal courts from granting a habeas petition if a state court has already evaluated the merits of the habeas claim. Federal courts may grant a habeas petition only if the state court decision was contrary to, or involved an unreasonable application of, clearly established federal law as determined by the U.S. Supreme Court.

In Andrade's case, the California Court of Appeal rejected the *Solem v. Helm* analysis, stating that the Court's subsequent decision in *Harmelin v. Michigan* made the validity of the *Solem* proportionality test questionable. Instead, the court compared the facts of Andrade's case to that of *Rummel.* Like Rummel, Andrade had an extensive criminal record that was composed of mostly property offenses. His most recent offense, theft of videotapes, was comparable to Rummel's offense of obtaining $120.75 by false pretenses. Because they were recidivist offenders subject to sentencing enhancement, their punishments were roughly equivalent as well. Rummel received a mandatory life sentence with parole and Andrade received two mandatory 25-year-to-life sentences with the possibility of parole occurring after he serves the initial minimum term. Using the Supreme Court's analysis in *Rummel,* the California Court of Appeal concluded that Andrade's sentence was not grossly disproportionate.

In his appeal to the Ninth Circuit, Andrade argued that the California court's decision reflected an unreasonable application of federal law because it decided the case on the basis of *Rummel,* not *Solem.* The Ninth Circuit Court of Appeals agreed with him, stating that the California Court of Appeal had made a clear error by not applying the *Solem* proportionality test. Although lower courts routinely acknowledged that Justice Kennedy's concurring opinion in *Harmelin* modified the *Solem* test, the Ninth Circuit declared that Kennedy's opinion did not dispute the main holding of *Solem.* The Ninth Circuit Court of Appeals concluded that although the state court reviewed the sentence for gross disproportionality it did not apply the specific criteria identified in *Solem* and therefore reached the wrong conclusion about Andrade's sentence.

The state of California appealed the ruling to the U.S. Supreme Court, arguing that the California Court of Appeal correctly applied the law and that the restrictions on habeas corpus appeals established by the AEDPA should have precluded the Ninth Circuit from reviewing the case. In granting the certiorari petition, the U.S. Supreme Court chose to examine only this particular issue and bypassed the question of whether the California Three Strikes law was constitutional. That specific issue was addressed in the companion case, *Ewing v. California,* which was argued before the Court on the same day.

The Ninth Circuit claimed that it had a right to grant Andrade's habeas petition because the California Court of Appeal had decided the case contrary to clearly established law. Yet, in a 5–4 opinion, the Court disagreed with the Ninth Circuit's assessment. In her opinion for the Court, Justice O'Connor repeated the theme that emerged during oral arguments: there is no clearly established law when it comes to determining the constitutionality of prison terms. In fact, she noted the only clear principle that emerges from *Rummel, Solem,* and *Harmelin* is that the Constitution forbids sentences that are grossly disproportionate to the crime. Furthermore, the Court acknowledged that its cases failed to clearly identify those factors that would indicate gross disproportionality. Therefore, it rejected the Ninth Circuit's assessment that the case was decided contrary to clearly established law because the California court did evaluate the case using the gross disproportionality standard.

The Court also concluded that the Ninth Circuit incorrectly interpreted the AEDPA stipulation that a habeas court may grant a review if the state court unreasonably applied the law. Instead, the Ninth Circuit asserted its right to review the case because the California court made a "clear error" by applying *Rummel* instead of *Solem.* The Supreme Court stated that those two standards are not interchangeable; "unreasonable application" is not the same thing as "clear error." Unreasonable application would occur when a court clearly understood the correct precedent yet unreasonably applied it to the facts of the case. The Court declared that the California court understood from its previous cases that the legislature was entitled to certain deference in the setting of criminal sentences; therefore, it was not "objectively unreasonable" for the California court to uphold Andrade's sentence. The Court concluded that its previous decisions established the tenet that "the gross disproportionality principle reserves a constitutional violation for only the extraordinary case."[31]

Justice Souter disagreed with the Court's decision and filed a dissent joined by Justices Stevens, Ginsburg, and Breyer. He expressed his belief that the California Court of Appeal should have used *Solem* to reach the conclusion that Andrade's sentence violated the Eighth Amendment. Not only did he consider *Solem* to be the appropriate precedent to use, Justice Souter added that he believed the facts of Andrade's case were more similar to those in *Solem* than they were to those in *Rummel.* Specifically, he noted that Andrade was convicted of a property offense for his most recent offense and had previous convictions for property thefts, like the offender in *Solem.* He also indicated that Andrade's two consecutive sentences should be viewed as a single 50-year-to-life sentence, and that for Andrade, this represented a true lifetime sentence. The California court's failure to view Andrade's two sentences as a single punishment in its proportionality analysis resulted in an unreasonable application of the law. Therefore, he felt that the Ninth Circuit Court of Appeals decision to grant Andrade's habeas review was appropriate and that its assessment of Andrade's sentence as being cruel and unusual was correct.

EWING V. CALIFORNIA (2003)

The constitutionality of California's Three Strikes sentencing law came under scrutiny in the companion case, *Ewing v. California* (2003). This case had facts similar to those found in the Andrade case, yet unlike Andrade, this case was granted review solely for the purpose of deciding whether the lengthy sentences imposed on recidivist offenders constituted a violation of the Eighth's Amendment prohibition against cruel and unusual punishment.

Gary Ewing was a four-time felon on parole from prison when he attempted to steal three golf clubs—each valued at $399—from a pro shop by concealing them in his pant leg. A shop employee, who became suspicious when she observed him limp out of the shop, called police. Officers apprehended Ewing shortly afterward and arrested him in the store parking lot.

Ewing was charged with felony grand theft, an offense that qualified him for an enhanced sentence under the California Three Strikes law. Although Ewing had accumulated nine misdemeanor offenses ranging from theft to drug possession to battery over his 16-year criminal career, his four serious felony convictions six years earlier made him eligible for the Three Strikes sentence. During a five-week period in 1993, Ewing targeted an apartment complex in Long Beach, California, and committed three burglaries and a robbery. In two instances, Ewing confronted the burglary victims with a weapon—once with a gun and another time with a knife. In both instances, the victims escaped unharmed. Finally apprehended in December 1993, Ewing was convicted of the four charges and was sentenced to nine years and eight months in state prison. He was released from prison on parole and was still on parole when he was arrested for stealing the golf clubs in 1999.

During his trial for the golf clubs, Ewing asked the judge to reduce his felony theft charge to a misdemeanor. In California, grand theft is considered a wobbler offense because the charge can wobble back and forth between a felony and a misdemeanor. When the property that is stolen has a value of $400 or more, the theft offense is typically charged as a felony. Nonetheless, Ewing could have still had his charge reduced to a misdemeanor if the judge had agreed to the reduction. At the sentencing hearing, however, the judge expressed concern over the aggravated nature of the Long Beach strike offenses, the number of criminal offenses on Ewing's record, and the fact that he was on parole when he committed this offense. After thoroughly considering Ewing's motion, she denied his request.

Ewing also asked the judge to use her discretion to dismiss a prior strike offense. This would allow the judge to temporarily vacate one or more of Ewing's prior strike convictions to keep him from the mandatory sentence. Under California's Three Strikes law, judges are permitted to do this if it would further the interest of justice. If the judge had agreed to Ewing's request, three of Ewing's strikes would be ignored during the sentencing hearing and he would be sentenced as a second-striker, subject to double the usual punishment instead of the mandatory minimum sentence of 25 years to life. Citing the same reasons as before, however, the judge denied this motion as well. Consequently, Ewing was sentenced as a third-striker to the mandatory minimum sentence.

On appeal, Ewing argued that his sentence violated the Eighth Amendment's prohibition against cruel and unusual punishment because his Three Strikes sentence was grossly disproportionate to his offense. In an unpublished opinion, the California Court of Appeal rejected his claim, stating that Ewing was sentenced more harshly because of his past offenses and that the law had a "legitimate goal" of deterring and incapacitating recidivist offenders. The California Supreme Court declined to review, and Ewing appealed to the U.S. Supreme Court.

In his brief to the U.S. Supreme Court, Ewing compared his circumstances to those in the case *Solem v. Helm* (1983) and urged the Court to overturn his sentence, just as it had done for Helm. He stated that his current offense of stealing golf clubs was similar to Helm's crime of writing a $100 no-account check. He also stated that their prior records were similar; Helm had also been previously convicted of several nonviolent felonies, three of which were burglaries. Finally, Ewing declared his sentence of 25 years to life to be comparable to Helm's life sentence; because of his age (38) and failing health, he, too, was likely to spend the rest of his life behind bars.

The state of California responded to Ewing's arguments by reminding the Court of the deference it had previously given to legislative enactments. It warned against a ruling that would replace legislative judgment with subjective judicial opinion, and it sought to reassure the Court that safeguards had been built into the law to prevent injustices from occurring. Specifically, the state noted that three-strikers needed to have at least two serious or violent felonies in their criminal past and that the third strike was required to be a felony; misdemeanor offenses would not be serious enough to trigger the Three Strikes sentence. Furthermore, the mandatory sentence offered parole, a key feature that allowed Ewing's sentence to be distinguished from the sentence in *Solem*. The state also pointed out that the law allowed judges to depart from the required sentence if they determined it to be in the interest of justice. The state concluded that while Ewing's sentence was lengthy, it "reflect[ed] a rational, graduated, and penologically-sound legislative response to the enhanced blameworthiness and substantial threat to public safety posed by serious or violent offenders who continue to commit felonies."[32]

As might be expected, the case generated much interest from outside organizations. In all, a total of five interest groups filed amici briefs with the Court. The states of Alabama, Indiana, Nebraska, Oklahoma, Oregon, Texas, Utah, Washington, and Wyoming filed a joint brief in support of the California legislation, as did the United States government. In addition, the California District Attorneys Association and the California-based Criminal Justice Legal Foundation submitted a brief urging the Court to uphold Ewing's sentence. Only the activist organization Families Against Mandatory Minimums submitted a brief on Ewing's behalf.

At oral argument, the Supreme Court justices voiced several themes that would later appear in their written opinions. Some of the justices disputed Ewing's characterization of his sentence as 25 years to life for the relatively minor crime of stealing golf clubs by pointing out that Ewing faced a longer-than-usual sentence because of his prior record. During the hearing Justice Scalia indicated his support of the sentence by suggesting that if the California law intended to incapacitate the small proportion of the population that committed a vast majority of the crime, then Ewing would be an appropriate candidate.

Other justices questioned how much of an enhancement an offender like Ewing should receive based on his prior record. Although Ewing's attorney conceded that recidivism could trigger a reasonable enhancement, the justices appeared to grapple with each other over how much enhancement was appropriate. One justice asked Ewing's attorney, Mr. Denvir, how much punishment would be appropriate for an offender who stole three golf clubs a hundred times previously. Mr. Denvir responded, "Your Honor, there's no doubt that the prior record … is relevant to the punishment for the present crime, and it does aggravate it. But there are limits to how aggravated shoplifting three golf clubs can be, no matter what has happened before."[33]

When Mr. De Nicola, attorney for the state of California, was questioned about his support for the Three Strikes law, Justice Breyer asked him to provide statistics that disproved that Ewing's sentence was unusual because it was much longer than what offenders in other states might receive. Mr. De Nicola admitted that he could not provide the statistics that Justice Breyer suggested but countered that the issue before the Court involved proportionality, not unusualness. Other justices questioned the wisdom of allowing any felony to count as a third strike, noting that what passes for a felony in California may be considered a misdemeanor elsewhere. However, Mr. De Nicola cautioned the Court not to second-guess the legislature, pointing out that it is not a judicial function to determine what should qualify as a felony offense.

Justice Souter also questioned the impact of the penological theory on the constitutional analysis, noting that if one state imposes a long punishment for the purpose of incapacitation, it makes it difficult to compare it with another state that advances another purpose, such as retribution. Mr. De Nicola conceded that it would be difficult to make a direct comparison but urged the Court to examine both the types of crimes found in the prior record and the sentence itself, which in this case provided for the possibility of parole.

Many constitutional scholars hoped that the Three Strikes issue would provide the Court with the opportunity for finally resolving the *Rummel-Solem-Harmelin* conflict. However, when the Court handed down its decisions in March 2003, it was clear that it had yet to come to an agreement over how the constitutionality of prison sentences ought to be determined. In a fractured 5–4 decision, the Court voted to uphold the California Court of Appeal decision affirming the constitutionality of Ewing's Three Strike sentence. Despite the decision to uphold the sentence, the Court failed to agree on an approach that would clear up the confusion. Justice O'Connor wrote the plurality opinion of the Court, which was joined by Chief Justice Rehnquist and Justice Kennedy. Justice Scalia and Justice Thomas agreed with the Court's decision, but each offered his own concurring opinion explaining his reasons for doing so. Justice Stevens filed a dissenting opinion that was joined by Justices Souter, Ginsburg, and Breyer. Justice Breyer also offered a separate dissenting opinion that was joined by Justices Stevens, Souter, and Ginsburg.

In announcing the decision of the Court, Justice O'Connor based her analysis on Justice Kennedy's concurring opinion in *Harmelin v. Michigan.* In that opinion, Justice Kennedy argued that the Eighth Amendment contained a narrow proportionality principle that applied to noncapital sentences. In

determining whether a sentence exceeded the boundaries established by this
narrow principle, Justice Kennedy recommended that a proportionality review process include the following considerations: the appropriate judicial
deference to the legislature, the legitimacy of a variety of penological schemes,
the nature of our federal system, the need for objective factors to guide the
review process, and an assumption that sentences will be upheld unless they
are grossly disproportionate to the offense. Justice O'Connor proceeded to
use Justice Kennedy's recommended criteria to review Ewing's claim of cruel
and unusual punishment.

In her consideration of the legislative prerogative to set criminal sentences,
Justice O'Connor stated that California's Three Strikes law represented a de-
liberate attempt by the legislature to tackle the problem of recidivism by imposing tougher sentences on repeat felons. This strategy of targeting career
criminals was borne out of public frustration with rising crime rates, and this
particular approach to crime control had been replicated in states across the
nation. She noted that while Three Strikes laws were relatively new, the judiciary had a long-standing tradition of "deferring to legislatures responsible for
enacting and implementing such important policy decisions."[34]

Justice O'Connor also reiterated Justice Kennedy's earlier observation
that the Constitution does not require states to adopt any particular penological justification for their sentencing systems. States may choose to
structure their sentences according to the theory of incapacitation, deterrence, retribution, or rehabilitation, yet this policy decision to adopt one
approach over another belongs to the legislatures, not the courts. In this
case, California had implemented a law that was designed to incapacitate
and deter offenders who had proven to society through their serious or
violent records that they were incapable of conforming to the requirements of the law. O'Connor concluded that since crime committed by
career criminals presented a real threat to the safety and well-being of society, Californians were justified in adopting a law drawn from principles
of incapacitation and deterrence.

To assess whether Ewing's sentence was grossly disproportionate to his
offense, Justice O'Connor first examined the seriousness of Ewing's offense
and the severity of his criminal history. Ewing was convicted of felony grand
theft for stealing property valued at nearly $1,200. In his brief to the U.S.
Supreme Court, Ewing emphasized the fact that grand theft is a wobbler offense in California, which means that it could be treated as either a felony or
a misdemeanor. Justice O'Connor, however, dismissed the importance of this
designation, noting that the offense is presumed to be a felony. In fact, she
noted that the federal government and most states would also categorize this
conduct at the felony level. Furthermore, Ewing's offense could be treated

as a misdemeanor only if the prosecutor or the judge agreed to reduce the charge. Because neither was willing to do so, Ewing was properly convicted and sentenced as a felon.

Justice O'Connor also noted that Ewing's sentence was based in part on his status as a repeat felon. This enhanced sentence for offenders with two or more serious or violent felonies represented a specific goal of the legislature to target career criminals, and the Court was obligated to take this intent into account in its proportionality review. Justice O'Connor felt that because Ewing had accumulated nine misdemeanor convictions, four felony strike convictions, and nine terms of incarceration, his sentence was "justified by the State's public-safety interest in incapacitating and deterring recidivist felons."[35] In summarizing the decision of the Court, Justice O'Connor emphasized that Ewing's sentence reflected a "rational legislative judgment, entitled to deference, that offenders who have committed serious or violent felonies and who continue to commit felonies must be incapacitated."[36] While acknowledging that Ewing's sentence was long, the Court declared that the 25-year-to-life sentence was not grossly disproportionate to the crime of felony grand theft.

Justice Scalia and Justice Thomas agreed with the Court's decision to uphold Ewing's sentence but offered different reasons for their decision. Justice Scalia reiterated his view—first stated in *Harmelin*—that the Eighth Amendment prohibits only certain forms of punishment. He expressed his opposition to any form of proportionality review because the concept of proportionality is tied specifically to the penological theory of retribution. When the goal of sentencing is to incapacitate or deter offenders, the proportionality analysis becomes impossible to apply. Justice Thomas also rejected the analysis offered by the plurality and stated his opinion that the Eighth Amendment contained no proportionality principle.

The justices in dissent focused on the role of the judiciary in determining the proportionality of the punishment and the specific factors present in this case that would have them rule in favor of upholding Ewing's claim. In his dissenting opinion, Justice Stevens argued that the proportionality principle is inherent in the Eighth Amendment, as demonstrated by the Court's treatment of excessive bails and fines as well as cases limiting the use of capital punishment. Moreover, Justice Stevens denied that the lack of a clear standard makes application of the proportionality principle impossible. Judges typically use their discretion to interpret vague laws in a variety of contexts; therefore, judges should "exercise their wise judgment in assessing the proportionality of all forms of punishment."[37] Prior to determinate sentencing reforms, judges were responsible for selecting sentences that were proportionate to the crime. Consequently, they should be able to determine when the proportionality principle has been violated.

In a separate dissent, Justice Breyer reviewed Ewing's sentence, the conduct for which he was sentenced, and the nature of his criminal record and concluded that the facts of Ewing were similar enough to those of *Solem* to warrant a similar finding of gross proportionality. Justice Breyer argued that the conduct represented by Ewing's current offense—stealing golf clubs valued at less than $1,200—was not substantially different, when adjusted for inflation, from Helm's offense of passing a no-account check worth $100. Their prior crimes are also similar; Ewing committed nine misdemeanors and four felonies, three of which were for burglary. Helm committed six felonies, three of which were for burglary. Finally, Breyer noted that while Helm's lifetime sentence was longer, Ewing's sentence of 25 years to life represented a life sentence because Ewing, sentenced at age 38, would likely die in prison.

Despite the similarities, Justice Breyer conceded that the sentence length differences between the two prompted a comparison with other sentences within the jurisdiction and in other jurisdictions according to the criteria established in *Solem v. Helm* and reiterated by Justice Kennedy in *Harmelin v. Michigan*. In comparing Ewing's sentence to others within the state of California, Justice Breyer found that apart from the Three Strikes law, Ewing would have likely received a sentence for 2–4 years for the theft of the golf clubs. Sentence enhancements based on his recidivist statute would have likely added an additional 3–4 years. Furthermore, apart from the Three Strikes law, the only other 25-year-to-life sentence authorized under California law is for nonrecidivist murderers.

Justice Breyer also compared the sentences authorized in other jurisdictions for the same offense. He found that in 33 other states and in federal courts, Ewing would have served no more than 10 years for his offense. In four other states, he would have faced a maximum of 15 years in prison; another four would have capped his sentence at 20 years. Nine other states authorized a sentence of 25 years or more, but Justice Breyer admitted that he could not confirm that anyone actually received a sentence that long.

As a result of his comparative analysis, Justice Breyer determined that Ewing's sentence was two to three times longer than the typical sentence for his crime—even after recidivism was factored in. He expressed particular concern that low-level property offenses, like grand theft, could trigger the Three Strikes sentence. Rationalizing that Ewing's long sentence could not be justified by any particular criminal justice concern, Justice Breyer concluded that Ewing's sentence was grossly disproportionate to his offense and thus violated the Eighth Amendment.

IMPLICATIONS OF THE RULINGS

Although the Supreme Court rulings in the cases challenging the California Three Strikes law may not have established any new precedents for evaluating

Eighth Amendment claims, they will likely reduce the number of success-ful challenges by future Three Strikes offenders. First, the ruling in *Andrade* sent a clear message to the federal courts that the AEDPA precluded them from reviewing cases already decided by state courts. Unless the state court violated clearly established law, or unreasonably applied the law, the federal courts may not get involved. Merely believing that the court made an error or should have reached a different result is not sufficient to overcome the requirements established by the AEDPA. The Supreme Court's firm rebuke of the Ninth Circuit Court of Appeals in the *Andrade* case will likely reduce the willingness of federal courts to entertain habeas claims by Three Strikes offenders who allege that their sentences are unconstitutional.

Second, the *Ewing* ruling reinforced the Court's position that criminal sentences are presumed to be constitutional. By emphasizing the role of the legislature in the sentencing process, the Court appears reluctant to give the judiciary the task of deciding how much punishment is enough—or how much is too much. Furthermore, the Court's decision further undermined the legitimacy of the *Solem* test by declaring that such proportionality reviews should be rare and infrequent. While the *Solem* ruling has not been explic-itly overturned by a majority on the Court, the justices continue to distance themselves from its requirements. Additionally, the Court's decision to up-hold Ewing's sentence means that Three Strikes defendants will likely be un-successful in contesting the constitutionality of their sentences in the future. The fact that the Court refused to strike down a 25-year-to-life sentence for a nonviolent offender convicted of stealing golf clubs means that one of two things will have to happen for an offender to be successful with his Eighth Amendment claim. Either the offender will have to present an even greater discrepancy between an offense and the sentence than what was demonstrated in *Ewing* or the Court will have to change its mind about the standard that should be used to judge the constitutionality of a noncapital sentence. In the meantime, lower courts are likely to interpret *Ewing* as upholding any prison sentence for repeat offenders as long as parole is available.

NOTES

1. *Witte v. United States,* 515 U.S. 389 (1995).
2. *Price v. Georgia,* 398 U.S. 323 (1970).
3. *Gryger v. Burke,* U.S. 334 728 (1948).
4. *Williams v. Oklahoma,* 358 U.S. 576 (1959).
5. *Monge v. California,* 524 U.S. 721 (1998).
6. Ibid., 624.
7. *Weems v. United States,* 217 U.S. 349 (1910).
8. *Pervear v. Massachusetts,* 72 U.S. 475 (1866).
9. *Wilkerson v. Utah,* 99 U.S. 130 (1878).

10. *O'Neil v. Vermont,* 144 U.S. 323, 339–40 (1892).

11. *Weems v. United States,* 367.

12. Ibid., 373.

13. Ibid., 377.

14. *Trop v. Dulles,* 356 U.S. 86, 100 (1958).

15. Ibid., 101.

16. *Furman v. Georgia,* 408 U.S. 238 (1972).

17. *Hudson v. McMillan,* 503 U.S. 1 (1992).

18. *Coker v. Georgia,* 433 U.S. 584 (1977).

19. *Enmund v. Florida,* 458 U.S. 782 (1982).

20. *Rummel v. Estelle,* 445 U.S. 263 (1980).

21. Ibid., 284.

22. Ibid., 288.

23. *Solem v. Helm,* 468 U.S. 277 (1983).

24. *Harmelin v. Michigan,* 501 U.S. 957 (1991).

25. Ibid., 965.

26. Ibid., 994–95.

27. Ibid., 1001.

28. *Lockyer v. Andrade.*

29. *Antiterrorism and Effective Death Penalty Act of 1996,* Pub. L. No. 104–132, 110 Stat. 1214 (Apr. 24, 1996).

30. *Ewing v. California*

31. *Lockyer v. Andrade,* 77.

32. *Ewing v. California,* Brief for Respondent, 8.

33. *Ewing v. California,* Transcript of Oral Argument, 26.

34. *Ewing v. California,* 24.

35. Ibid., 29.

36. Ibid., 30.

37. Ibid., 33.

5

Implementation and Impact of Three Strikes Laws

After Three Strikes laws were enacted, criminal justice professionals, scholars, and other observers became concerned about the possible negative impacts that the laws would have on the overall justice system. Mandatory sentences, which had become commonplace by the mid-1990s, usually affected a smaller, more narrowly defined group of offenders, such as narcotics abusers or gun users. Moreover, their impact on the overall system itself was often minor in that many of the mandatory penalties imposed only moderate sentence enhancements on offenders. Massachusetts, for example, imposed a relatively short one-year mandatory penalty for the crime of gun carrying, and Michigan imposed a two-year sentence enhancement on felons who used guns during the commission of their crimes. A few states, such as New York and Michigan, imposed lengthy mandatory penalties on drug offenders, but these laws usually affected a narrow class of criminals. Three Strikes policies, on the other hand, required lengthy sentences to be imposed on a potentially broad segment of the offending population. As a result, some predicted that the combination of these two features would have a substantial impact on the functioning of the justice system.

Scholars have found, however, that the potential influence of any law is dependent on the degree to which it is implemented. Previous research has shown that legislation that is not enforced will not have much of an impact at all. In the case of mandatory sentencing laws, offenders receive the required penalties only if prosecutors and judges comply with the terms of the law. If they do not use the law, or if they somehow adapt the law to maintain the status quo, then the law will have little to no effect on the way the justice system functions. On the other hand, if prosecutors and judges fully implement the law, then it can greatly affect how the whole system functions. Assuming that Three Strikes laws would be implemented as written, many feared that the laws would produce a number of negative side effects. First, it was expected that in many states, court dockets would become overloaded as more strike defendants sought acquittal—and thus escape from the mandatory sentence—through the trial process. This, in turn, would lead to jail overcrowding and increased workloads for those in the criminal justice system. Second, many were concerned that Three Strikes laws would exacerbate the problem of minority overrepresentation in the prisons because they would capture a larger percentage of minority defendants. Third, it was predicted that Three Strikes laws would crowd prisons and cost the states millions, or even billions, of dollars each year to incarcerate repeat offenders for longer periods. More money would be needed to build more prisons and to pay for the cost of incarcerating inmates for a longer time.

Early reports indicated that some of the predictions about case workload, impact on minority groups, and prison overcrowding had initially come true. However, three to four years after implementation, the negative effects began to dissipate, and these concerns became less compelling over time. In particular, criminal and civil case backlogs disappeared, workload levels decreased, and the number of new prisoners stabilized. Some suggested that the rapid reduction in the nation's crime rate was responsible for the nonexistent side effects in that fewer felony offenses means that there are fewer Three Strikes offenders. Others suggested that the system adapted to Three Strikes laws by reducing the degree of implementation to a more manageable level. Regardless of the reason, evidence suggests that the laws are causing fewer overall problems today than what was originally anticipated.

CONCERN #1: VOLUME OF THREE STRIKES CASES MAY OVERLOAD LOCAL SYSTEMS

Will Three Strikes Increase the Number of Criminal Trials?

Although the United States prides itself on the constitutional due process rights available to criminal defendants, few offenders actually take advantage of their most prominent right—the right to trial by jury. Instead, national statistics show that nearly 90 percent of all criminal cases end in negotiated plea bargains, wherein the offender pleads guilty, forfeiting his right to a jury trial, in exchange for a reduced sentence. Today, criminal trials are typically reserved for those offenders who are accused of very serious crimes and those who are facing long prison sentences (or the death penalty). Offenders also exercise their right to trial by jury when they believe that they have a reasonable chance of being acquitted. For everyone else, the prosecution and defense teams are quick to negotiate a deal—a guilty plea in exchange for a lighter sentence—in which the sentence is usually based on the established going rate for that crime in that jurisdiction. Because plea bargaining allows cases to be settled quickly, it is considered by the courtroom work group to be an indispensable tool for the swift processing of criminal cases. Without it, cases would take longer to resolve, and a backlog of pending cases would threaten the functioning of the entire system.

Despite its widespread use and apparent necessity for the smooth functioning of the judicial system, plea bargaining has frequently been the target of criticism and scorn. Many members of the public—and some lawmakers—believe that plea bargaining allows the offender to "get away with something" because the negotiations often revolve around sentence reductions for offenders. Consequently, when the public wants to get tougher with criminals, plea bargaining is often restricted or prohibited altogether. This was the case with most of the Three Strikes laws that were enacted by the states. All but four states (Arkansas, Connecticut, Kansas, and Nevada) made Three Strikes sentences mandatory while other states, such as California, included language in the statutes that specifically prohibited plea-bargaining practices.[1] As a result, the restriction on plea bargaining was expected to increase the number of Three Strikes cases going to trial because prosecutors would no longer be able to offer sentence reductions in exchange for guilty pleas. This, in turn, would lead to courtroom delays for other criminal and civil cases.

One of the first studies to estimate the impact of Three Strikes on the court system was commissioned by the Board of Supervisors for the County of Santa Clara, California. Using 1992 baseline statistics, county representatives projected that Three Strikes-related cases would soon constitute 28 percent of their felony case filings and would affect 2,315 offenders. Furthermore, they predicted that all strike offenders, including those accused of their first strike, would likely take their case to trial because of the long-term consequences that strike convictions would produce. Accordingly, they estimated that offenders would request 385 more trials each year, constituting a 200 percent increase over previous levels. They also estimated that court-related hearings to contest various issues, such as the admissibility of evidence, would increase by 85 percent, accounting for an extra 50,000 days of court processing time. Finally, authorities concluded that the workload associated with jury selection would increase, as more jurors would be needed for the additional criminal trials.[2]

Another study of the impact of Three Strikes in Los Angeles County, California, revealed that within the first two years of the law's enactment, the number of criminal cases going to trial increased substantially. Before Three Strikes went into effect, approximately 70 percent of all criminal cases in Los Angeles County ended in a plea-bargained sentence. Another 25 percent of the cases were dismissed because of evidence problems, and the remaining 4 percent to 5 percent were resolved through the trial process. However, after the Three Strikes law was implemented, 25 percent of the defendants eligible for the sentencing enhancement began to insist on a jury trial, hoping, perchance, that a sympathetic jury might acquit them of the charges.[3] Perhaps what is even more significant is that the remaining 75 percent of Three Strikes cases did *not* go to trial. Statistics provided by the county indicated that 19 percent were dismissed by prosecutors or judges for lack of evidence, and 11 percent resulted in charge reductions that carried a less severe, non–Three Strikes sentence. The remaining 45 percent of Three Strikes cases were resolved through a negotiated settlement, despite the official ban on plea bargaining.[4]

Although scholars attributed the substantial plea-bargaining activity to the increased workload and pressure on prosecutors to resolve backlogged cases, the Los Angeles County District Attorney's Office defended its plea-bargaining practices as being consistent with the parameters established by California law. Before Three Strikes had been in effect for very long, deputy prosecutors were admonished by the department's administrative leaders to exercise their discretion to dismiss prior strike convictions only in extreme cases. But prosecutors soon discovered that the situations that would typically warrant the dismissal of prior strikes happened more frequently than they had originally anticipated. In fact, the Los Angeles County District Attorney's Office estimated that 40 percent of all third-strike cases involved either minor drug offenses or felony petty thefts, which were two crimes that they considered to be undeserving of the 25-year-to-life mandatory sentence. Thus, prosecutors explained, the 45 percent figure was consistent with their authorized use of discretion to dismiss prior strike offenses in the furtherance of justice.[5]

To help courts handle the increased volume of cases going to trial, some counties established special courtroom teams that worked only on Three Strikes cases. County officials in San Diego County, California, attempted to handle the growing backlog of criminal cases by identifying certain judges, prosecutors, and public defenders as Three Strikes experts. Members of this special courtroom workgroup worked exclusively on Three Strikes cases to resolve them quickly and efficiently. Additionally, the dedicated team helped county officials avoid two specific problems. First, it helped them to comply with California speedy trial rules that required cases to go before a judge for an initial examination within 60 calendar days of arraignment. If this deadline was not met because judges were backed up with other cases, authorities would be obligated under law to let the offender go free. Second, it helped them avoid case delays for civil complaints. Before Three Strikes was enacted, county officials had worked diligently to reduce the wait time for civil cases from four years to about 12–15 months, and they wanted to ensure that the new law did not undermine this progress.[6]

By 1995, the California Legislative Analyst's Office (LAO) indicated that many of the predictions about the increased workload brought about by Three Strikes cases had begun to materialize.[7] Statewide data indicated that within the first eight months of enactment only 14 percent of two-strike cases and 6 percent of three-strike cases were resolved through plea bargaining. In many counties, the added pressure to accommodate more jury trials resulted in a growing backlog of criminal cases. In some counties, district attorneys had decided to forgo prosecution of misdemeanor cases to concentrate on serious ones. Civil cases, too, had experienced backlog-related delays after just a few months of the law's enactment. Within seven months, for example, no civil cases filed in Los Angeles went to trial in 3 of the county's 10 courthouse facilities, and more than half of the court-rooms regularly dedicated to civil matters were converted for use in criminal trials. Additionally, county officials predicted that eventually between two-thirds and three-fourths of all courtrooms would be used to handle criminal cases. The LAO further noted that civil parties would likely turn to other arrangements, such as arbitration, to resolve their cases. This would mean that the county would forfeit filing and other court-related fees, reducing the amount of incoming revenue that the court system relied on to defray some of its operating costs.[8]

Even two years after the law went into effect, California courts reported that they were struggling to keep up with the additional workload demand. A statewide survey found that in 28 percent of the county courts, accounting for more than half of the state's felony filings, Three Strikes had increased overall workload by more than 10 percent. Courts also reported that strike cases were more likely to go to trial: only 4 percent of nonstrike cases went to trial, whereas at least 9 percent of second-strike cases and 41 percent of third-strike cases were sent to trial. Furthermore, court officials reported that the administrative workload had also increased because more staff time was needed to prepare records and certify prior convictions, collect data on two- and three-strike cases, and certify cases for appeal. As a result, courts were forced to shift resources away from civil disputes to criminal matters, causing a backlog of civil cases in at least 17 of the 58 counties.[9] In response to the growing demands on the courts, the California legislature authorized in 1996 an additional $3.5 million in state funding for the judicial system so that courts could hire more help for the extra cases. Up to 30 retired judges were brought back on a temporary basis to help county courts resolve the extra cases produced by the large number of two- and three-strike filings.[10]

In contrast, officials in Georgia did not expect the law to produce many courtroom delays because the scope of its Three Strikes law was fairly narrow. In fact, in three of the state's most populous counties, strike cases accounted for only 3 percent to 7 percent of all felony filings, with most of this increase accounted for by first-strike offenders. Consequently, the courtroom delays produced by Three Strikes were minimal. Although Three Strikes defendants, like those in California, were more likely to take their cases to trial, the overall impact on the court system was very small because relatively few offenders faced the possibility of receiving the lengthy mandatory sentences.[11]

Will Three Strikes Increase the Local Jail Population?

With the increase in the number of serious offenders awaiting trial, many feared that local jails would become overcrowded as well. Typically, city or county jails are responsible for housing offenders for brief periods while their cases are pending before the courts. Serious offenders who have been denied bail, or cannot afford to post bail, are held almost exclusively in local jail facilities while they are on trial. However, jails also imprison less serious offenders who have already been tried, convicted, and sentenced to short prison terms. Because jails perform this dual function, they often become overcrowded—especially since authorities often have a difficult time estimating in advance how many offenders will be housed at any given time.

Prior to Three Strikes, severe overcrowding conditions had prompted federal judges to temporarily take over management of some facilities to alleviate conditions that were viewed as cruel and unusual. Some of the judges relieved the overcrowding pressure by requiring officials to find alternative housing for inmates or by ordering the release of inmates back into the community. After Three Strikes was enacted, officials became even more concerned about the overcrowding problem, given that most jail facilities had little room to accommodate the additional offenders who would be housed while awaiting trial. Consequently, many feared that they would have to once again release other inmates early to make room for Three Strikes offenders.

In some California counties, preliminary reports indicated that local officials were, in fact, resorting to early release to accommodate the extra inmates. In 28 of the 58 counties, jail officials were already under federal orders to maintain strict enrollment caps, so when Three Strikes inmates were brought in for holding, other offenders had to be released to make room for the new felons. In many jurisdictions, such as Los Angeles County, local officials released misdemeanor offenders who were serving their sentences to make room for Three Strikes inmates awaiting trial. County officials estimated that within the first few months under the new Three Strikes law, misdemeanor offenders served 20 percent less time than they had prior to Three Strikes. San Bernardino County also reported that it had to turn away offenders arrested for misdemeanor offenses because the growing number of strike offenders awaiting trial had led to overcrowded jail facilities.[12]

Georgia also experienced jail overcrowding, but researchers concluded that the overcrowded conditions were not caused by the Three Strikes law. Although the total number of jail admissions in two of its most populous counties increased after the law went into effect on January 1, 1995, the additional volume was not produced by Three Strikes.[13] In fact, Three Strikes cases accounted for fewer than 1 percent of all jail inmates in these two counties. Furthermore, researchers concluded that even without the Three Strikes sentencing law, these defendants, who were accused of very serious crimes, would have been detained in jail anyway while they waited for their trials to end. Moreover, two of the three counties showed no signs of case-processing delays, which meant that Three Strikes inmates were not staying longer than usual while waiting for their case to be resolved. Only Fulton County experienced case delays, but much of this was attributable to the extra arrests that police made during the 1996 Summer Olympic Games in Atlanta. Finally, researchers noted that the increase in jail admissions after Three Strikes was part of a larger trend that began in the late 1980s, several years before the Three Strikes law was enacted.[14]

CONCERN #2: THREE STRIKES MAY DISPROPORTIONATELY AFFECT MINORITY OFFENDERS

As states began to enact tough Three Strikes laws targeting repeat offenders, some expressed the concern that the new sentencing legislation would disproportionately affect minority groups. In the past, nationwide statistics revealed that more minority offenders faced arrest, conviction, and incarceration when compared to nonminority offenders. This finding held true for property offenders, violent offenders, and repeat offenders. Prior to the civil rights movement, much of this discrepancy could be explained by the presence of overt bias in the system. However, many of the sentencing reforms that were adopted in the 1970s and 1980s were designed to root out this prejudice. As a part of this reform process, mandatory sentencing laws, which eliminated discretion over the sentencing decision, were enacted so that all eligible offenders would receive identical penalties. Judges would no longer have an opportunity to favor one group of offenders over another.

Today, minority offenders are still overrepresented in the criminal justice system, but much of that imbalance is attributed to socioeconomic disparities and differences in offending patterns. To simplify much research, scholars have found that crime is often correlated with poverty and that racial and ethnic minority groups suffer from economic hardship more frequently than whites. Thus, crime is higher in the poorest areas, and impoverished communities are more likely to be populated minority groups. Additionally, law enforcement agencies often target high-crime neighborhoods for rigorous enforcement. This usually results in more minorities being apprehended and prosecuted, which, in turn, increases the number of minorities in the prison system. This cycle tends to repeat itself as offenders who have been convicted of and sentenced for a crime are more likely to be sentenced to prison if convicted of subsequent offenses.[15]

Although much of the overt bias levied against minority offenders in the criminal justice system has been eliminated in recent years, research has shown that race is still correlated with harsher treatment. Black offenders, for example, often receive less favorable treatment by prosecutors when it comes to charging decisions. They also often receive harsher sentences by judges when the court has discretion over the sentencing decision. Yet, researchers have also found that the correlation between race and harsher treatment is usually attributable to offending status, not race itself.[16] Once a person has been arrested and convicted, his status as a repeat offender usually means that he will be treated more severely by prosecutors and judges. Prosecutors are less likely to reduce the charges in plea-bargaining negotiations, and judges are less likely to sentence repeat offenders to probation or suspend their sentences to help them avoid incarceration. Thus, sentences like Three Strikes may be applied more often to minority offenders because a disproportionate number of minority offenders have a prior record.

However, not all observers are convinced that the system is devoid of explicit racial bias. The fact that more minority defendants are arrested and convicted in the first place raises suspicion with some that police may be targeting minorities in their law enforcement practices. Recent revelations of policing practices that utilize forms of racial profiling have only enhanced these concerns. Because of these findings, scholars and community activists following the implementation of Three Strikes policies have expressed concern that bias might also be present in the charging and sentencing of minority offenders.

Although only a few studies have examined the impact of Three Strikes laws on minority populations, all of the published reviews to date have found that racial and ethnic minorities are overrepresented among offenders who have received the mandatory sentences. Florida's habitual offender law, which many viewed as a precursor to current Three Strikes policies, was found to incarcerate 22 percent of black defendants as habitual offenders but only

12 percent of whites. Researchers compiling the statistics indicated that the discrepancies could not be explained by differences in the offenders' prior criminal record or the nature of the most current offense.[17]

One of the first reviews of the impact of California's Three Strikes law on minority defendants found that within the first six months of implementation, black defendants in Los Angeles County were charged with the sentencing enhancement at a higher rate than white defendants. The Los Angeles County Public Defender's Office reported that although blacks made up 10 percent of the general population, they were involved in 30.5 percent of felony case filings and 57.3 percent of third-strike cases. In comparison, non-Hispanic whites comprised 36.6 percent of the general population, yet they were charged in only 19.7 percent of felony cases and were involved in 12.6 percent of the county's third-strike cases.[18]

A follow-up report on California's Three Strikes law found that two years after the law was enacted, blacks were still overrepresented in the groups of offenders who were arrested and sentenced under the law. Statewide statistics collected by the California Department of Corrections determined that as of 1996, black defendants made up 23 percent of those who were arrested for felony offenses, 31 percent of the general prison population, and 43 percent of the offenders who were sentenced to the minimum 25-year-to-life sentence. These figures were considered highly disproportionate considering that blacks made up only 7 percent of the statewide general population. In contrast, non-Hispanic whites constituted 53 percent of the general population but comprised only 33 percent of felony arrestees, 29.5 percent of prison inmates, and 24.6 percent of third-strike offenders. This meant that blacks were arrested for felony offenses at 4.7 times the rate of non-Hispanic white offenders and were incarcerated at 7.8 times the rate of non-Hispanic whites. They were also imprisoned for third-strike offenses at 13.3 times the rate of non-Hispanic whites.[19]

Although observers have not alleged that overt bias was responsible for these discrepancies, they have suggested that subtle biases might influence the treatment of defendants at various points in the process. Judge Theodore A. McKee, a California circuit judge for the Third Circuit Court of Appeal, made news in 1996 by proposing that individual acts of discretion might be the cause of minority overrepresentation in the Three Strikes population. He speculated that bias could be introduced during the decision to arrest a person, the decision to prosecute an offender, the decision to file a Three Strikes sentencing enhancement against him, or any combination of these. Because prosecutors have the ability to exercise discretion to decide who gets the mandatory minimum sentence and who does not, he encouraged district attorneys to promote more minority prosecutors to supervisory positions to prevent bias from influencing the decision-making process.[20]

Needless to say, the suggestion that California's Three Strikes law specifically targeted minority offenders generated much controversy. In the past, some criminologists had described the overrepresentation of minorities as an unfortunate reality of urban crime, but in this situation, the availability of prosecutorial (and later, judicial) discretion to dismiss prior strikes in the furtherance of justice led some to propose that prosecutors were not doing all that they could to remedy racial imbalances.[21] Prosecutors, in response, bristled at the suggestion that their decisions to pursue Three Strikes sentences were biased against minority defendants. Gregory Totten, Executive Director of the California District Attorneys Association in 1996, argued that such reports were flawed. Furthermore, he dismissed the suggestion that prosecutors made decisions that were racially motivated. He noted that prosecutors were "ethically bound to be colorblind" in their decision making and that the Three Strikes law had done much to protect members of the minority community who were often victimized by repeat offenders.[22]

Although more offenders are sentenced under California's Three Strikes law than in any other state, reports from other areas indicated that some minority groups were overrepresented in those jurisdictions as well. Washington State, for example, had a black population of approximately 4 percent, but in 2001, blacks made up 22.5 percent of the prison population and 37 percent of the state's Three Strikes offenders.[23] Yet, supporters of the Washington Three Strikes law have insisted that the law is fair in its function and application. To highlight this point, they cite government statistics that show that other minority groups are underrepresented in the pool of Three Strikes offenders. For example, in 2001, Hispanics made up 6.2 percent of Washington's general population and 12.3 percent of the state prison population, but only 3 percent of the Three Strikes population. The state's Asian residents made up 5.9 percent of the general population but constituted only 2.6 percent of the prison inmate population and 1 percent of the Three Strikes population. In contrast, non-Hispanic whites represented 88.7 percent of the general population, 70.8 percent of the total prison population, and 55 percent of the state's Three Strikes offenders.[24] John Carlson, author of Washington's Three Strikes law, argued that statistics like these prove that the law does not target race but instead targets only those who commit serious and violent crime.[25]

Additional data from California revealed that although the imbalances were not as skewed as they had been in 1994, blacks and Hispanics in California were still overrepresented among the state's Three Strikes offenders nearly 10 years after the law went into effect. As with other criminal justice policies, statistics indicated that minority offenders were incarcerated under Three Strikes at higher rates than nonminority offenders. Specifically, the rate of incarceration for third-strike offenses was 12 times higher for blacks than it was for non-Hispanic whites, and the combined rate of incarceration for second- and third-strike offenses was over 10 times higher for blacks than it was for non-Hispanic whites. Furthermore, there were also differences in the rates of incarceration between Hispanics and non-Hispanic whites. The rate of incarceration on a third-strike offense was 45 percent higher for Hispanics than it was for non-Hispanic whites; when second- and third-strike offenses were combined, the rate of incarceration for Hispanics was over 78 percent higher than the rate for non-Hispanic whites.[26]

Statistics compiled by the California LAO confirmed again in October 2005 that minorities were overrepresented in the strike offender population. However, it did not find any evidence to suggest that Three Strikes was making the problem worse. Specifically, the LAO reported that although blacks represented 37 percent of two- and three-strike offenders, Hispanics represented 33 percent, and non-Hispanic whites represented 26 percent, this racial and ethnic breakdown was nearly identical to the composition of the entire prison population. This finding suggests that Three Strikes had not exacerbated the problem of disproportional representation in the state's prison system; instead, minorities were being sentenced under the law at nearly the same rate as they had been under other criminal justice policies. The only statistical anomaly to contradict this conclusion was found in the rate of incarceration for black offenders. In general, blacks represented approximately 30 percent of all prison inmates, but they accounted for approximately 45 percent of the state's three-strike offenders.[27]

A study of Oregon's mandatory sentencing policy, Measure 11, which was adopted in 1994 at the same time the Three Strikes movement was sweeping the nation, also found that while minorities were overrepresented in the state's prison system, the change in the sentencing structure did not make the problem worse. Although Oregon's law was not considered a Three Strikes policy because the sentences applied to all offenders, not just repeat offenders, it featured lengthy mandatory sentences for certain felony offenses—just like Three Strikes. Furthermore, prosecutors were found to use their charging discretion to bypass the law for those offenders who were considered to be undeserving of the sentences, as many prosecutors also did under Three Strikes policies. Researchers found that even though discretion was used regularly to mitigate the effects of the law, it was not used in a racially biased manner. Overall, minority offenders fared no worse under the new law than they had under the previous sentencing scheme.[28]

CONCERN #3: THREE STRIKES MAY LEAD TO PRISON OVERCROWDING

Will Three Strikes Produce Prison Overcrowding in California?

When the California Three Strikes law was first introduced, the general understanding was that inmate populations would increase and that the extra inmates would cost the state more money to house. Yet, people still supported the measure because they believed that the increase in prison-related expenditures would be worth the concomitant reduction in crime. However, when the RAND Corporation released its predictions in October 1994, shortly before Californians went to the polls to vote on Three Strikes, most were surprised by the magnitude of the projected increases. According to RAND researchers, the broad strike zone created by the statutory version of Three Strikes (and proposed by the initiative version) would result in explosive growth in the state's prison population. They predicted that the combined effect of large numbers of two- and three-strikers serving lengthy sentences would double the prison population from approximately 125,000 in 1994 to 250,000 inmates in 1998. Furthermore, they predicted that the state prison population would nearly triple in 10 years to 350,000 inmates. This increase in the number of prisoners would cost taxpayers an average of $5.5 billion per year, with most of the increase allocated for prison operating costs. In fact, they estimated that the state's current budget allocation for the Department of Corrections would have to increase by more than 100 percent, swelling the agency's share of the state budget from 9 percent to 18 percent. This would mean taxpayers would have to choose between suffering large tax increases—unlikely, given California's anti-tax political climate—or imposing drastic reductions in spending for higher education and health and welfare programs.[29] Five-year projections by the California Department of Corrections (CDC) confirmed RAND's conclusion. It estimated that its prison population would more than double from approximately 120,000 in mid-1994 to nearly 250,000 by June 1999, far outstripping the prison capacity of 170,000 inmates.[30]

Since then, supporters of the Three Strikes law have pointed out that the predictions of both inmate population growth and associated costs had been severely overestimated. Although the prison system did experience modest growth during the first five years, increasing from 124,813 inmates in 1994 to 162,064 in 1999, the number of inmates stabilized at the 162,000 level through 2001 and then actually declined to approximately 158,000 inmates in 2002.[31] Only in 2004 and 2005 did the prison populations exceed 162,000; in 2004, the population was 163,500 and in 2005, it increased to 164,179.[32] Correspondingly, supporters also point out that the predictions about budgetary problems caused by Three Strikes also failed to come true. Instead of doubling in size, the state Department of Corrections budget shrunk by one-third, from 9 percent of the overall state spending in 1994 to just 6 percent in 2004.[33]

Researchers have since admitted that some of the parameters that guided their original analyses failed to account for decreasing crime rates and the use of prosecutorial (and later, judicial) discretion that reduced the number of strike offenders sentenced under the law. They have also acknowledged that the enactment of Proposition 36 in 2000, which required nonviolent drug offenders to be sentenced to treatment instead of prison, diverted some strike offenders away from the prison system. Substantial decreases in the state's crime rate also meant that fewer people overall were being sentenced under the law, which also reduced the strain on the state's correctional system.[34] Still, critics point out that within the first 10 years, Three Strikes was responsible for significant increases in the state prison population. Specifically, the prison population grew by 22.6 percent, from 125,473 in 1994 to 153,783 in June 2003, and the percentage of two- and three-strikers in the institution increased from 3.5 percent in 1994 to 27.2 percent in June 2003. They argued that this upward trend, especially if it increased as fast as it had in the past, would place a substantial financial burden on the state's budget. Not only does each additional strike offender cost the state $27,000 per year in prison operating costs, but strike offenders stay in prison much longer, which also serves to increase prison-related costs. At a time when the state's budget is in a precarious position, this type of cost increase, they point out, is even harder to bear.[35]

Still, supporters of the law contend that the costs associated with incarcerating repeat offenders are inconsequential next to the costs associated with high crime rates. Instead of viewing incarceration-related expenses as a taxpayer burden, supporters of Three Strikes view these expenses as an investment in the social and financial well-being of the people. In his four-year assessment of Three Strikes, California Attorney General Dan Lungren credited Three Strikes with reducing the state's crime rate and estimated that the law was responsible for saving the state almost $6 billion in tangible (measurable) costs, which included lost productivity, medical care, public safety services, property damage losses, and victim services, and another $10.5 billion in intangible (immeasurable) losses, such as reduced quality of life, pain and suffering, and mental anguish. When compared to the relatively small cost of incarcerating a serious felon, the attorney general concluded that the investment was well worth the benefit. He argued that the people should question not whether the state could afford to maintain Three Strikes, but rather whether the state could afford to abandon Three Strikes.[36]

Will Three Strikes Cause Prison Overcrowding in Other States?

When the Three Strikes law was approved in Washington in November 1993, officials estimated that between 40 and 75 offenders would be sentenced to life in prison under its provisions each year. Although these numbers did not threaten to overwhelm the prison system, the cost of incarcerating that many offenders for life would not be inconsequential, either. In reality, though, far fewer inmates were sentenced under Three Strikes than originally anticipated. Three and a half years after the law was implemented, fewer than a hundred offenders (97) had been sentenced under the Three Strikes law.[37] By 2004, 10 years after implementation, only 209 offenders had been sentenced to life in prison under its provisions.[38] This averages out to slightly more than 20 offenders per year and fewer than two offenders per month. Washington prison officials noted that their original projections had assumed that drug-trafficking offenses would qualify as prior strikes, but the final version of the law contained no such provision. Additionally, their initial calculations were based on the number of strikes committed each year, not the number of strike offenders. Because strike offenders often commit multiple offenses, fewer persons were responsible for those crimes than originally anticipated.[39]

Nationwide, prison admission figures have consistently increased since states adopted an overall get-tough approach in the 1980s and 1990s, but budget surpluses allowed policy makers to defray the costs without having to cut services in other sectors. But, with declining tax revenues impacting states across the nation, prison costs have recently begun to negatively affect state budgets in other areas. As a result, state officials have expressed concern over the increase in health care expenditures for inmates given that prisons now hold many more aging prisoners.[40]

Although it would seem as though Three Strikes states would be facing more of these prison-related problems than non–Three Strikes states, recent statistics have shown that Three Strikes jurisdictions are no worse off than other areas of the country. In fact, Louisiana was the only Three Strikes state to make the top five list of states that posted the highest incarceration rates per resident population in 2003. Furthermore, there appears to be no observable trend between Three Strikes states and non–Three Strikes states with regard to prison population changes. This holds true even for those states that frequently invoke their Three Strikes laws. California, for example, recorded only a small increase (1.1% to 5%) in the number of state prisoners in 2002–2003, while Georgia reported that its inmate numbers remained virtually the same as the year before.[41] Additionally, three of the Three Strikes states posted moderate to significant decreases in the number of inmates (–14.9% to –1.1% decrease); seven states reported static numbers (–1.0% to 1.0% change); 11

states reported low to moderate increases in their prison populations (1.1% to 5.0% increase); and four Three Strikes states, Florida, Indiana, Montana, and North Dakota, reported moderate to significant increases in the number of prison inmates (5.1% to 11.4% increase). In comparison, four non–Three Strikes states reported decreases, three states reported static numbers, nine states reported low to moderate increases, and seven non–Three Strikes states recorded moderate to significant increases in their prison populations. Thus, these recent statistics show that Three Strikes states appear to be doing as well as, if not better than, non–Three Strikes states in keeping their prison admission numbers under control.

Similarly, there appears to be no observable pattern between Three Strikes states and non–Three Strikes states with regard to prison-related costs, since both groups reported comparable figures with regard to budget expenditure increases for the 2004–2005 fiscal year.[42] California led the states in increased expenditures, posting a 15.8 percent increase for the year, but most of the states that posted increases reported much smaller percentages. The national average was 4.9 percent, and 17 of the 25 Three Strikes states reported increases lower than that average. Seven states, including California, had higher percentage changes than the national average, and one state, New Jersey, posted a rate equal to the national average. In comparison, 17 non–Three Strikes states also posted an increase less than the national average; seven states posted increases higher than the national average, including Wyoming, which reported a one-year double-digit increase of 13.1 percent; and one state, Kentucky, could not provide data.[43]

DEGREE OF IMPLEMENTATION

Despite the initial concerns about the impact of Three Strikes policies on the nation's criminal justice system, it became clear within the first few years that in some areas the predicted impacts never materialized, and in other areas they appeared initially but then quickly vanished. As researchers and statisticians analyzed the initial data, they found that only a handful of states were actually using their laws on a regular basis, even though policy makers assumed that the laws would be routinely enforced for all eligible offenders. California led the nation in the number of cases prosecuted and sentenced under its Three Strikes law, but as shown in Table 5.1, only a few states used their laws to any measurable degree within the first 10 years of implementation. Georgia has used the law with some regularity, as have Florida, Virginia, and Nevada, but many states that adopted Three Strikes laws have rarely used them. In fact, by 2004 nearly half of the original 24 states had sentenced fewer

Table 5.1

Number of Offenders Sentenced under Three Strikes Laws as of 2004

State	Strike Zone Defined	Strikes Needed	Required Sentence	Number of People Sentenced
Alaska	All strikes must be serious felonies	Three	40–99 years in prison	1*
Arkansas	Murder, kidnapping, robbery, rape, terrorist act	Two	Minimum 40 years in prison; no parole	
	1st-degree battery, firing a gun from a vehicle, use of prohibited weapon, conspiracy to commit murder, kidnapping, robbery, rape, 1st-degree battery, 1st-degree sexual abuse	Three	Range of no-parole sentences, depending on offense	5
California	Any felony if one prior felony conviction is serious or violent felony	Two	Double the presumptive sentence	
	Any felony if two prior felony convictions are serious or violent felonies	Three	Indeterminate life sentence, with no parole eligibility for 25 years	42,322
Colorado	Any Class 1 or 2 felony, or any Class 3 felony that is violent	Three	Mandatory life in prison; parole eligibility after 40 years	4
Connecticut	Murder, attempted murder, assault with intent to kill, manslaughter, arson, kidnapping, aggravated sexual assault, robbery, 1st-degree assault	Three	Up to life in prison	1
Florida	Any forcible felony, aggravated stalking, aggravating child abuse, lewd or indecent conduct, escape	Three	Life if 3rd strike is 1st-degree felony, 30–40 years if 2nd-degree felony; 10–15 years if 3rd-degree felony	1,628
Georgia	Murder, armed robbery, kidnapping, rape, aggravated child molesting, aggravated sodomy, aggravated sexual battery	Two	Mandatory life without parole	
	Any felony	Four	Mandatory maximum sentence	7,631

Table 5.1
(Continued)

State	Strike Zone Defined	Strikes Needed	Required Sentence	Number of People Sentenced
Indiana	Murder, rape, sexual battery with a weapon, child molesting, arson, robbery, burglary with a weapon or resulting in serious injury, drug dealing	Three	Mandatory life without the possibility of parole	38
Louisiana	Murder, attempted murder, manslaughter, rape, armed robbery, kidnapping, serious drug offenses, serious felony offenses	Three	Mandatory life in prison without possibility of parole	N/A
	Any four felony convictions with at least one on above list	Four	Mandatory life in prison without possibility of parole	
Maryland	Murder; rape; robbery; 1st- or 2nd-degree sexual offense; arson; burglary; kidnapping; car jacking; manslaughter; use of firearm in felony; assault with intent to murder, rape, rob, or commit sexual offense. Separate prison terms required for each offense.	Four	Mandatory life in prison without parole	330 (approx.)
Montana	Deliberate homicide, aggravated kidnapping, sexual intercourse without consent, ritual abuse of a minor	Two	Mandatory life in prison without parole	0
	Mitigated deliberate homicide, aggravated assault, kidnapping, robbery	Three	Mandatory life in prison without parole	
Nevada	Murder, robbery, kidnapping, battery, abuse of children, arson, home invasion	Three	Life with parole possible after 10 years, or 25 years with parole after 10 years	304
New Jersey	Murder, robbery, carjacking	Three	Mandatory life in prison without parole	10

(Continued)

Table 5.1
(*Continued*)

State	Strike Zone Defined	Strikes Needed	Required Sentence	Number of People Sentenced
New Mexico	Murder, shooting at or from vehicle and causing harm, kidnapping, criminal sexual penetration, armed robbery resulting in harm	Three	Mandatory life in prison with parole eligibility in 30 years	0
North Carolina	47 violent felonies; separate indictment and finding that offender is "violent habitual offender"	Three	Mandatory life in prison without parole	22
North Dakota	Any Class A, B, or C felony	Two	If 2nd strike is Class A felony, court may sentence to life; if Class B felony, up to 20 years; if Class C felony, up to 10 years.	10
Pennsylvania	Murder, voluntary manslaughter, rape, involuntary deviate sexual intercourse, arson, kidnapping, robbery, aggravated assault	Two	Enhanced sentence of up to 10 years	50 (approx.)
	Same offenses	Three	Sentence of up to 25 years	
South Carolina	Murder, voluntary manslaughter, homicide by child abuse, rape, kidnapping, armed robbery, drug trafficking, embezzlement, bribery, certain accessory and attempt offenses	Two	Mandatory life in prison without parole	14
Tennessee	Murder, aggravated kidnapping, robbery, arson, or rape; rape of a child. Prior prison term required.	Two	Mandatory life in prison without parole	14
	Same as above, plus rape, aggravated sexual battery. Separate prison terms required.	Three	Mandatory life in prison without parole	
Utah	Any 1st- or 2nd- degree felony	Three	3 years to life without parole; judge has discretion	N/A

Table 5.1
(Continued)

State	Strike Zone Defined	Strikes Needed	Required Sentence	Number of People Sentenced
Vermont	Murder; manslaughter; arson causing death; assault and robbery with weapon causing injury; aggravated assault, sexual assault, and domestic assault; kidnapping; maiming; lewd conduct with a child	Three	Court may sentence up to life in prison	16
Virginia	Murder, kidnapping, robbery, carjacking, sexual assault; conspiracy with above crimes	Three	Mandatory life in prison without parole	328
Washington	Murder, manslaughter, rape, child molestation, robbery, aggravated assault, explosion with threat to humans, extortion, kidnapping, vehicular assault, arson, attempted arson, burglary, any felony with deadly weapon, treason, promoting prostitution, leading organized crime	Three	Mandatory life in prison without parole	209
Wisconsin	Murder, manslaughter, vehicular homicide, aggravated battery, abuse of children, robbery, sexual assault, taking hostages, kidnapping, arson, burglary	Three	Mandatory life in prison without parole	9
Federal government.	Murder, voluntary manslaughter, assault w/intent to commit murder or rape, robbery, aggravated sexual abuse, abusive sexual contact, kidnapping, aircraft piracy, carjacking, extortion, arson, firearms use, serious drug crimes	Three	Mandatory life in prison without parole	35**

*As of August 1998. **As of September 1996.
Sources: Austin et al., *"Three Strikes and You're Out": Implementation and Impact*; Dickey, *"Three Strikes" Five Years Later*; Schiraldi, et al., *Three Strikes and You're Out: An Examination of the Impact.*

than two dozen offenders to the required mandatory sentence, and seven of those states had sentenced fewer than 10 offenders. Furthermore, two states, Montana and New Mexico, reported no Three Strikes convictions at all.[44]

Because only a few states have regularly used their Three Strikes laws, the impact of the legislation is less than what was originally anticipated. This may be due in part to the fact that crime fell much faster than analysts had predicted. Most experts used 1992–1993 crime data—which included record-high figures—to calculate how many Three Strikes offenders might be sentenced under the new law. However, because crime quickly declined from these peak levels, there were fewer offenders who were eligible for the new mandatory sentences.

Implementation was also affected by the overlap of Three Strikes with other preexisting sentencing laws. Because repeat offenders were already subject to longer prison sentences in most states, the adoption of Three Strikes legislation did not radically change the treatment of recidivist offenders. In fact, in many jurisdictions, the differences between the prior laws and the new Three Strikes laws were subtle; some states expanded the list of offenses that would be subject to additional punishment while others extended sentences that were already lengthy.[45] For example, before Louisiana adopted its Three Strikes law, it already required a mandatory life sentence without parole for offenders convicted of a fourth felony. When it adopted its Three Strikes policy, the legislature kept the life sentence requirement but dropped the stipulation that two of the prior offenses had to be either serious drug offenses or violent crimes. Additionally, Maryland maintained the same sentencing scheme that it had under its previous law but added carjacking and armed carjacking to the list of eligible strike offenses. Similarly, when Virginia enacted Three Strikes, it included drug distribution offenses to its list of eligible crimes that triggered the extra punishment. Thus, because many of the sentencing laws were similar to previous laws, prosecutors and judges may have not thought the new policy worth pursuing because the end result was largely the same. Additionally, most states repackaged their previous habitual offender laws in such a way that the zone of eligibility continued to be narrowly drawn. This, in turn, kept the number of potential offenders low and minimized the impact that Three Strikes cases would have on the states' justice systems.[46]

Finally, fewer offenders may have received the mandatory minimum sentences because prosecutors and judges used their discretion to bypass the law for a number of offenders. Previous research has shown that when prosecutors and judges believe a sentence to be too harsh or too restrictive, they will often engage in avoidance practices to mitigate the sentence for a particular offender. Prosecutors might charge a defendant with a less serious crime to avoid the mandatory sentence, or judges might sentence the offender to either a different sentence (e.g., probation instead of prison) or a lesser sentence in defiance of the law. In some cases, prosecutors or judges have been known to dismiss the charges altogether to avoid the mandatory penalty.

In Georgia, state officials became concerned about possible avoidance practices when an audit revealed that prosecutors and judges were often failing to apply the Three Strikes enhancement. Some prosecutors and judges cited their ignorance of the law as the reason they did not apply it. Others indicated that they had forgotten to use it, and still others noted that their failure to apply the enhancement was intentional. Prosecutors and judges have complained that Georgia's law, which requires an automatic 10-year sentence for first-time offenders who are convicted of one of the seven strike offenses, is too severe for first-time offenders. Prosecutors have also objected to the provision that excludes first-time offenders from parole consideration. This restriction has eliminated the incentive for offenders to participate in rehabilitation programs, increasing the likelihood that they will recidivate once they are released from prison. Because of these objections, some prosecutors in Georgia admitted to bypassing the Three Strikes law for first-time offenders so that they would not receive the automatic penalty.[47]

Some states allow judges to have some discretion over the imposition of a Three Strikes sentence. In Kansas, for example, the state authorizes judges to double the sentence for a two-time violent felon or triple the sentence for a third-striker, but it also gives them the discretion to choose an alternate sentence instead. Similarly, Nevada gave judges a range of possible Three Strikes sentencing options to choose from, including life without parole, life with parole after a minimum of 10 years, or 25 years with possible parole after a minimum of 10 years.[48] Because judges have been given this discretion, not all eligible Three Strikes offenders in these states necessarily receive a Three Strikes sentence. Thus, the projected impact of the laws in these jurisdictions may be less than what was originally predicted.

Discretion has also been officially incorporated into the functioning of California's Three Strikes law. Although the use of discretion has been controversial because of the potential inconsistency with which it is applied, it has nevertheless resulted in a substantial number of three-strike offenders escaping the mandatory 25-year-to-life sentence. Statewide statistics on the frequency of use are not available, but research has shown that in San Diego County during the first several years of the law's implementation, prosecutors exercised their discretion to dismiss prior strike convictions in the furtherance of justice in 27 percent of eligible three-strike cases. Furthermore, after judges were granted the same discretion in 1996, discretion was exercised in another 28.5 percent of the cases. Thus, when the two sources of discretion were combined, more than half (55.5%) of the eligible third-strikers actually received a penalty that was less than the mandatory sentence.[49]

SUMMARY

When Three Strikes laws first debuted in the mid-1990s, most practitioners and criminal justice professionals expressed concern that a tidal wave of Three Strikes cases would threaten the stability of the nation's criminal justice system. Increased sentences and plea-bargaining restrictions would increase the number of cases going to trial, and local jails would struggle to find room for inmates awaiting trial. After conviction, the additional Three Strikes offenders being sentenced to prison would cause the prison populations to dramatically increase, forcing states to make stark choices about their budgetary priorities.

Once the laws were implemented, however, many of the dire predictions never came true. California counties experienced a brief surge in Three Strikes-related problems, but within a few years, the negative side effects had dissipated. Substantial reductions in crime, coupled with more frequent use of discretion by prosecutors and judges, worked together to reduce the number of Three Strikes cases that were fully sentenced under the law. Still, California and a few other states are presently experiencing increases in prison-related expenditures that may be attributed to the rising health costs associated with larger numbers of aging prisoners. However, this phenomenon is not just found in Three Strikes states. Other states have had to grapple with increases in prison costs, rising prison admission numbers, and a large group of geriatric prisoners who will likely grow old and die in prison.

As states struggle with tough budgetary choices, the effectiveness of the laws becomes the all-important issue. If the laws are costly but effective in keeping crime low, then state lawmakers may decide to increase taxes or cut costs elsewhere to keep the laws fully functional. However, if the laws are not proven to be effective, then policy makers will likely act to either repeal the laws or reform them so that they present less of a tax burden to the people.

NOTES

1. Clark et al., *"Three Strikes and You're Out": A Review of State Legislation.*

2. Center for Urban Analysis, Office of the County Executive, Santa Clara County, California, *Assessing the Impact of AB971.*

3. Since Three Strikes cases accounted for 13 percent of all felony filings, the number of additional trials represented a sixfold increase over the previous two-year period.

4. Alan Abrahamson, "25% of Three-Strikes Cases Go to Trial, Straining Courts," *Los Angeles Times,* July 2, 1996.

5. Ibid.

6. Tony Perry, "'Three-Strikes' Law Spawns Specialist System in San Diego County," *Los Angeles Times,* March 14, 1995.

7. Legislative Analyst's Office, *Status Check: The "Three Strikes and You're Out" Law—A Preliminary Assessment* (Sacramento, Calif.: Legislative Analyst's Office, 1995).

8. Ibid.

9. Judicial Council of California, Administrative Office of the Courts, *"Three Strikes" Summary* (San Francisco: Judicial Council of California, 1998).

10. James Austin, John Clark, Patricia Hardyman, and D. Alan Henry, *"Three Strikes and You're Out": The Implementation and Impact of Strike Laws* (Washington, D.C.: U.S. Department of Justice, National Institute of Justice, 1999).

11. Ibid.

12. Legislative Analyst's Office, *Status Check.*

13. Austin et al., *"Three Strikes and You're Out": Implementation and Impact.*

14. Ibid.

15. John H. Kramer and Jeffrey T. Ulmer, "Sentencing Disparity and Departures from Guidelines," *Justice Quarterly* 13, no. 1 (1996), 81–106.

16. Joan Petersilia and Susan Turner, "Guideline-Based Justice: Prediction and Racial Minorities," *Crime and Justice: A Review of Research* 9 (1987), 151–81 .

17. Reynolds Holding, "Behind the Nationwide Move to Keep Repeaters in Prison," *San Francisco Chronicle,* December 8, 1993.

18. Vincent Schiraldi and Michael Godfrey, *Racial Disparities in the Charging of Los Angeles County's Third "Strike" Cases* (San Francisco: Center on Juvenile and Criminal Justice, 1994).

19. Greg Krikorian, "More Blacks Imprisoned Under '3 Strikes,' Study Says," *Los Angeles Times,* March 5, 1996.

20. Ibid.

21. Ibid.

22. Ibid.

23. Scott Sunde, "Blacks Bear Brunt of '3 Strikes' Law," *Seattle Post-Intelligencer*, February 20, 2001.

24. Ibid.

25. John Carlson, "Three-Strikes Law Works," *Seattle Post-Intelligencer*, March 1, 2001.

26. Scott Ehlers, Vincent Schiraldi, and Jason Ziedenberg, *Still Striking Out: Ten Years of California's Three Strikes* (Washington, D.C.: Justice Policy Institute, 2004).

27. Brian Brown and Greg Jolivette, *A Primer: Three Strikes. The Impact after More than a Decade* (Sacramento, Calif.: Legislative Analyst's Office, 2005).

28. Nancy Merritt, Terry Fain, and Susan Turner, *Oregon's Measure 11 Sentencing Reform: Implementation and System Impact* (Santa Monica, Calif.: RAND Corporation, 2004).

29. Greenwood et al., *Three Strikes and You're Out: Estimated Benefits and Costs.*

30. Austin et al., *"Three Strikes and You're Out": Implementation and Impact;* Legislative Analyst's Office, *The "Three Strikes and You're Out" Law: An Update* (Sacramento, Calif.: Legislative Analyst's Office, State of California, 1997).

31. California Department of Corrections, "Fall 2003 Population Projections, 2004–2009" (Sacramento, Calif.: Population Projections Unit, Estimates and Statistical Analysis Section, Offender Information Services Branch, Department of Corrections, September 2003).

32. California Department of Corrections and Rehabilitation, "Spring 2006 Adult Population Projections, 2006–2011" (Sacramento, Calif.: Population Projections Unit, Estimates and Statistical Analysis Section, Offender Information Services Branch, Department of Corrections and Rehabilitation, February 2006).

33. Recent budget calculations are available at http://govbud.dof.ca.gov/Budget-Summary.

34. Austin et al., *"Three Strikes and You're Out": Implementation and Impact;* Ehlers et al., *Still Striking Out.*

35. Ehlers et al., *Still Striking Out.*

36. Dan Lungren, *"Three Strikes and You're Out"—Its Impact on the California Criminal Justice System after Four Years* (Sacramento: California Attorney General's Office, 1998). Lungren's argument that Three Strikes is responsible for the drop in crime is debated in chapter 6.

37. Austin et al., *"Three Strikes and You're Out": Implementation and Impact.*

38. Vincent Schiraldi, Jason Colburn, and Eric Lotke, *Three Strikes and You're Out: An Examination of the Impact of 3 Strike Laws 10 Years after Their Enactment* (Washington, D.C.: Justice Policy Institute, 2004).

39. Austin et al., *"Three Strikes and You're Out": Implementation and Impact.*

40. Arturo Perez, "States Wrangle with Corrections Budgets," *State Legislatures* 31, no. 5 (2005),19–20.

41. Ibid., The change in Georgia was included in the category that posted a change in the number of inmates of –1.0 percent to 1.0 percent.

42. Ibid.

43. Ibid.

44. Austin et al., *"Three Strikes and You're Out": Implementation and Impact.*

45. Clark et al., *"Three Strikes and You're Out": A Review of State Legislation.*

46. Ibid.

47. Austin et al., *"Three Strikes and You're Out": Implementation and Impact.*

48. Clark et al., *"Three Strikes and You're Out": A Review of State Legislation.*

49. Walsh, "Dismissing Strikes 'In the Furtherance of Justice.'"

6

Effectiveness of Three Strikes Laws

Three Strikes laws impose severe sentences on repeat offenders to reduce crime through deterrence and incapacitation. Supporters of the laws believe that deterrence may be achieved in two ways. First, mandatory sentences are likely to convince the habitual offender to abandon his criminal career to avoid the lengthy Three Strikes sentence. Second, the mandatory penalties are severe enough that they are likely to discourage other would-be offenders from pursuing a life of crime. Incapacitation, on the other hand, would reduce crime by isolating from the rest of society known career criminals, who may be responsible for committing dozens—even hundreds—of crimes per year. Although these offenders might still try to commit crimes from within the prison institutions, their criminal reach would be short, and they would not affect the safety and well-being of the law-abiding public.

In the more than 12 years since Three Strikes laws were enacted, the question frequently asked by lawmakers and members of the public is: Do the laws work? Government statistics reveal that crime across the nation has decreased significantly since 1994, which is the year that many Three Strikes laws took effect. In fact, the nation's crime rate plummeted in some places to 30-year lows. Supporters of Three Strikes were quick to attribute the decreasing crime rate to the effectiveness of the laws, but critics of Three Strikes argue that the decrease in crime may have been caused by other factors, such as demographic and economic changes, that make crime less likely. To assess which interpretation is correct, researchers have conducted numerous studies, ranging from inmate interviews to sophisticated statistical analyses, to determine if the laws are responsible for this decrease in crime. However, with all of the variables and possible permutations that these studies can include, the results have been somewhat contradictory. Consequently, both sides have claimed that the data support their position.

EVIDENCE OF CRIME REDUCTION

The one fact that both supporters and opponents of Three Strikes laws agree on is that crime dramatically decreased after the laws were passed. Statistics collected by local, state, and federal government agencies confirm that beginning in 1994, crime began a precipitous drop from its record-high levels. In many areas of the country the crime rates did not stop their decline until after the turn of the century.

Annual crime statistics are provided by the Federal Bureau of Investigation (FBI) through its *Uniform Crime Report* (UCR) program. In its annual report, the FBI compiles the number of major violent and property crimes reported to local police agencies across the nation. The offenses represented in the UCR, called Index Crimes, include violent offenses, such as murder, voluntary manslaughter, forcible rape, robbery, and aggravated assault. Property crimes, including burglary, larceny/theft, and motor vehicle theft, are recorded also. Statistics from the UCR show that the nation's crime rate dropped considerably between 1993 and 2004 for both violent and property crimes. During this period, violent crime decreased by 38 percent and property crime dropped by 26 percent.[1] By 2004, the national violent crime rate was at its lowest point since 1973, and property crime had not been lower since 1969. Many states recorded similar results. Even the nation's most populated states, which typically have the highest crime rates, posted considerable decreases in the number of offenses reported to police. As seen in Table 6.1, California's violent crime rate decreased by 49 percent and property crime declined by 36 percent. In New York, violent crime decreased by a stunning 59 percent and property crime declined by an impressive 51 percent. At almost 2,200 property crimes per 100,000 residents, the rate in New York was at its lowest point since modern record keeping began in 1960. Texas posted the least dramatic reductions of the four most populous states, but the decrease still reached double-digit percentage levels.[2]

Analysis of Crime Reduction

The aggregate figures reported by the FBI are useful because they identify how much crime has occurred and whether crime levels have increased

Table 6.1
Crime Rates of Most-Populous States*

	California		Florida		New York		Texas	
	Violent	Property	Violent	Property	Violent	Property	Violent	Property
Rates in 1993	1,077.8	5,379.1	1,206.0	7,415.0	1,073.5	4,477.8	762.1	5,677.0
Rates in 2004	551.8	3,419.0	711.3	4,179.7	441.6	2,198.6	540.5	4,494.0
Percentage of rate reduction from 1993–2004	49	36	41	44	59	51	29	21
Year of last lowest rate	1972	1962	1977	1968	1967	Pre-1960	1984	2000

*The rates are expressed as number of crimes per 100,000 people. The government excludes the murder and nonnegligent homicides that occurred as a result of the events of September 11, 2001.

Source: Bureau of Justice Statistics, www.ojp.usdoj.gov/bjs/.

or decreased. Yet, the UCR cannot explain *why* crime rates are going up or going down. Rather, that task is delegated to statisticians, economists, criminal justice professionals, and social scientists who analyze different variables to discover why crime has either increased or decreased. A definitive answer is often difficult to obtain, however, because analyses with different data and different variables will many times yield different results. Researchers are confident, though, that as more studies are done over time, the reasons for crime reduction can be deduced.

Most of the research studies that examine the effectiveness of Three Strikes laws attempt to accomplish two objectives. First, studies typically analyze the crime rates for jurisdictions that have adopted Three Strikes laws to verify that crime has indeed decreased. This is an important first step because if crime rates *increased* in areas that enacted Three Strikes laws, then it would be difficult to attribute any crime control effectiveness to those measures. So far, all of the studies completed to date have found substantial reductions in crime in those jurisdictions that have adopted a Three Strikes policy. Second, researchers may then try to determine if the decrease in crime is attributable to the Three Strikes law. Usually, this type of analysis is done with statistical computations that allow researchers to simultaneously consider how Three Strikes laws and several other crime-related variables have affected the crime rate. This technique helps the researcher to determine if the decrease is attributable to the law, or if the decline is related to one of the other factors included in the study. Some studies have also attempted to determine if the laws have produced a measurable deterrent or incapacitation effect that has contributed to the decrease in crime.

Although the Three Strikes movement impacted half the states, most of the studies have focused on the effectiveness of California's law. With more than 40,000 offenders sentenced thus far, researchers have plenty of data to work with. A few studies, though, have attempted to cull data from other states to study the effectiveness of the laws in those jurisdictions as well. Some of the findings support the premise that Three Strikes laws are effective, whereas others dismiss claims that the laws are responsible for the decrease in crime. In combination, however, the research to date seems to confirm that Three Strikes laws are responsible for *some* of the recent crime reduction—but not all. Analysts have concluded that other factors, such as demographic changes, may have also played a part in bringing crime levels down to historic lows.

HAVE THREE STRIKES LAWS LOWERED CRIME RATES?

One of the first publicized reports examining the effectiveness of Three Strikes laws was released in 1998 by California Attorney General Dan Lungren.

He noted that after California's law was implemented in early 1994, the state's crime rate began to drop significantly. By 1998, murder had decreased by 40 percent, rape had declined by 17 percent, the number of robberies dropped by 39 percent, assault declined by 19 percent, the rate of burglary fell by 32 percent, and even the number of car thefts was reduced by 33 percent. He attributed much of the crime reduction to the success of Three Strikes, although he acknowledged that states without Three Strikes policies, such as New York and Massachusetts, had also experienced large reductions in crime. However, he attributed those decreases to other types of criminal justice policies enacted in those states, such as New York's zero tolerance policy against social disorder offenses (e.g., panhandling and loitering) and to the widely lauded community policing programs adopted in Boston and other cities in Massachusetts.[3]

He also reported that California's reduction in crime between 1994 and 1997 was substantially larger than that experienced by the rest of the country. The rest of the states experienced a 17.4 percent drop in overall levels of crime, but California's drop was 30.8 percent. Similarly, the rest of the 49 states experienced a drop in violent crime of 18.2 percent, but California's drop of 26.9 percent was much greater. Lungren rejected the possibility that the reduction in crime was caused by other factors, such as demographic or economic changes. He noted that the size of the state's largest crime-producing group, 15- to 24-year-olds, had stabilized even while crime continued to decline. He also pointed out that evidence supporting the link between economic cycles and crime increases or decreases was not sufficiently compelling. He concluded that the only change that appeared to be responsible for the dramatic decrease in crime was the adoption of get-tough sentencing legislation in the early 1990s.[4]

However, an early study conducted by researchers Lisa Stolzenberg and Stuart J. D'Alessio contradicted the conclusion that California's Three Strikes law was responsible for the rapid decrease in the state's crime rate. Utilizing a methodological design known as interrupted time-series and monthly UCR data from California's 10 most populous cities in 1994 and 1995, they compared crime trends before and after the Three Strikes law went into effect. Although the UCR statistics revealed that the number of serious crimes in these cities had decreased, the authors' statistical analysis concluded that the decrease in crime in 9 of the 10 cities had no relationship with the enactment of the Three Strikes law. The reduction in crime, they determined, was part of a preexisting downward trend that began shortly before the law was passed. Only data from the city of Anaheim presented a possible relationship between the policy and the subsequent reduction in crime. However, the authors also acknowledged that their analysis may have been too premature to account for an incapacitation effect. Because California already punished repeat offenders more harshly for their recidivist behavior, the extra sentence reflected in the Three Strikes law could not be measured until after the offenders' original sentence would have ended. The authors also noted that their study did not measure the change in behavior of individual offenders; therefore, they could not test for a deterrence effect either.[5]

More recent studies have confirmed that the reduction in crime following the mid-1990s was indeed significant, but debate continues over the reasons for the decline. In its 2004 retrospective, the California District Attorneys Association (CDAA) noted that in the 10-year period following the adoption of Three Strikes, California's crime rate fell by 45 percent to its lowest point since 1965. This translated into 1,500 fewer crimes per 100,000 residents. Additionally, they reported that homicide levels dropped by 40 percent between 1994 and 2002, decreasing the number of murders per year from 4,600 to 2,500—a net savings of 2,100 lives. Although they acknowledged that other factors may have contributed to the decrease in crime, they asserted that it would be "counterintuitive" to believe that the Three Strikes law was not responsible for a portion of that reduction.[6]

In contrast, another 10-year review of the Three Strikes movement by the Justice Policy Institute concluded that the laws had made little impact on the nation's violent crime rate. By analyzing UCR data between 1993 and 2002, the institute found that states that had enacted Three Strikes laws recorded larger overall reductions in crime than the non–Three Strikes states (26.8% vs. 22.3%); however, much of this decline was accounted for by larger reductions in the number of property offenses. Non–Three Strikes states had slightly greater reductions in violent crime rates (34.3% vs. 33.0%) and substantially higher reductions in homicide rates (43.9% vs. 38.2%). Similarly, when California, the largest Three Strikes state, and New York, the largest non–Three Strikes state, were removed from the crime rate calculations, the results remained largely the same. Overall crime reductions were higher in Three Strikes states (22.6% vs. 17.4%), with much of the difference accounted for by the reduction of property crime (21.9% vs. 15.8%). Non–Three Strikes states posted greater reductions in the area of violent crime (28.5% vs. 27.3%) and homicide (38.2% vs. 33.7%).[7]

ASSESSING A DETERRENT EFFECT: ARE OFFENDERS SCARED OF THREE STRIKES?

When Three Strikes laws were enacted, policy makers were hopeful that mandatory sentencing laws would deter crime because offenders would be fearful of receiving lengthy prison sentences. This deterrence could be achieved specifically with the target population of repeat offenders, or more generally with first-time offenders or those at-risk for committing a crime. In the case of specific deterrence, policy makers would look for the law to deter more experienced offenders, who would be subject to the sentencing enhancement if they were caught committing another crime. General deterrence would be achieved if the enhanced punishment imposed on others persuaded would-be or first-time offenders to abandon their criminal ways before they, too, became ensnared by the law.

Since the laws were enacted, researchers and policy makers have been curious to see if either form of deterrence has been achieved. Consequently, a number of research studies have attempted to determine whether the laws have convinced current offenders or would-be criminals to change their ways. Assessing a deterrent effect, however, is difficult because much is still unknown about how and why people make decisions. Although a popular technique is to measure crime rate changes over time to infer a deterrent effect, such measures usually offer insufficient explanation because they cannot account for individual decisions or behavior, nor can they accurately account for other possible explanations. Other studies that try to find a deterrent effect fail to consider long-term ramifications of the policy, or they fail to account for the informal changes to the policy that often occur when it is implemented by the criminal justice system.[8]

Despite these limitations, researchers have tried to gauge whether Three Strikes has had a measurable deterrent effect on crime. One early indication that offenders might be fearful of receiving Three Strikes sentences was reported by the California Department of Corrections (CDC). The CDC noted that immediately after the Three Strikes law was enacted in 1994, the number of parolees asking to leave the state increased dramatically—signaling, perhaps, that offenders were afraid of getting caught on a third-strike offense. Since 1976, more parolees had asked to come in to California to finish their period of parole supervision than had asked to leave the state. However, beginning in 1994, this trend reversed itself; more California parolees requested to leave the state than asked to come in. By 1997, the CDC reported that California had a net loss of more than 1,000 parolees.[9] California Attorney General Dan Lungren noted that this development was even more remarkable considering that state law prohibited parolees from leaving California until all remaining obligations, such as restitution and fines, had been satisfied.[10]

Another possible indicator that offenders are scared of the laws is found in the tendency of three-strike defendants to fake mental illness so that they might escape lengthy prison sentences. A study by forensic psychiatrists Mark Jaffe and Kaushal Sharma found that nine defendants facing a 25-year-to-life sentence under the California Three Strikes law fabricated psychiatric symptoms prior to sentencing. None of these defendants had a history of previous mental illness, and all were observed to exhibit behavior that was consistent with individuals who pretend to be mentally ill. The behaviors the psychiatrists observed included exaggeration of symptoms, selective amnesia about their crimes and criminal histories, and specific requests to be sent to a mental hospital instead of prison. The psychiatrists concluded that the defendants pretended to be mentally ill to have the court declare them in-competent, which would postpone their sentencing, or help them to establish mitigating circumstances that might convince prosecutors or judges to use their discretion to dismiss a prior strike. Jaffe and Sharma noted that their conclusions corresponded with unpublished findings from a psychologist at a well-known California mental hospital that three-strike candidates are more than twice as likely as other defendants to fake psychiatric illness to avoid their mandatory minimum sentences.[11]

Yet another study, this time of younger offenders, attempted to measure the impact of California's Three Strikes law on juvenile offenders in California.[12] Because FBI statistics show that teenagers and young adults under 25 commit nearly half of the serious felonies, deterring these would-be repeat offenders would significantly reduce the crime rate. To see if juveniles have been "scared straight" by the prospect of one day encountering a Three Strikes sentence, a survey was administered to 523 juveniles in an all-male residential juvenile facility in southern California. The participants ranged from under 10 to over 20, with most of the juveniles falling between 11 and 20 years of age. Most of the respondents indicated that they had had some high school education, but only 13 percent had graduated from high school. Almost half the partici-pants (47%) indicated that they had been raised by both parents; 43 percent stated that they had come from a single-parent home, and 10 percent stated that they had been raised by someone other than a parent. Over half the participants (52%) stated that they had established gang membership, and one-quarter of the participants responded that they had fathered children of their own.[13]

Some of the juveniles participating in the survey had already earned strikes and would therefore be eligible for the enhanced sentence if they committed another strike offense as an adult. For specific deterrence to work, these of-fenders would have to indicate their willingness to change their behavior to avoid the consequences of the law. Other offenders in the facility had not yet earned a strike offense, so their willingness to learn from the negative example of others and avoid the same fate is an important component of general deter-rence. When asked various questions about the California Three Strikes law, over three-fourths (78%) of the participants stated that they understood the provisions of the law. Furthermore, 61 percent stated that they would change their behavior and not commit another serious or violent crime if they faced a two-strike (doubled) sentence. Additionally, 70 percent of the respondents indicated that they would not commit a serious or violent crime if they faced a three-strike (minimum 25-year-to-life) sentence. Both of these response figures indicate that the law achieved a specific deterrent effect among these juvenile inmates. However, this effect appeared to be mitigated when the young offenders were asked about their likely future behavior in general. One-third (33%) of the respondents stated that they would kill their victims if they were facing a third-strike sentence since they were going to spend the rest of their life in prison anyway. Also, only 46 percent stated that the Three Strikes law would likely keep them from committing a serious or violent crime.[14]

The respondents also expressed less certainty about the law's ability to deter others. For example, only 32 percent stated that another person would change their behavior if they faced a two-strike (doubled) sentence, 31 percent stated that a person would not change their behavior, and the majority of respondents (37%) said that a person might change his behavior. Nonetheless, 48 percent of the respondents indicated that they believed the Three Strikes law would prevent someone from committing a serious or violent crime. Another 33 percent said that it would not keep someone from committing a major felony, and the rest (19%) indicated that it might work.[15]

Not all adult inmates believe that Three Strikes will have a deterrent effect, either. Interviews with 33 inmates in California prisons presented contradictory opinions about whether the law works to stave off crime. Some inmates said that the law was not having an effect at all, given that violent offenders already do a substantial amount of prison time. Other inmates, however, thought that Three Strikes increased the level of violence because offenders were fearful of being apprehended. Suspected three-strikers would be more likely to flee from police or shoot at officers to avoid arrest. They also differed on whether Three Strikes deterred crime. Some noted that their friends had stopped peddling drugs or had moved to other states to avoid the law, while others doubted that any sentencing law could make certain offenders stop their behavior. Seven of the inmates interviewed said that fear of the law had caused them to change from committing robberies to committing thefts; however, none of the offenders realized that the California strike zone was so broad that felony thefts could also count as the last strike. Ultimately, all seven of these offenders were apprehended and sentenced under the law despite their attempts to avoid it.[16]

Another study examined whether third-strike offense arrests had decreased in California in the age group most likely affected by the law. Researchers Mike Males and Dan Macallair hypothesized that Three Strikes laws most often affect older offenders (e.g., those in their 30s and 40s) because they have longer criminal histories. Therefore, if Three Strikes had a deterrent effect, the crime and arrest rates for this age group would decline faster than the rates for the younger age groups, which would not be as affected by the provisions of the new law. To test this theory, the authors compared the felony offense rates of all age groups for four years prior to the law and four years after the law. Their findings revealed that offense rates declined for the younger age groups (20–24 and 25–29) but showed an increase for the over-30 age group, which is the group that should have been deterred the most. Thus, based on this finding, the authors concluded that the California Three Strikes law had no deterrent effect among potential third-strike offenders.[17]

In a more sophisticated study, Eric Helland and Alexander Tabarrok measured the arrest rates of two groups of California offenders released from prison in 1994. All of the offenders in the first group had two prior strikes and thus were at risk for a 25-year-to-life sentence upon conviction of any third felony. The offenders in the second group also had prosecutions for two prior strike offenses but convictions for only one; for these offenders, the second strike offense had been plea-bargained to a nonstrike offense. The results of the comparison indicated that offenders facing a third possible strike conviction in California had an arrest rate that was 17 percent to 20 percent lower than offenders who faced only a second strike. The authors found that the arrest rate for two-time offenders was also lower in Texas, which has an older recidivist statute similar to Three Strikes. This comparison is significant considering that offenders with two prior convictions in Illinois and New York (non–Three Strikes states) have the same likelihood of being arrested as offenders with only one prior conviction. Consequently, Helland and Tabarrok concluded that offenders who are eligible to receive an enhanced sentence upon conviction of a third strike are deterred from crime.[18]

Even if three-strikers are deterred from committing more offenses, researchers studying the felony arrest and crime rate data in a three-city sample in California (Los Angeles, San Diego, and San Francisco) concluded that the number of strikers in that category is so small that the practical effect on the state's overall crime rate is almost negligible. In their study, Franklin Zimring, Sam Kamin, and Gordon Hawkins estimated that recidivist offenders accounted for only a little more than 10 percent of the crime committed in 1993, and that only 3.3 percent of the offenders in their sample were eligible for the third-strike sentence. Thus, if the law deterred all recidivist offenders targeted by the law, the researchers suggested that the subsequent impact on the crime rate would be a reduction of only 10%. However, the authors also stated that this was a best-case scenario; in their study, they found no measurable deterrent effect at all. Instead, their analysis suggested that offenders targeted by the law in these three cities exhibited no differences in behavior than other types of offenders. Additionally, they found no spillover deterrence in other offending groups. Even nonstrike felony offenders in their sample group did not exhibit any change in behavior after the law went into effect. As a result, they concluded that the decreases in crime experienced in California were not produced by the Three Strikes law.[19]

In another recent study, Joanna Shepherd created an economic model of crime to evaluate whether the increased cost of punishment would affect the types of crimes that people committed. Specifically, she predicted that criminals would commit fewer crimes that the state identifies as strikes so as to avoid the lengthy mandatory sentences. Using California data from 1983 to 1996, Shepherd found that the law had the greatest deterrent effect on new criminals. In particular, she found that offenders avoided those serious and/or violent crimes that could count as first-strike offenses.[20] However, she found no deterrent effect among other felony offenses, which can trigger a mandatory sentence for two- and three-strike offenders. She concluded that new offenders fear the first strike; therefore, they commit fewer serious and/or violent offenses. That does not mean that these offenders refrain from all crime, though. Instead, many potential first-strike offenders substitute nonstrike offenses for strike offenses. For example, a person might choose to commit larceny or auto theft instead of residential burglary or robbery because larceny and auto theft are not counted as strikes for the first-time offender. Additionally, Shepherd found that deterrence is linked to the extra penalty an offender will receive for a particular crime, which explains why she found only a small deterrent effect for the crime of murder and virtually no deterrent effect for the crime of rape. Because these offenses are already heavily punished, when an offender decides to commit those crimes, he is already aware that he will receive a lengthy prison sentence if he is caught and convicted. The extra sentence that he would receive under the Three Strikes law is unlikely to be significant enough to convince him to change his mind about committing those particular crimes.

Additionally, the study found that the deterrent effects of California's Three Strikes law were not specific to any particular counties. Although some counties apply the law more frequently than others, criminals are typically not aware of issues related to jurisdiction. They may not know what county they are in, or they may not understand how counties decide which one will have jurisdiction over a crime. Therefore, aggressive enforcement policies in one county will also produce deterrent effects in neighboring counties so that the whole state benefits from the application of the law.

Shepherd also concluded that the full deterrent effect of the Three Strikes law is responsible for a significant number of crimes being prevented and a large net cost savings to California residents. Specifically, she calculated that within the first two years of enactment, the law was responsible for deterring eight murders, nearly 4,000 aggravated assaults, 10,672 robberies, and almost 400,000 burglaries. The cost savings to residents was equal to nearly $900 million. However, she noted that because offenders began substituting theft offenses for serious or violent strike offenses, the number of larceny crimes increased to 17,700 in the first two years, at a cost to victims of nearly $7 million.[21]

Criminal justice scholars have expressed concern that when the costs of crime are increased too much, there will be an effect opposite to that of deterrence. In other words, certain crimes will *increase*—not decrease—because the law imposes such severe sanctions. Although Shepherd found that offenders were substituting less serious theft offenses for robberies and burglaries, other researchers have suggested that offenders might also be inclined to commit more serious crimes, such as murder. Their assumption is that when an offender is likely to receive the same penalty for a more severe crime than he is for a less severe crime, he will commit the more severe crime if it increases his chances of escaping detection. For example, a repeat offender who holds up a convenience store and robs five patrons could receive a life sentence if convicted under a typical Three Strikes law. The offender might calculate that his sentence would not be much greater, if greater at all, if he murdered the victims after he robbed them. Since most offenders would receive life in prison for murder—just as they would for robbery if sentenced in a typical Three Strikes state—there would be little incentive not to kill their victims. Letting them live would only increase the likelihood that they would cooperate with police, which in turn would increase the likelihood of capture.[22]

To test this premise, Thomas Marvell and Carlisle Moody used statewide data from all 50 states over a 29-year period (1970–1998) to compare the homicide rates in states with Three Strikes laws against the rates in states without Three Strikes laws. They found that the homicide rate in Three Strikes states was higher by 10 percent to 12 percent, and they projected an even greater increase of 20 percent to 29 percent over a long-term period. They estimated that the initial increase led to an additional 1,400 homicides during the first few years of the law's enactment and could potentially generate an additional 3,300 homicides nationwide in the future. However, the authors acknowledged that this effect disappears in states that have harsh Three Strikes laws. For example, California, which has one of the strictest Three Strikes law, shows the least amount of increase in homicide. Furthermore, Georgia, which has the second most severe law, shows the second least amount of increase.[23]

Although Marvell and Moody speculated that the law may not have as much of an effect on homicide rates in California and Georgia because of possible deterrent or incapacitation effects, Shepherd believes that the example of these two states reveals an error in the authors' analysis. Only a few states, including California and Georgia, have used their laws to any substantial degree. The remaining Three Strikes states have used their laws infrequently or not at all. Therefore, it would be illogical for offenders in states other than California or Georgia to kill their victims to keep from receiving the extra punishment; they need not fear Three Strikes sentences in these states because they are rarely applied.[24] If suspects were killing their victims to avoid receiving the severe mandatory penalty, then the largest increase in homicide rates should be in states like California and Georgia where offenders face the greatest risk of receiving extra punishment for their crimes. Because Marvell and Moody's analysis revealed that the homicide increase is actually the smallest in these states, Shepherd suggested that the cause-and-effect relationship might be reversed. It is possible that high homicide rates prompted lawmakers to pass Three Strikes laws in the first place, and this is why rates appear to be higher in these jurisdictions.[25]

MEASURING THE INCAPACITATION EFFECT OF THREE STRIKES LAWS

Because Three Strikes laws are designed to reduce crime through deterrence and incapacitation, researchers believe that they ought to test for both effects independently before determining if the laws are effective.[26] However, this has proven difficult because the two phenomena are naturally intertwined. A sentence enhancement like Three Strikes can produce a deterrent effect while simultaneously promoting an incapacitation effect. Therefore, if crime is reduced, it could be attributable to either deterrence or incapacitation, or it could be caused by both forces working together. For example, some offenders may no longer commit crime because they have been deterred by the law, while others may no longer offend because they have been incapacitated by longer prison sentences. Consequently, separating how much of the reduction in crime is attributable to deterrence and how much has been caused by incapacitation is a formidable, but important, methodological task. If researchers find that there is no incapacitation effect, then a policy of incarcerating prisoners for long periods would be ineffective and an unwise way to use valuable state resources. Moreover, if analyses reveal that Three Strikes laws have only an incapacitation effect, which prevents current habitual offenders from committing new crimes but does nothing to deter a new wave of offenders, then policies of warehousing inmates to reduce crime are also likely to be considered a costly and ineffective use of resources. However, if a deterrent effect is present, then the increases in the number of inmates subject to lengthy incarceration will be offset by a lower number of new offenders, thus keeping prison costs down and crime low.[27]

Daniel Kessler and Steven Levitt have suggested that the two effects can be measured independently at different points in time. Reductions that occur immediately after the law is enacted are likely attributable to deterrence, whereas additional reductions that are experienced over time are likely attributable to incapacitation. The incapacitation effect takes longer to manifest itself because an offender is not considered to be incapacitated by the Three Strikes law until after his original sentence, which he would have received under the old law, has ended. Any reduction in crime that occurs during the term of the offender's original sentence should be attributable to a deterrent effect on other offenders, not the incapacitation of this particular offender. Only the crime that is prevented *after* the original sentence has ended and the enhancement has begun may be attributable to an incapacitation effect.[28] For instance, a California Three Strikes offender who would have been released after five years in prison under the old law but now is confined for 25 years will be prevented from committing any new crime in that subsequent 20-year period. Thus, crime reduction that is found during the initial 5-year sentence should be attributable to deterrence, whereas the additional crime reduction that is experienced during the following 20 years—the period imposed by the new policy—is likely produced by the ongoing incapacitation of the offender.

Because of these time-ordering issues, researchers had to wait until enough time had passed before trying to assess whether Three Strikes laws have been successful in reducing crime through the incapacitation of repeat offenders. However, now that the laws have been active for more than a decade, researchers have sufficient data to test for incapacitation. One of the first studies to examine the possibility of an incapacitation effect was a study by John Worrall that used a series of statistical models to estimate how much crime was prevented by the California Three Strikes law. Using countywide data from 1989 to 2000, Worrall analyzed whether the law had a measurable deterrent and incapacitative effect that was responsible for the reduction in crime during this period. Once he included data on the level of Three Strikes enforcement in each county, his model found no incapacitation effect and only a weak deterrent effect. Out of all felony index crimes represented in his study, only the crime of larceny was found to be deterred. In fact, his study suggests that the California Three Strikes law has had a neutral effect on the crime rate; it has neither caused it to go up (as suggested by Marvell and Moody) nor caused it to go down (as suggested by Shepherd). Worrall attributes the difference between his results and the results from previous studies to the variables that were included in his model. Previous studies, like the one conducted by Marvell and Moody, did not take into consideration different levels of enforcement, and other analyses, like the one completed by Shepherd, did not include a measurement of incapacitation.[29]

However, another study testing for deterrence and incapacitation found that the law produced a clear effect in both areas. After dividing the categories of crime into two main groups—instrumental crimes, which are planned in advance (e.g., burglary and robbery), and violent crimes, which are usually spontaneous (e.g., aggravated assault and rape)—Juan Ramirez and William Crano ran three separate analyses using UCR and arrest data. In their first analysis, they replicated and expanded the original time-series analysis conducted by Stoltzenberg and D'Alessio in 1997. Although they were equipped with more data than the previous researchers, Ramirez and Crano found similar results: Three Strikes did not appear to have either a short-term or long-term deterrent effect on crime. However, they acknowledged that the technique they used in this first analysis presumed that the law had an immediate and long-term impact on crime. This rarely occurs in real-world conditions; instead, effects develop over time, resulting in a cumulative impact on crime rates. In their second analysis, Ramirez and Crano corrected for this fictional assumption, but still saw no appreciable change in the results.[30]

In their final analysis, Ramirez and Crano, adjusting their statistical techniques to improve the accuracy of their model, found that the California Three Strikes law clearly reduced crime through a short-term deterrent effect and a long-term incapacitative effect. However, the magnitude of the effects differed for each crime category. The law had the biggest impact on instrumental crimes, which are offenses that are planned in advance. The authors found that the number of instrumental crimes decreased immediately by 9 percent in the first month that the law went into effect. Furthermore, the number of instrumental crimes continued to drop for a total reduction of 45 percent over the duration of the study period, which extended from March 1994 to December 1998. The authors reported similar findings with their arrest data; there was an immediate 15 percent decrease in the number of arrests for instrumental crimes and a long-term decrease of 42 percent.

When they analyzed the impact of California's Three Strikes law on violent crime, the authors saw no immediate reduction attributable to deterrence but found a cumulative decrease of 36 percent. Their results for minor crimes were also mixed. An analysis of minor-crime data suggested that the law produced an immediate decrease of 7 percent and a long-term reduction of 34 percent. Yet, the analysis using arrest data suggested that a short-term decrease of 8 percent and the long-term decrease of 25 percent had begun in advance of the 1994 enactment and appeared to be slowing down by the end of 1998.

In interpreting the significance of these results, Ramirez and Crano concluded that the California Three Strikes law had produced a significant deterrent and incapacitation effect just as its authors had hoped. They also concluded that the effect of the law extended beyond the serious crimes targeted by the law to minor offenses as well. They speculated that the two offense groups could be linked together because offenders who commit serious crimes also commit minor crimes. Thus, when offenders are incapacitated from one, they cannot commit the other, either. Ramirez and Crano suggested that it could also be that offenders are uncertain as to which crimes count as strikes; therefore, they choose to abstain from both. Finally, the authors acknowledged that they found no incapacitative effect on drug arrests and hypothesized that these crimes are impervious to increasingly severe sentences.[31]

In another study, researchers Tomislav Kovandzic, John Sloan, and Lynne Vieraitis used nationwide data to see if deterrence and incapacitation had produced a decrease in crime in selected U.S. cities. They compared the crime rates of cities within Three Strikes states with similar cities in non–Three Strikes states and hypothesized that if a deterrent effect was present, then crime rates in only the Three Strikes cities should exhibit an immediate reduction. If incapacitation were also present, then the crime rates in those cities should experience a gradual ongoing reduction in crime as well. To test their theory, the authors tracked changes in the rates of the UCR Index offenses, which include homicide, robbery, rape, assault, burglary, larceny, and motor vehicle theft.[32]

Their initial results suggested that Three Strikes cities experienced a gradual reduction in crime that surpassed the decline experienced in non–Three Strikes cities; therefore, the authors suggested that the decline could be caused by an incapacitation effect. However, their more sophisticated analysis linked the reduction to increases in prison populations that occurred before these states adopted Three Strikes laws. Furthermore, they found no deterrent effect in operation in Three Strikes states. Instead, cities in Three Strikes states experienced increases in homicide rates, which supported the conclusion reached earlier by Marvell and Moody that Three Strikes offenders were more likely to kill their victims to improve their chances of escape.

When Kovandzic and his coresearchers evaluated the changes in crime rates on a state-by-state basis, they also found mixed results. In some states, the authors found that Three Strikes had produced statistically significant decreases in crime, whereas in others, they found that the law had caused increases in crime. Some of this effect may be related to frequency of enforcement, as had been suggested by other researchers in previous studies. States that have high enforcement policies, such as California, also demonstrated the most reduction attributable to Three Strikes. California, for example, showed an incapacitation effect on six out of seven crime categories. However, Georgia, which also routinely enforces its Three Strikes law, showed an increase in the rates of five out of seven crimes.

The authors explained that these insignificant findings may be attributable to the fact that many of the offenders affected by the law are older and already have a relatively low rate of offending. Incapacitating these offenders for longer periods is not likely to have a substantial impact on the crime rate because they have already slowed their rates of reoffending. Second, the authors noted that strike offenders are either unconcerned with getting caught or incapable of thinking about the consequences of their actions because they are under the influence of drugs or alcohol. Third, the authors suggest that offenders sentenced under Three Strikes are replaced by new offenders entering the crime market because Three Strikes laws are failing to deter would-be offenders. Last, they acknowledge that many of the states enacting Three Strikes laws already had sentencing enhancements available to use against repeat offenders; therefore, the increase in punishment is usually not significant enough to produce a measurable deterrent or incapacitation effect.[33]

Finally, Kathleen Auerhahn examined the ability of California's Three Strikes law to capture the most dangerous offenders. Because one of the primary motivations behind the law was to lock up violent felons before they could strike again, the law targets those offenders who have accumulated one or more serious and/or violent felony convictions. If this selection strategy is effective, then offenders who are still left in society should be less dangerous than those who have been incarcerated under the law. To test this proposition, Auerhahn measured the dangerousness of offenders who have been arrested against those who are in jail, on probation, on parole, or in prison. She measured dangerousness on an 11-point scale, with various points given according to age, gender, number of prior convictions, violent tendencies, and severity of the current offense. On Auerhahn's scale, for example, young males with two or more violent prior convictions are considered the most dangerous, whereas older female offenders with no serious or violent prior offenses are considered the least dangerous.[34]

In comparing the dangerousness of various offending populations, she found that the dangerousness of those who were arrested declined by 9 percent between 1980 and 1998. The dangerousness of the jail population decreased by 6 percent, and the level of danger presented by the probation population first increased by 31 percent between 1980 and 1987 and then later declined by 9 percent between 1987 and 1998. Parolees showed no change in their level of dangerousness to the community. Surprisingly, Auerhahn found that the average dangerousness of prisoners also declined by 8 percent during this period, despite public policies that were designed to incarcerate those offenders who presented the greatest risk to the public. Although she acknowledged that the data may be too premature to measure an incapacitation effect due to Three Strikes, her models predicting the future dangerousness of prison offenders also showed no incapacitation effect attributable to the law.[35]

SUMMARY

For policy makers and members of the public, evaluating the effectiveness of Three Strikes sentencing laws can be a dizzying task. Some studies have found, for example, that the Three Strikes movement is responsible for much of the decline in crime experienced in the last several years. Other researchers have found that the decline in crime is not solely attributable to the Three Strikes movement. Additionally, some recent studies have found that a widely enforced Three Strikes law, like the one in California, can produce a deterrent and incapacitation effect. Yet, others offer findings that question whether the effects are large enough to be significant. Taken together, it appears as though Three Strikes laws *can* have some deterrent or incapacitation effect if the laws are enforced. States that enacted Three Strikes laws but never use them are not likely to find that crime has been substantially reduced just because the law is listed in their penal codes. However, policy makers in states like California, where the law is widely applied, may rest a little easier knowing that there is likely some crime-control benefit at work.

The effectiveness of these laws will continue to be of significance as lawmakers in states around the country begin to question whether Three Strikes and other get-tough policies have outlived their usefulness. Crime is no longer the problem that it once was, and other domestic concerns have crowded the political agenda. Because state budgets are now pressed on other issues, such as increasing energy costs, homeland security costs, and hurricane recovery expenditures, some lawmakers have suggested that their get-tough policies should be scaled back to save on incarceration-related costs. Supporters of these get-tough policies warn, however, that a return to leniency may trigger the very problems that prompted the Three Strikes movement in the first place. Thus, the findings regarding the effectiveness of the laws and their utility in a tight budgetary environment are all the more important to the ongoing debate.

NOTES

1. Bureau of Justice Statistics Crime and Justice Data Online, http://www.ojp. usdoj.gov/bjs/.
2. Ibid.
3. Lungren, *"Three Strikes and You're Out"—Its Impact.*
4. Ibid.
5. Lisa Stolzenberg and Stewart J. D'Alessio, "'Three Strikes and You're Out': The Impact of California's New Mandatory Sentencing Law on Serious Crime Rates," *Crime & Delinquency* 43 (1997), 457–69.
6. CDAA, *Prosecutors' Perspective.*

7. Schiraldi et al., *Three Strikes and You're Out: An Examination of the Impact.*

8. Daniel S. Nagin, "Criminal Deterrence Research at the Outset of the Twenty-First Century," *Crime & Justice* 23 (1998), 1–42.

9. This trend continued until 2002. CDAA, *Prosecutors' Perspective.* See also http://www.corr.ca.gov/ReportsResearch/OffenderInfoServices/Annual/CalPris/ CALPRISd2004.pdf.

10. Lungren, *"Three Strikes and You're Out"—Its Impact*

11. Mark Evan Jaffe and Kaushal K. Sharma, "Malingering Uncommon Psychiatric Symptoms among Defendants Charged under California's 'Three Strikes and You're Out' Law," *Journal of Forensic Science* 43, no. 3 (1998), 549–55.

12. John R. Schafer, "The Deterrent Effect of Three Strikes Law," *FBI Law Enforcement Bulletin* (April 1999), 6–10.

13. Ibid.

14. Ibid., Unfortunately, the survey did not ask the offenders about their willingness to avoid all felonies, since California's Three Strikes law allows any felony offense to trigger the mandatory sentence.

15. Ibid.

16. Austin et al., *"Three Strikes and You're Out": Implementation and Impact.*

17. Mike Males and Dan Macallair, "Striking Out: The Failure of California's 'Three Strikes and You're Out' Law," *Stanford Law & Policy Review* 11, no. 1 (1999), 65–74.

18. Eric Helland and Alexander Tabarrok, "Does Three Strikes Deter? A Non-Parametic Estimation," *Journal of Human Resources* (forthcoming).

19. Franklin E. Zimring, Sam Kamin, and Gordon Hawkins, *Crime and Punishment in California: The Impact of Three Strikes and You're Out* (Berkeley: Institute of Governmental Studies Press, University of California, Berkeley, 1999).

20. These crimes are the "strikable" felonies identified in Cal. Penal Code §667.5(c), §1129.7(c), and §1129.8.

21. Joanna M. Shepherd, "Fear of the First Strike: The Full Deterrent Effect of California's Two- and Three-Strikes Legislation," *Journal of Legal Studies* 31 (2002), 159–201.

22. In this analysis, the authors do not discuss the impact that moral sensitivities may have on the offenders' decisionmaking process. It is possible that offenders would *not* murder their victims because of moral sensibilities, even if this would increase the likelihood of apprehension.

23. Thomas B. Marvell and Carlisle E. Moody, "The Lethal Effects of Three-Strikes Laws," *Journal of Legal Studies* 30 (2001), 89–106.

24. Shepherd, "Fear of the First Strike."

25. Ibid.

26. Daniel Kessler and Steven D. Levitt, "Using Sentence Enhancements to Distinguish between Deterrence and Incapacitation," *Journal of Law and Economics* 42, no. 1 (1999), 343–63.

27. Ibid.

28. Ibid.

29. John L. Worrall, "The Effect of Three-Strikes Legislation on Serious Crime in California," *Journal of Criminal Justice* 32 (2004), 283–96.

30. Juan R. Ramirez and William D. Crano, "Deterrence and Incapacitation: An Interrupted Time-Series Analysis of California's Three Strikes Law," *Journal of Applied Social Psychology* 33, no. 1 (2003), 110–44.

31. Ibid.

32. Tomislav V. Kovandzic, John J. Sloan, III, and Lynne M. Vieraitis, "'Striking Out' as Crime Reduction Policy: The Impact of 'Three Strikes' Laws on Crime Rates in U.S. Cities," *Justice Quarterly* 21, no. 2 (2004), 207–39.

33. Ibid.

34. Kathleen Auerhahn, *Selective Incapacitation and Public Policy: Evaluating California's Imprisonment Crisis*, SUNY series in New Directions in Crime and Justice Studies (Albany: State University of New York Press, 2003).

35. Ibid.

7

Attempts to Reform Three Strikes Laws

Although Three Strikes laws were initially very popular with legislators and members of the public, subsequent criticisms about the fairness of the policies and questions about their cost-effectiveness prompted some interest groups to lobby for reform just a few years after the laws went into effect. Falling crime rates has made amending the laws somewhat more palatable, since public pressure to get tough on criminals has begun to ease. However, in most states lawmakers nonetheless appear to be a bit hesitant in casting Three Strikes laws aside for fear of being labeled soft on crime by a public that is still supportive of these types of sentencing measures. Yet, reform may still be imminent. Crime has reached historic lows in recent years, so the public may now be willing to tolerate less stringent sentences for offenders, especially if states' budgetary woes continue to prompt debate about the government's funding priorities.

SUGGESTIONS TO REFORM THREE STRIKES AND YOU'RE OUT

Over the past 12 years, the Three Strikes movement has been the target of much criticism and opposition. Some opponents object to the laws because their mandatory nature prohibits judges from adjusting the sentences to fit the unique circumstances presented in individual cases. Others object to the laws because they believe that the sentences are too severe. They believe that lifetime sentences—or near lifetime sentences—should be reserved for society's worst offenders, not merely those who have engaged in repeated, but relatively inconsequential, behavior. While some critics would like to see the legislation repealed outright, others have suggested a number of reforms that would fix some of the potential flaws associated with the legislation. Those reform recommendations range from shortening the severity of the sentences to narrowing the list of offenses that can count as strikes. Other recommendations include expanding the use of discretion to improve the fairness of the sentencing and restoring a system of parole that would facilitate the release of geriatric prisoners.

Reform Suggestions for Mandatory Sentences in General

Some of those who oppose Three Strikes laws object to mandatory penalties in general because of the inflexible and impersonal way in which they are applied. Although these critics usually urge lawmakers to repeal the laws outright, there is a growing recognition that the political popularity of the laws has made them a mainstay in our penal systems. As a result, some have suggested ways in which the policies could be modified so that mandatory sentencing laws would be more palatable. First, the laws could be changed so that they operate more like sentences imposed under presumptive guidelines systems. Mandatory penalties could be identified as presumptive or default sentences, but judges would have the ability to impose lesser sentences for offenders who presented compelling mitigating circumstances.[1] This would allow the symbolic value of the laws to remain intact while providing enough flexibility to accommodate unforeseen circumstances. It would also allow judges and prosecutors to use their discretion openly, rather than trying to skirt the law through unconventional practices and procedures.

Although most of the Three Strikes laws prohibit traditional uses of discretion, California's law gives prosecutors and judges the ability to temporarily overlook a prior strike conviction to prevent injustices from occurring with the mandatory sentencing requirement. Nonetheless, critics point out that further reform is still needed because the California legislature has failed to identify or explain the circumstances that would lead to an appropriate exercise of discretion. Consequently, because there are no statewide criteria, opponents fear that Three Strikes sentences could result in sentencing disparity for similarly situated offenders. Mandatory sentencing laws that incorporate some form of a discretionary bypass system would also need to structure that discretion so that it is used fairly and consistently.

Michael Vitiello, an outspoken critic of California's Three Strikes law, agrees that inconsistent application of the law can lead to "uneven justice" across jurisdictions.[2] Consequently, he has suggested reforming the law so that discretion for judges and prosecutors is much more structured. For example, judges could be allowed to assign points to an offender based on the number of prior convictions; the number of points would determine how long a sentence the offender would serve. Similarly, the legislature could offer guidelines that would instruct prosecutors on circumstances that would prompt an appropriate use of discretion. Restructuring the way that discretion is used would introduce flexibility into the application of the sentence so that prosecutors and judges could respond to individual circumstances without sacrificing the consistency of uniformity of the sentencing outcomes.[3]

Another idea that has been offered to reform Three Strikes and other mandatory sentencing laws is to attach so-called sunset provisions to the legislation when it is enacted. This technique, which is often used with tax legislation, would allow the policy to automatically expire unless it is specifically renewed by the legislature. Realizing that mandatory penalties are often political responses to temporary passions, sunset clauses would allow laws like Three Strikes to die quietly without the fierce political fighting that often accompanies suggestions for repeal or reform.[4] Policy makers could then enact legislation to make a symbolic stand on a particular problem without fearing political fallout if they later change their minds. For example, when policy makers rushed to enact Three Strikes laws in 1994 and 1995, such policies were considered the best solution for the problem at the time. Now that crime has decreased dramatically, and states are facing increased budgetary pressures, some lawmakers are questioning the wisdom and the necessity of such strict legislation. Policy makers might now wish to repeal the laws, but reversing course on a policy as popular and symbolic as Three Strikes might inflict political damage if they are labeled by opponents as soft on crime.

Reform Suggestions for Three Strikes Laws

Scholars who have studied the effects of Three Strikes laws often make recommendations on how the laws might be improved. After studying the potential deterrent effect of mandatory sentencing laws, Daniel Kessler and Steven Levitt concluded that Three Strikes laws are not as effective as they could be because in most states they are drawn too narrowly. Previous research has established that offenders are deterred more by the certainty of punishment than they are by the severity of punishment, which means that a repeat offender would be less likely to commit another crime if he knew for certain that he would receive a sentencing enhancement—even if it were shorter than a typical Three Strikes sentence. Conversely, a very long Three Strikes sentence is meaningless to a defendant who is not subject to its provisions. Consequently, Kessler and Levitt recommended that states reduce the severity of their Three Strikes sentences but increase the scope of the law so that more offenders are subjected to the enhancements.

Often, scholars use simulation models to see which version of Three Strikes might reduce crime to the greatest degree for the least amount of cost. This, in turn, allows them to recommend changes to the law that would improve the law's overall efficiency. RAND researchers engaged in this type of simulation analysis when California voters were preparing to vote on the Three Strikes law. From their models, they concluded that the Three Strikes version that the voters approved offered the greatest crime-reduction potential, but also cost the most. Other alternatives, such as restricting strikes to violent offenses only, or using just a two-strike provision, cost less money but also were less effective in reducing crime. The version that the researchers recommended was actually not a Three Strikes proposal at all. Rather, they concluded that requiring offenders to serve their full sentences for all crimes would offer the most crime reduction for the least amount of cost.[5] Despite their recommendations, California voters opted to stay with the more stringent Three Strikes version enacted by the legislature, even though it would potentially cost more in the long run.

In another simulation study, Jonathan Caulkins concluded that Three Strikes sentences should be kept short to maximize their utility. He found that shorter sentences are usually more cost-efficient than longer sentences; therefore, he recommended that states shorten their sentences for two- and three-strike offenders. Specifically, he suggested that two-strikers should be sentenced to 6 years in prison and three-strikers should spend no more than 10 years in prison. The shorter sentences would be almost as effective in reducing crime but would cost the state much less. For states that need to incorporate a system of incapacitation, Caulkins recommended sentencing only violent offenders to lengthy mandatory sentences, as this would be more efficient than sentencing a broad range of offenders to life in prison. Furthermore, he suggested that states expand their sentences for first-strike offenders because this is more efficient than imposing very lengthy sentences for the second and third offense.[6]

Kathleen Auerhahn, who has studied the incapacitative effect of California's Three Strikes law, has expressed concern that the policy has ensnared too many nonviolent offenders. Because the sentences under Three Strikes are so long, she predicted that California's prison budget will be soon consumed by costs associated with warehousing geriatric prisoners who pose little threat to the public. In her study, Auerhahn ran simulation models to see if various Three Strikes reforms would be effective in reducing the number of offenders who were unnecessarily incapacitated by lengthy mandatory sentences. She found that variations that restricted the third strike to only violent offenses but would allow the first two strikes to remain as they are currently defined would increase the number of violent offenders in prison. It would also, however, lead to an aging prison population that presented little threat to the public. A second alternative would be to apply the lengthy sentence to repeat offenders who have been convicted of a violent strike and also to offenders with two or more convictions who have a history of violence. Although this version would feature a broader strike zone than the violent third-strike-only proposal, Auerhahn estimated that the proportion of violent offenders in prison would increase and the number of nonviolent property and drug offenders would decrease. Therefore, she suggested that a reform like this would help to improve the incapacitative benefit of Three Strikes by focusing the law on more dangerous offenders.[7]

She also noted the law could be changed to allow early release for geriatric offenders, age 55 years and older. Allowing older inmates to be released before the end of their mandatory term would result in significant cost savings caused by a reduction in the number of inmates who have expensive health-related costs. It would also be consistent with a philosophy of selective incapacitation in that geriatric offenders represent little danger to society at large. Although Auerhahn acknowledged that many of these offenders would still require assistance from the state in the form of halfway houses, income assistance, or even nursing home care, the costs associated with these services are far less costly when they are provided outside the prison setting.[8]

Last, a number of scholars, observers, newspaper editorial boards, and policy makers have suggested redrawing the strike zones more narrowly so that they would affect fewer offenders each year. This recommendation is often directed at the California Three Strikes law because its strike zone is the broadest in the nation. In particular, one of the main criticisms of California's policy has been that it allows minor felonies to trigger the mandatory sentence; other states require all strikes to be serious or violent felonies. Therefore, opponents have spent much time and energy lobbying the legislature to modify the law so that the last strike is restricted to only serious or violent felonies. This change would reduce the number of offenders who receive the enhanced sentence, which would also reduce the cost of the law, while at the same time preserving the lengthy sentence that supposedly deters and incapacitates offenders. Other suggestions directed at California's policy include revising the serious and/or violent offense list to remove nonviolent crimes, such as residential burglary, so that an offender can no longer strike out without having caused or threatened harm to another individual.

ATTEMPTS TO REFORM THREE STRIKES AND YOU'RE OUT

In the early 1990s, politicians noted that circumstances required that they act tough on crime. Today, policy makers acknowledge that a tough-on-crime strategy may no longer be fiscally possible. Increasing prison populations, combined with tighter state budgets from reduced tax revenues, have prompted lawmakers to declare that they have to be "smart on crime" instead.[9] Accordingly, legislators in many states across the nation have begun to discuss ways in which sentencing laws might be modified to best fit the needs of their states. Some states have decided to reform their sentencing laws by exempting drug offenders from mandatory sentences or providing treatment in the place of punishment. Other states, like California, have focused their sentencing reform efforts on Three Strikes specifically, but without much success. Still others have not considered Three Strikes reform to be a high priority given that the laws are infrequently used. Moreover, other states, like Florida, are concentrating their current sentencing reform efforts on incapacitating high-risk sex offenders who present ongoing threats to the community. Regardless of the approach, it is clear that lawmakers are looking beyond Three Strikes for solutions to ongoing crime problems. Although their experimentation with other sentencing strategies does not mean that Three Strikes laws are on the verge of becoming obsolete, lawmakers' willingness to look for other ways to improve the government's response to crime may mean that their long-term viability is less certain than it once was.

Proposition 66: An Attempt to Narrow California's Strike Zone

In November 2004, voters in California were presented with an opportunity to redraw the strike zone of the nation's toughest and most controversial sentencing law. Through Proposition 66, entitled the Three Strikes and Child Protection Act of 2004, proponents of reform sought to revise the state's Three Strikes policy in four key areas. First, the initiative proposed to narrow the qualifications for the last strike offense so that only crimes identified as serious and/or violent in the penal code could trigger the mandatory two- or three-strike sentences. This change would mean that *all* strikes would have to be serious and/or violent; no longer would any felony count as a second- or third-strike offense. Second, the proposition sought to narrow the strike zone by removing some of the serious and/or violent felonies that previously could count as strike offenses. Specifically, the initiative proposed to eliminate residential burglary, attempted burglary, nonresidential arson, conspiracy to commit assault, threats to commit criminal acts, interference with a trial witness, participation in gang-related felonies, and unintentional infliction of significant personal injury while committing a felony from the eligible strike list. Third, the proposition included language that would make the changes retroactive to 1994, which would mean that all offenders currently in prison under a Three Strikes sentence who would no longer qualify based on the proposed changes would be eligible for resentencing. Consequently, offenders who qualified for a resentenced term that was less than what they had already served would be immediately released from prison. Fourth, the proposition also included provisions that would prohibit a defendant from earning more than one strike at each trial. Offenders charged with multiple counts would earn multiple strikes only if each strike was charged and tried in a separate proceeding. Under the original version of the law, for instance, an offender charged with committing two robberies could be tried for both robberies in the same proceeding and earn two strikes upon conviction. Under the provisions of Proposition 66, prosecutors would be required to try the two robberies separately—a costly undertaking—if they wanted to pursue separate strike allegations against the defendant.[10]

In their ballot argument, supporters of Proposition 66 emphasized that voters in 1994 had been misled to believe that Three Strikes targeted violent offenders, such as rapists and kidnappers. Instead, they argued, voters approved a law that allowed offenders to strike out on minor property offenses. Supporters stressed that because of the wide strike zone, offenders were sentenced to 25 years to life for petty crimes, such as stealing T-shirts, videotapes, and even food. This represented a waste of valuable taxpayer revenue and resulted in unfair sentences for the offenders. Proposition 66, they argued, would correct these problems by remaking Three Strikes according to voters' original intent. Furthermore, supporters argued that the law would impose tougher sentences on child molesters because another section of the proposition would raise the sentence for child molesters to 6, 8, or 12 years on the first offense and would require a mandatory 25-year-to-life sentence upon conviction of a second offense.[11]

Just getting a Three Strikes reform measure before the voters represented a symbolic victory for the law's opponents since language included in the original Three Strikes law stipulated that the policy could be changed only by a two-thirds vote of the state legislature or through another ballot initiative approved by a majority of the voters. Interest groups, such as Families Against California Three-Strikes (FACTS), first tried to work with the legislature to amend the law; however, numerous reform measures introduced between 1997 and 2003 either died in committee or failed to garner enough support to meet the two-thirds approval requirement.[12] Two proposals that were approved by the legislature would have commissioned state-sponsored studies of the effects of Three Strikes; however they were subsequently vetoed by Governor Pete Wilson, Republican, in 1998 and Governor Gray Davis, Democrat, in 1999.[13] Both governors explained that studies were not necessary to demonstrate the effectiveness of Three Strikes; the dramatic reduction in crime was evidence enough that the law was working. As Governor Wilson explained, "There are many mysteries in life, the efficiency of 'Three Strikes,' however, is not one of them."[14]

The drive to put Proposition 66 on the general election ballot also seemed headed for failure until a $1.56 million donation by Sacramento insurance company owner Jerry Keehan provided the funds needed to gather the required number of signatures.[15] Once the proposition was qualified for the November 2004 general election ballot, supporters began a public relations campaign to convince voters to change the law. Initially, their job looked as though it would be easy, as the timing for a Three Strikes reform initiative appeared to be right. In June 2004, just after the initiative was certified for the November ballot, the Field Institute found that 76 percent of California voters—80 percent of Democrats and 74% of Republicans—favored the reform ideas included in Proposition 66.[16] Moreover, the level of support remained high throughout the summer despite attempts by opponents to characterize the proposition as a "fatal blow" to Three Strikes. Even by early October, public support for Proposition 66 was strong: 65 percent of voters said that they would vote yes on Proposition 66; only 18 percent indicated that they would vote no.[17]

Although a number of victims associations and taxpayer groups rallied against the proposed changes to Three Strikes, the public campaign against Proposition 66 was nonexistent for much of the election season. However, a sizable 11th-hour donation to the "No on 66" organization gave opponents the opportunity to launch a last-minute campaign blitz that featured a virtual who's who of current and former California politicians. With the election just three weeks away, the No on 66 campaign ran around-the-clock TV and radio ads featuring Governor Arnold Schwarzenegger and four of California's former governors: Gray Davis (Democrat), Pete Wilson (Republican), George Dukemejian (Republican), and Jerry Brown (Democrat).[18] In addition, Democratic Attorney General Bill Lockyer voiced his opposition to the reform measure, as did all 58 county district attorneys and the California District Attorneys Association (CDAA).

The CDAA's opposition to Proposition 66 represented a reversal of the organization's position on the original law, as the CDAA had been one of the most vocal opponents of Three Strikes when it was introduced in 1994. Fearing that the law would cause massive delays in the criminal processing system and result in thousands of offenders being sentenced unjustly, the association originally lobbied for a more narrowly tailored measure. After a decade of use, however, the CDAA argued that Three Strikes was an effective crime-fighting tool that had contributed to the dramatic decrease in crime. Marc Klaas, Polly Klaas's father, also reversed his position on Three Strikes. In 1994, Klaas denounced the original Three Strikes measure, arguing that it captured the wrong type of offender. However, he admitted that he had changed his mind on the law after seeing how discretion allowed prosecutors and judges to pass over undeserving offenders while using the law effectively to stop those criminals with violent tendencies. Through his work with criminal justice officials in Virginia, he also reported that he had witnessed how often DNA evidence collected from inmates serving time for nonviolent theft offenses is linked to other unsolved crimes. Thus, he concluded that incarcerating offenders for property offenses may be useful in saving lives because many of those offenders have committed violent crimes as well.[19]

Throughout its brief campaign, the No on 66 advocates emphasized two main points in their advertisements against the measure. First, opponents argued that the current version of Three Strikes was working so well that there was no need to fix it. Crime rates had declined substantially and prison costs had remained stable for much of the previous decade. Opponents of Proposition 66 also reminded voters that prosecutors and judges had the ability to bypass the law for offenders who were truly undeserving of the mandatory sentence. Second, the campaign emphasized that as many as 26,000 Three Strikes offenders would be eligible for early release if Proposition 66 was enacted.[20] Some of these offenders had extremely violent histories despite the fact that their triggering offenses were nonserious or nonviolent offenses. Under the heading "Meet Your New Neighbors," the No on 66 campaign profiled several of the offenders who would be eligible for release if Proposition 66 was enacted. One of the offenders, Rudolph Casillas, had previously strangled his former girlfriend and mother of his child and left her for dead. Later, he threatened to kill her if she reported him to police. Prior to this crime, he had accumulated eight prior strike convictions. His latest convictions for commercial burglary, resisting arrest, spousal abuse, heroin possession, and felony possession of a firearm would not be considered eligible third-strike offenses if Proposition 66 was approved by voters; therefore, his 25-year-to-life sentence would be revoked and Casillas would be eligible for immediate release. Another offender, Robert Boyce, would also be eligible for immediate release if Proposition 66 was passed. Boyce had five prior strike convictions for rape and was sentenced to 25 years to life for illegal possession of a firearm—a nonviolent felony.[21]

Just a week after nonstop advertising from the No on 66 forces, public opinion began to change. Instead of favoring Three Strikes reform, voters were evenly split on the measure, with just a week to go before election day. Additional campaign funds donated from Governor Schwarzenegger allowed for one last final advertising push in the weekend before the election. Days before the election, public opinion appeared to turn against the reform measure and by election day, Californians rejected the measure by a vote of 47.3

percent in favor to 52.7 percent opposed. Based on its polling data, the Field Institute estimated that 1.5 million voters changed their minds in the last 10 days of the campaign season—the fastest reversal of public opinion in decades.[22] A breakdown of votes by county, presented in Table 7.1, reveals that Three Strikes support appeared to be more politically motivated than practically inspired. Voters in politically liberal counties with high crime rates, like San Francisco and Los Angeles, supported the reform measure. However, voters in more conservative areas with lower crime rates, including Orange and Ventura Counties, rejected Proposition 66 by wide margins.

Sentencing Reform in Other Areas

In the 1990s, most states were enjoying the same economic boom that pushed Wall Street into record-high territory. Budgets were comfortable and lawmakers could easily afford to enact expensive legislation without having to pass tax increases along to state residents. But after the decline of the stock market, and corresponding decreases in tax revenues, state lawmakers began to worry that their long-term financial commitments would be difficult to meet without substantial tax increases. As a result, lawmakers, faced with tough fiscal choices, began to consider ways in which budgetary obligations might be trimmed. Since criminal justice–related costs represent a sizable percentage of most state budgets, lawmakers began to look for ways to pare down prison costs without endangering public safety.

In some states, lawmakers recently decided to allocate more money for reentry programs that focus on providing job skills, technical training, and even education for inmates, in the belief that these programs will keep recidivism rates low. In Oregon, for example, lawmakers have funded a halfway house pilot program that helps inmates find jobs, secure housing, and complete substance abuse treatment. Similar programs were implemented in 2004 in Louisiana, Colorado, Oklahoma, and Kentucky. Lawmakers in Tennessee directed prison officials to provide guidance and instruction on employment and family and child support issues to inmates being released into the community. Illinois made changes that eased the way for former inmates to secure occupational licenses.[23] Even Texas, which has a reputation for being tough on criminals, is relying on drug courts and reentry programs to reduce recidivism.[24]

In addition, state lawmakers have begun to change their policies with regard to drug users. Before Three Strikes laws became popular, mandatory sentencing laws were most often used to punish drug offenses. Threatened by the crack cocaine epidemic and related gang violence, state lawmakers used severe sentences to deter and incapacitate drug-related offenders. Although the laws were successful in capturing some of the offenders responsible for the buying

Table 7.1
Distribution of Proposition 66 Votes by County

County	Yes (%)	No (%)	Violent Crime	County	Yes (%)	No (%)	Violent Crime
Alameda	60.5	39.5	675.7	Orange	38.1	61.9	273.8
Alpine	62.6	37.4	—	Placer	36.1	63.9	202.2
Amador	36.2	63.8	—	Plumas	46.9	53.1	—
Butte	51.7	48.3	326.3	Riverside	39.1	60.9	518.8
Calaveras	41.1	58.9	—	Sacramento	43.6	56.4	581.5
Colusa	36.8	63.2	—	San Benito	27.1	72.9	—
Contra Costa	49.4	50.6	417.1	San Bernardino	36.5	63.5	542.8
Del Norte	51.1	48.9	—	San Diego	42.7	57.3	468.5
El Dorado	36.6	63.4	286.0	San Francisco	69.5	30.5	732.5
Fresno	37.5	62.5	590.7	San Joaquin	43.1	56.9	860.1
Glenn	42.1	57.9	—	San Luis Obispo	53.1	46.9	247.8
Humboldt	63.9	37.0	304.5	San Mateo	54.1	45.9	294.8
Imperial	49.3	50.7	503.3	Santa Barbara	57.2	42.8	270.3
Inyo	42.9	57.1	—	Santa Clara	52.1	47.9	309.0
Kern	43.5	56.5	521.7	Santa Cruz	65.4	34.6	489.2
Kings	39.7	60.3	312.9	Shasta	47.1	52.9	435.9
Lake	49.3	50.7	—	Sierra	49.1	50.9	—
Lassen	45.1	54.9	—	Siskiyou	54.9	45.1	—
Los Angeles	50.4	49.6	842.7	Solano	47.0	53.0	534.5
Madera	36.6	63.4	645.3	Sonoma	54.6	45.4	381.6
Marin	59.7	40.3	221.3	Stanislaus	43.1	56.9	635.5
Mariposa	40.0	60.0	—	Sutter	36.7	63.3	—
Mendocino	60.6	39.4	—	Tehama	45.6	54.4	—
Merced	41.3	58.7	695.1	Trinity	51.1	48.9	—
Modoc	40.0	60.0	—	Tulare	35.1	64.9	653.1
Mono	48.3	51.7	—	Tuolumne	41.0	59.0	—
Monterey	59.1	40.9	490.4	Ventura	38.7	61.3	253.9
Napa	44.7	55.3	290.3	Yolo	50.7	49.3	571.1
Nevada	42.8	57.2	—	Yuba	39.2	60.8	—

Note: Rates are expressed as crimes per 100,000 residents. Crime rates are not available for counties with populations less than 100,000.
Source: California Secretary of State: http://www.ss.ca.gov/elections/sov/2004_general/contents.htm.

and selling of illegal narcotics, many of the people sentenced under the laws were nonviolent drug addicts.[25] Furthermore, without treatment, drug users would almost always reoffend. One study estimated that offenders who were addicted to drugs committed, on average, over 60 crimes per year.[26] As a result, lawmakers in the late 1990s began to question the wisdom of punishment-only policies, since they appeared to be ineffective at deterring the average drug user. Consequently, some states, like New York, shortened sentences for drug users, and Michigan repealed its notorious mandatory minimum drug sentencing laws.[27]

Other states, such as Delaware and California, used federal funds to implement drug court programs that diverted first-time nonviolent drug users from the traditional criminal justice system. Drug court programs are usually characterized by a process that integrates substance abuse treatment with criminal case processing. Offenders are placed in treatment services and receive care for their addictions while they are under the supervision of the court. Judges work closely with prosecutors and defense attorneys in a coordinated strategy to ensure that the offender completes the treatment program and subsequently remains drug-free. Additionally, judges have greater supervisory oversight over their offenders and can threaten to send the offender to prison if they refuse to complete their drug treatment programs.[28]

Yet, the move toward more programming-based prison alternatives does not signal a philosophical shift away from incarceration and longer sentences. Lawmakers and Texas and Idaho, for example, have argued that tough sentencing laws are still needed to keep crime under control.[29] In fact, some states have passed even tougher legislation for violent offenders. In Oklahoma, offenders convicted of violent offenses have to register their whereabouts with the state Department of Corrections or a local police agency for 10 years after being released from prison. The state also requires personal identification, including address, fingerprint information, and even DNA markers, to be kept in a violent-offender registry.[30]

Sex offenders have also been at the center of recent reforms, as parents have expressed continuing concern over the predatory nature of violent pedophiles. California and other states now release information about the whereabouts of registered sex offenders, including their home addresses, to the public on the state's Web site. Arizona requires local authorities to notify personnel, such as school administrators, when registered sex offenders move into a nearby area. In 2004, Georgia exempted sex offenses from any type of sentencing leniency normally given to first-time offenders, and Maine and Washington passed additional sentencing enhancements for dangerous pedophiles.[31] However, the toughest measure to date is the Jessica Lunsford Act, passed in Florida in 2005 after the abduction, assault, and murder of 9-year-old Jessica Lunsford by a registered sex offender. The law mandates a 25-year-to-life sentence for offenders convicted of sexually assaulting children under 12 years of age. It also requires sex offenders to be monitored for life using satellite tracking equipment. Sex offenders currently on probation would also be electronically monitored for the duration of their supervision period.[32] Similarly, in November 2006, 70 percent of Californians approved a law that would increase penalties for sex offenders, forbid them from living within 2,000 feet from a school or park, and require them to be monitored by satellite tracking equipment for life.

As supporters of Jessica's Law and other mandatory sex offender sentencing laws can attest, the get-tough movement is still alive and well, more than a decade after the initial Three Strikes laws swept the nation. In fact, the governor of Arizona just recently approved a Three Strikes law on April 18, 2006. Arizona is now the 26th state in the nation to enact a Three Strikes law. The legislator sponsoring the law, introduced as Senate Bill 1444, stated that he proposed the policy to protect crime victims and the community through the identification and removal of offenders who continue to threaten public safety. The law imposes a mandatory life sentence on any offender who has been convicted of two previous strike offenses, which are defined as violent or aggravated felonies. Crimes on the eligible strike list include first- and second-degree murder, aggravated assault, drive-by shooting, kidnapping, violent sexual assault, child molestation, sexual abuse of a child, child prostitution, sexual exploitation of a minor, residential burglary of an occupied dwelling, armed robbery, participation in organized crime or a criminal street gang, terrorism, and acts of germ warfare. Offenders sentenced under the Three Strikes law will be ineligible for parole, probation, pardon, or any other release provision for at least 35 years.[33]

Is the Public Ready for Reform?

The role of public opinion was instrumental in getting Three Strikes enacted in the first place, and lawmakers will likely take public opinion into consideration before proposing or endorsing Three Strikes reforms. Although time has passed since a wave of frustration and fear swept the nation in the mid-1990s and crime rates have fallen substantially from their record-high levels, it is not yet clear that the public is willing to be more forgiving of offenders who repeatedly break the law. The drug court reform movement is one indication that public opinion may have softened for those who have committed victimless crimes, but the public still appears to be supportive of punitive measures for violent or repeat offenders. Unless a consensus for change emerges over the handling of recidivist offenders, or the public loses confidence in the ability of the government to handle the problem, then the current penal scheme will likely remain in place for some time.[34] However, if the public loses confidence in the government's ability to control crime or if the people demand real change from the legislature, then policy makers will likely respond by another series of reforms.

The public may also decide that reform is necessary if discussions center on Three Strikes cases. Research has shown that the public is largely supportive of Three Strikes laws in general, but that support begins to waver when people are introduced to actual Three Strikes scenarios. For example, when researchers asked voters in Ohio about their general support for a Three Strikes bill that was pending in 1995, they found that 52.1 percent of the residents who were surveyed strongly supported the Three Strikes measure. An additional 36.3 percent said that they supported the law "somewhat," and only 11.5 percent indicated that they were opposed to the bill.[35] However, when researchers gave residents a series of vignettes that described an offender's current crime and past convictions and asked them to select an appropriate punishment from a wide range of penalty options, only a few people chose the proposed Three Strikes sentence of life in prison. Instead, the majority of respondents supported much shorter sentences for the hypothetical offenders instead.[36]

Additionally, a large majority of the respondents stated that they supported a Three Strikes law that allowed exceptions to be made for certain offenders. For instance, 75.5 percent of the respondents supported discretion over the sentence when the third offense was relatively minor (e.g., stealing a slice of pizza); three out of five also favored granting exceptions to offenders who were mentally retarded. The respondents also appeared to be evenly split in their support for exceptions to Three Strikes sentences for nonviolent offenders (48.7% supported exceptions) or for offenders who are rehabilitated after participating in treatment programs (54.1% supported exceptions).[37] However, only a few respondents supported the idea of granting exceptions to solve financial or institutional problems; fewer than one out of five supported exceptions for Three Strikes sentences just to save tax revenues or to alleviate prison overcrowding.[38] Thus, proposals that emphasize the cost-savings nature of various reform proposals may not be successful in persuading the public to abandon a policy that they otherwise support.

Possible Three Strikes Reforms

In early 2005, Washington State Senator Adam Kline introduced two bills that proposed to modify the state's Three Strikes law. The first proposal, Senate Bill 5760, would allow persistent offenders sentenced under the law to be released after serving a minimum of 15 years in prison, provided that the offenders have not been convicted of violent Class A felonies. Proponents of the change argue that a geriatric release provision will not jeopardize public safety because older offenders typically have low recidivism rates. Furthermore, releasing inmates early will help to defray some of the health care expenditures that would be required for aging prisoners. The second proposal, Senate Bill 5284, would eliminate second-degree robbery as an eligible offense. Criminal defense attorneys claim that the offenses should be excluded from the list of strike offenses because second-degree robberies are less serious offenses. Usually they begin as shoplifting or petty theft events, but because the defendant pushes or shoves an attendant or clerk in an attempt to get away, prosecutors are able to charge it as a strike. The bill also would allow previously sentenced offenders to be resentenced under the new requirements. Estimates are that 50 strike offenders would be eligible for immediate release and an additional 40 offenders would be eligible for release a few years later.[39] Although Kline's proposals won the support of some members in the justice system, both bills were defeated in committee during the 2005 legislative cycle. Kline reintroduced them in January 2006, but the bills appear to be headed for another legislative defeat.

Although Proposition 66 was rejected just a short time ago, California voters may once again be asked to consider proposals to amend the Three Strikes law. Recently, there were two competing ballot initiatives in circulation that would have revised the way the current Three Strikes law is structured. The first proposal, drafted by Los Angeles County District Attorney Steve Cooley and Los Angeles attorney Brian Dunn, sought to narrow the strike zone by removing the mandatory 25-year-to-life sentence for three-strike offenders convicted of a nonserious or nonviolent felony. These offenders would receive a doubled sentence instead. This would give the offender a much shorter sentence, thus curtailing much of the criticism that has been levied against California's Three Strikes law. The proposed initiative would have also authorized the resentencing of offenders under this same formula but would have eliminated certain felony crimes from resentencing consideration. For example, otherwise eligible offenders that had previous strikes for murder, firearm use, and specific drugs and/or sex crimes would have been exempt from the shorter sentence. Unlike Proposition 66, this proposal would have done nothing to alter the serious and/or violent strike list under Cal. Penal Code §1192.7(c), nor would it have restricted the number of strikes that an offender could earn during a single trial.[40]

Steve Cooley began his quest for Three Strikes reform shortly after the law was enacted. As head deputy of the busy San Fernando branch of the Los Angeles County District Attorney's Office, Cooley developed a regional policy of charging third strikes only against defendants who committed serious and/or violent offenses. Although this strategy sometimes upset his supervisors, who adopted a tougher no-bargaining approach, Cooley's policy won him the support of local judges.[41] When he campaigned against incumbent Gil Garcetti in fall 2000, Cooley pledged to make this Three Strikes policy a cornerstone of his prosecution strategy. Shortly after his victory, he issued a directive to deputy prosecutors instructing them to use their discretion to dismiss prior strikes against those offenders who are accused of nonserious or nonviolent third-strike crimes. Supervisors would be allowed to approve deviations to this policy, but they would have to be justified by objective factors in the offender's record.[42]

Although Proposition 66 also proposed to restrict the third strike to serious and/or violent felonies, Cooley vigorously opposed that initiative because it would have automatically released thousands of two- and three-strike offenders at a considerable risk to public safety. His support for reform now is grounded in his belief that the current law has the potential to create disproportionately severe sentences. Furthermore, he has acknowledged that reform is inevitable but expresses concern that future measures like Proposition 66 would go too far and strip the law of its ability to fight crime. Consequently, Cooley noted that his Three Strikes motto is "fix it or lose it."[43] For Cooley to have been successful in getting his proposal on the November 2006 ballot, he would have needed to obtain almost 350,000 valid signatures. Although it failed to qualify this time around, he has pledged to try again.

Cooley may also receive some future assistance in his reform efforts from the state legislature. In spring 2006, California Senate Majority Leader Gloria Romero (D) introduced Senate Bill 1642 that would have placed Cooley's proposal directly on the November 2006 ballot, thus sidestepping the expensive signature-gathering process. The bill, which Cooley supported, also earned the support of leading law enforcement officials. Los Angeles Police Chief William Bratton called the reform measure a "balanced approach," and Los Angeles County Sheriff Lee Baca voiced his support for legislative involvement in Three Strikes reform.[44] Their support, however, put them at odds with other law enforcement groups, including the CDAA. Although the CDAA originally opposed the Three Strikes proposal in 1994, the organization has since become one of the law's strongest supporters. With 2006 primary elections just days away, the CDAA successfully lobbied the rest of the legislature to reject the bill. In particular, the CDAA argued that because the bill would be applied retroactively, up to 4,400 strike offenders would be resentenced, and many of those would likely be immediately released.[45] Although Romero's proposal failed to win enough votes in the legislature to pass the measure, Cooley and other supporters may ask the legislature to try again in the new term.

In addition to Cooley's proposal, another Three Strikes reform initiative, authored by Steve Ipsen, President of the Association of Deputy District Attorneys, also attempted to qualify for the November 2006 ballot. Ipsen was instrumental in helping defeat Proposition 66, but like Cooley, he believes that Three Strikes reform is likely. Ipsen's proposal, however, extended beyond the removal of the controversial minor strike provision. Rather, Ipsen's measure sought to reclassify the state's felony offense designations into three categories. Violent felonies would be considered Class A offenses, serious felonies would be labeled as Class B crimes, and other felonies would be identified as Class C offenses. Offenders would continue to earn strikes for Class A and Class B offenses, but for final strike offenses, courts would be given additional discretion to impose shorter sentences on offenders convicted of Class C crimes. Like Cooley's proposal, Ipsen's initiative also failed to collect enough valid signatures to qualify for the November 2006 ballot.

Although both initiatives failed to qualify for the ballot in this most recent election cycle, it is possible that they will be successful in attracting more supporters in the future. Much of that success will depend on their ability to convince influential organizations, such as the CDAA, to back their efforts. Initially, the CDAA was resistant to any type of reform that would potentially weaken the law, but the consistent lobbying by Los Angeles County District Attorney Steve Cooley may be significant enough to convince other district attorneys to change their minds. It is also possible that interest groups who have consistently opposed Three Strikes will support Cooley's future efforts to reform the law, believing, perhaps, that some reform is better than none. Fearing that future reform would neuter the law, Three Strikes supporters might also adopt Cooley's rationale and conclude that a little reform might improve the chances that the law will be left largely intact for years to come.

SUMMARY

Despite criticism from scholars, some criminal justice professionals, policy makers, and interest groups, Three Strikes laws appear as though they are here to stay. Lawmakers have been hesitant to suggest outright repeal of the laws even though their prison budgets are quickly inflating due to health-related costs of aging prisoners. Furthermore, violent crimes, such as the abduction and murder of Jessica Lunsford in Florida, still happen frequently enough to remind voters that tough laws are still needed for dangerous offenders. At the same time, there appears to be a new movement to reduce penalties for drug users and to utilize rehabilitation and treatment programs for less-serious offenders. Interest is also growing among lawmakers to allocate funds to assist former inmates in reintegrating with their families and communities to reduce the number of parole violations and to lower the rate of recidivism. Providing former inmates with job training, housing assistance, and even income assistance until they are able to provide for themselves is seen by some as a wise—and cost-effective—investment.

If public sentiment continues to favor rehabilitation and treatment over incarceration, lawmakers need not formally repeal Three Strikes laws to render them obsolete. Use of discretion by prosecutors and judges could produce the same effect, in that laws that are routinely ignored are no different in practical terms than laws that are repealed. To some degree, this may have already happened. As statistics have shown, only a handful of states actually use their Three Strikes laws to any measurable degree. California leads the way with over forty thousand offenders sentenced under its provisions, but reformers have been working diligently to substantially reduce that number. Georgia and Florida have also used their Three Strikes laws on a regular basis, but budgetary pressures may discourage aggressive enforcement. Other states, which have used their laws even less frequently, might choose to forgo lengthy mandatory sentences in favor of shorter enhancements if expanding prison populations become too great a concern.

As for now, it appears as though Three Strikes laws still hold symbolic value with voters who perhaps have not completely forgotten a time when crime rates were high and acts of random violence prompted quick legislative action. Although fears of crime have recently declined, and enforcement of some mandatory sentencing laws may have eased, recently released statistics show that violent crime rates are once more on the rise.[46] If this trend continues, the public may prompt policy makers to get tough once again.

NOTES

1. Tonry, "Mandatory Penalties."

2. Michael Vitiello, "Reforming Three Strikes' Excesses," *Washington University Law Quarterly* 82 (2004), 33.

3. Ibid., 1–42.

4. Tonry, "Mandatory Penalties."

5. Greenwood et al., *Three Strikes and You're Out: Estimated Benefits and Costs.*

6. Jonathan P. Caulkins, "How Large Should the Strike Zone Be in 'Three Strikes and You're Out' Sentencing Laws?" *Journal of Quantitative Criminology* 17, no. 3 (2001), 227–46.

7. Auerhahn, *Selective Incapacitation and Public Policy.*

8. Kathleen Auerhahn, "Selective Incapacitation, Three Strikes, and the Problem of Aging Prison Populations: Using Simulation Modeling to See the Future," *Criminology & Public Policy* 1, no. 3 (2002).

9. Fox Butterfield, "With Cash Tight, States Reassess Long Jail Terms," *New York Times,* November 10, 2003.

10. Official Voter Information Guide, California General Election, November 2, 2004. Available at http://vote2004.ss.ca.gov/voterguide/propositions/prop66-title. htm. Accessed June 15, 2006.

11. http://vote2004.ss.ca.gov/voterguide/propositions/prop66-arguments.htm. Accessed June 15, 2006.

12. The various proposals to narrow Three Strikes were introduced as AB1076 (1997), AB 2447 (1999), AB 1790 (2002), SB 1517 (2002), and AB 112 (2003). Another bill, SB 331, sought to strengthen Three Strikes was also introduced in 1996. This bill would have reversed the California Supreme Court's decision in the 1996 case *People v. Superior Court (Romero)* that extended discretion to judges to dismiss prior strike convictions. This bill also failed to clear the two-thirds vote requirement.

13. SB 2048 (1998) and SB 873 (1999).

14. Veto message for SB 2048, 1998. Available at http://www.leginfo.ca.gov. Accessed June 16, 2006.

15. Dan Morain, "Man Bankrolls Initiative to Change 3-Strikes Law," *Los Angeles Times,* May 31, 2004.

16. Dan Walters, "Apparent Flaws Mar Poll that Showed Voters Ready to Dilute 'Three Strikes,'" *Sacramento Bee,* June 25, 2004.

17. Bill Ainsworth, "Poll Finds Support for Proposition on 3 Strikes is Declining," *San Diego Union-Tribune,* October 30, 2004.

18. Dan Walters, "Voter Turnaround on Proposition 66 was a Dramatic Campaign Event," *Sacramento Bee,* November 16, 2004.

19. Bill Ainsworth, "'3 Strikes' Campaign Splits Klaas Family," *San Diego Union-Tribune,* July 14, 2004.

20. http://vote2004.ss.ca.gov/voterguide/propositions/prop66-arguments.htm. Accessed June 15, 2006.

21. See additional profiles at http://whyamidead.com. Accessed June 14, 2006.

22. Walters, "Voter Turnaround on Proposition 66."

23. Donna Lyons, *State Crime Legislation in 2004* (Denver, Colo.: National Conference of State Legislatures, 2005).

24. Donna Lyons, "Tough Times to Be Tough on Crime: An Edited Transcript of a Recent Discussion on Corrections and Sentencing Policy among Key State Legislators," *State Legislatures* 29, no. 6 (2003), 12–18.

25. Ibid., 12–18.

26. Richard S. Gebelein, *The Rebirth of Rehabilitation: Promise and Perils of Drug Courts* (Washington, D.C.: U.S. Department of Justice, Office of Justice Programs, National Institute of Justice, 2000).

27. Butterfield, "With Cash Tight, States Reassess Long Jail Terms."

28. Gebelein, *Rebirth of Rehabilitation.*

29. Lyons, "Tough Times to be Tough on Crime," 12–18.

30. Lyons, *State Crime Legislation in 2004.*

31. Ibid.

32. Abbie Vansickle, "Bush Signs Jessica Lunsford Act; Parents Watch Birth of Law to Spare Others Their Agony," *St. Petersburg Times,* May 3, 2005.

33. Associated Press, "'3 Strikes' Measure Goes to Governor, " *Arizona Republic,* April 14, 2006. Available online at http://www.azcentral.com/arizonarepublic/local/articles/0414three-strikes0414.html.

34. Zimring et al., *Crime and Punishment in California.*

35. Brandon K. Applegate, Francis T. Cullen, Michael G. Turner, and Jody L. Sundt, "Assessing Public Support for Three-Strikes-and-You're-Out Laws: Global versus Specific Attitudes," *Crime & Delinquency* 42, no. 4 (1996), 517–34.

36. Ibid., 517–34.

37. Ibid., 517–34.

38. Ibid., 517–34.

39. Tracy Johnson, "Bill Would Let Some 'Three Strikes' Convicts Seek Release After 15 Years," *Seattle Post-Intelligencer,* February 9, 2005.

40. Steve Cooley, "'Three Strikes' Must Be Reformed Statewide," *Sacramento Bee,* February 26, 2006.

41. Krikorian et al., "Front-Line Fights over 3 Strikes."

42. Memorandum from Steve Cooley, December 19, 2000.

43. Joe Domanick, "New Count for Three-Strikes Law," *Los Angeles Weekly,* January 13–19, 2006.

44. Peter Y. Hong, "Bratton, Baca Support Attempts to Reform Three Strikes Law," *Los Angeles Times,* March 3, 2006, B3.

45. "It's Politics: Romero Strikes Back," *Los Angeles Times,* June 3, 2006.

46. Anne Sweeney, "Violent Crime Makes Biggest Jump Since '91," *Chicago Sun-Times,* June 13, 2006.

Bibliography

Abrahamson, Alan. "25% of Three-Strikes Cases Go to Trial, Straining Courts." *Los Angeles Times,* July 2, 1996, sec. A.

Ainsworth, Bill. "'3 Strikes' Campaign Splits Klaas Family." *San Diego Union-Tribune,* July 14, 2004, sec. A.

———. "Poll Finds Support for Proposition on 3 Strikes Is Declining." *San Diego Union-Tribune,* October 30, 2004, sec. A.

Allen, Francis A. "Criminal Justice, Legal Values and the Rehabilitative Ideal." *Journal of Criminal Law, Criminology, and Police Science* 50 (1959): 226–32.

American Friends Service Committee. *Struggle for Justice.* New York: Hill and Wang, 1971.

Antiterrorism and Effective Death Penalty Act of 1996. Pub. L. No. 104–132, 110 Stat.1214 (Apr. 24, 1996).

Applegate, Brandon K., Francis T. Cullen, Michael G. Turner, and Jody L. Sundt. "Assessing Public Support for Three-Strikes-and-You're-Out Laws: Global Versus Specific Attitudes." *Crime & Delinquency* 42, no. 4 (1996): 517–34.

Ardaiz, James A. "California's Three Strikes Law: History, Expectations, Consequences." *McGeorge Law Review* 32, no. 1 (2000): 1–36.

Armstrong, Scott. "Nation's Toughest Three-Strike Law Being Reassessed." *Christian Science Monitor,* August 30, 1994.

Associated Press. "'3 Strikes' Measure Goes to Governor." *Arizona Republic,* April 14, 2006.

Auerhahn, Kathleen. *Selective Incapacitation and Public Policy: Evaluating California's Imprisonment Crisis.* Edited by Austin T. Turk, SUNY Series in New Directions in Crime and Justice Studies. Albany: State University of New York Press, 2003.

————. "Selective Incapacitation, Three Strikes, and the Problem of Aging Prison Populations: Using Simulation Modeling to See the Future." *Criminology & Public Policy* 1, no. 3 (2002): 353–88.

Austin, James, John Clark, Patricia Hardyman, and D. Alan Henry. *"Three Strikes and You're Out": The Implementation and Impact of Strike Laws.* Washington, D.C.: U.S. Department of Justice, National Institute of Justice, 1998.

Babus, Marc, Joseph Perkovich, and Vincent Schiraldi. *Big Time for Petty Crime: The Story of Petty Theft Offenders in California.* San Francisco: Center on Juvenile and Criminal Justice, 1995.

Baker, Michael. "'Three Strikes' convict charged with theft." *Fresno Bee,* December 13, 2003.

Balzar, John. "The Target: Repeat Offenders." *Los Angeles Times,* March 24, 1994, sec. A.

Beck, Allen J., and Bernard E. Shipley. *Recidivism of Prisoners Released in 1983.* Washington, D.C.: U.S. Department of Justice, Office of Justice Programs, Bureau of Justice Statistics, 1989.

Bennett, William J. "Yes on 593; Three Strikes and You're Out." *Seattle Times,* September 19, 1993, sec. B.

Brown, Brian, and Greg Jolivette. *A Primer: Three Strikes. The Impact After More Than a Decade.* Sacramento, Calif.: Legislative Analyst's Office, 2005.

Bureau of Justice Statistics Crime & Justice Data Online, www.ojp.usdoj.gov/bjs/.

Butterfield, Fox. "With Cash Tight, States Reassess Long Jail Terms." *New York Times,* November 10, 2003, sec. A.

California Department of Corrections, "Fall 2003 Population Projections, 2004–2009." Sacramento, Calif.: Population Projections Unit, Estimates and Statistical Analysis Section, Offender Information Services Branch, Department of Corrections, September 2003. Available online at http://www.cdcr.ca.gov/ReportsResearch/OffenderInfoServices/Projections/F03Pub.pdf

California Department of Corrections, "Second and Third Strikers in the Institution Population, December 31, 2001." Sacramento, Calif.: Data Analysis Unit, Estimates and Statistical Analysis Section, Offender Information Services Branch, California Department of Corrections, 2001. Available online at http://www.cdcr.ca.gov/ReportsResearch/OffenderInfoServices/Quarterly/Strike1Archive.html.

California Department of Corrections and Rehabilitation, "Second and Third Strikers in the Adult Institution Population, December 31, 2005." Sacramento, Calif.: Data Analysis Unit, Estimates and Statistical Analysis Section, Offender Information Services Branch, California Department of Corrections and Rehabilitation, 2005. Available online at http://www.cdcr.ca.gov/ReportsResearch/OffenderInfoServices/Quarterly/Strike1Archive.html.

California Department of Corrections and Rehabilitation. "Spring 2006 Adult Population Projections, 2006–2011." Sacramento, Calif.: Population Projections Unit, Estimates and Statistical Analysis Section, Offender Information Services Branch, Department of Corrections and Rehabilitation, February 2006. Available online at http://www.cdcr.ca.gov/ReportsResearch/OffenderInfoServices/Projections/S06Pub.pdf.

California District Attorneys Association. *Prosecutors' Perspective on California's Three Strikes Law: A 10-Year Retrospective.* Sacramento, Calif.: California District Attorneys Association, 2004.

Cameron, Mindy. "Black-White Campaigns on Issues Bathed in Gray." *Seattle Times,* October 31, 1993, sec. B.

Carlson, John. "Three-Strikes Law Works." *Seattle Post-Intelligencer*, March 1, 2001.

Carlson, Kenneth. *Mandatory Sentencing: The Experience of Two States.* Washington, D.C.: U.S. Department of Justice, National Institute of Justice, Office of Development, Testing, and Dissemination, 1982.

Casper, Jonathan D., David Brereton, and David Neal. *The Implementation of the California Determinate Sentencing Law.* Washington, D.C.: U.S. Department of Justice, National Institute of Justice, Office of Research Programs, 1982.

Caulkins, Jonathan P. "How Large Should the Strike Zone Be in 'Three Strikes and You're Out' Sentencing Laws?" *Journal of Quantitative Criminology* 17, no. 3 (2001): 227–46.

Center for Urban Analysis, Office of the County Executive, Santa Clara County, California. *Assessing the Impact of AB971 "Three Strikes, You're Out" on the Justice System in Santa Clara County, California.* Santa Clara, Calif.: Santa Clara County Board of Supervisors, 1994.

Church, Thomas. "Plea Bargaining, Concessions and the Courts: Analysis of a Quasi-Experiment." In *The Invisible Justice System: Discretion and the Law,* edited by Burton Atkins and Mark Pogrebin, 204–19. Cincinnati: Anderson, 1978.

Clark, John, James Austin, and D. Alan Henry. *"Three Strikes and You're Out": A Review of State Legislation.* Washington, D.C.: U.S. Department of Justice, Office of Justice Programs, National Institute of Justice, 1997.

Clear, Todd R., John D. Hewitt, and Robert M. Regoli. "Discretion and Determinate Sentence: Its Distribution, Control, and Effect on Time Served." *Crime & Delinquency* 25 (1978): 428–45.

Cohen, Jacqueline. "The Incapacitative Effect of Imprisonment: A Critical Review of the Literature." In *Deterrence and Incapacitation: Estimating the Effects of Criminal Sanctions on Crime Rates,* edited by Alfred Blumstein, Jacqueline Cohen, and Daniel Nagin, 187–243. Washington, D.C.: National Academy of Sciences, 1977.

Coker v. Georgia, 433 U.S. 584 (1977).

Cooley, Steve. "'Three Strikes' Must Be Reformed Statewide." *Sacramento Bee,* February 26, 2006.

Davis, Kenneth Culp. *Discretionary Justice: A Preliminary Inquiry.* Baton Rouge: Louisiana State University Press, 1969.

Dewar, Helen. "Republicans Are Racing to Collar Crime Issue Purloined by President." *Washington Post,* January 27, 1994, sec. A.

Dickey, Walter J. *"Three Strikes" Five Years Later.* Washington, D.C.: Campaign for an Effective Crime Policy, 1998.

Ditton, Paula M. *Truth in Sentencing in State Prisons.* Washington, D.C.: U.S. Department of Justice, Office of Justice Programs, Bureau of Justice Statistics, 1999.

Domanick, Joe. "Dumb Kid, Petty Crimes: A Life Term?" *Los Angeles Times,* July 24, 1998, sec. B.

———. "New Count for Three-Strikes Law." *Los Angeles Weekly,* January 13–19, 2006.

Ehlers, Scott, Vincent Schiraldi, and Jason Ziedenberg. *Still Striking Out: Ten Years of California's Three Strikes.* Washington, D.C.: Justice Policy Institute, 2004.

Eisenstein, James, Roy B. Fleming, and Peter F. Nardulli. *The Contours of Justice: Communities and Their Courts.* Lanham, Md.: University Press of America, 1999.

Enmund v. Florida, 458 U.S. 782 (1982).

Ewing v. California, 538 U.S. 11 (2003).

Feeley, Malcolm M., and Sam Kamin. "The Effect of 'Three Strikes and You're Out' on the Courts: Looking Back to See the Future." In *Three Strikes and You're Out: Vengeance as Public Policy,* edited by David Shichor and Dale K. Sechrest, 135–54. Thousand Oaks, Calif.: Sage, 1996.

Finucane, Martin. "Breyer Criticizes Mandatory Minimum Sentences." *washingtonpost.com,* September 22, 2003.

Fisher, Ian. "Why '3-Strike' Sentencing Is a Solid Hit This Season." *New York Times,* January 25, 1994, sec. B.

Frankel, Marvin E. *Criminal Sentences: Law without Order.* New York: Hill and Wang, 1972.

Frase, Richard S. "State Sentencing Guidelines: Still Going Strong." *Judicature* 78, no. 4 (1995): 173–79.

Freedman, Dan. "Polly's Dad Urges Clinton to Make America Safer." *Times-Picayune*(New Orleans), December 21, 1993, sec. A.

Furman v. Georgia, 408 U.S. 238 (1972).

Gebelein, Richard S. *The Rebirth of Rehabilitation: Promise and Perils of Drug Courts.* Washington, D.C.: U.S. Department of Justice, Office of Justice Programs, National Institute of Justice, 2000.

Gest, Ted. *Crime & Politics: Big Government's Erratic Campaign for Law and Order.* New York: Oxford University Press, 2001.

Gilmore, Susan. "Initiative Backers Try Again for Tough-Sentencing Plan." *Seattle Times,* January 7, 1993, section G.

Goldston, Linda. "Search for Missing Girl Called No Less Than Petaluma Miracle; Effort to Find Kidnapped 12-Year-old One of Largest Ever." *Houston Chronicle,* October 13, 1993, sec. A.

Gottfredson, Stephen D., and Don M. Gottfredson. "Accuracy of Prediction Models." In *Criminal Careers and "Career Criminals,"* edited by Alfred Blumstein, Jacqueline Cohen, Jeffrey A. Roth, and Christy A. Visher, Panel on Research on Criminal Careers, Committee on Research on Law Enforcement and the Administration of Justice, Commission on Behavioral and Social Sciences and Education, National Research Council, 212–90. Washington, D.C.: National Academy Press, 1986.

Greenwood, Peter, C. Peter Rydell, Allan F. Abrahamse, Jonathan P. Caulkins, James Chiesa, Karyn E. Model, and Stephen P. Klein. *Three Strikes and You're Out: Estimated Benefits and Costs of California's New Mandatory-Sentencing Law.* Santa Monica, Calif.: RAND, 1994.

Greenwood, Peter W., and Allan F. Abrahamse. *Selective Incapacitation.* Santa Monica, Calif.: RAND Corporation, 1982.

Griset, Pamala. *Determinate Sentencing: The Promise and the Reality of Retributive Justice.* Albany: State University of New York Press, 1991.

Gross, Jane. "Drive to Keep Repeat Felons in Prison Gains in California." *New York Times,* December 26, 1993, sec. 1.

Gryger v. Burke U.S. 334 728 (1948).

Gunnison, Robert B., and Greg Lucas. "Wilson Pushes Crime, Economy in State of the State Address." *San Francisco Chronicle,* January 6, 1994, sec. A.

Harmelin v. Michigan, 501 U.S. 957 (1991).

Harris, John, and Paul Jesilow. "It's Not the Old Ball Game: Three Strikes and the Courtroom Workgroup." *Justice Quarterly* 17, no. 1 (2000): 186–203.

Helland, Eric, and Alexander Tabarrok. "Does Three Strikes Deter? A Non-Parametic Estimation." *Journal of Human Resources* (forthcoming).

Heumann, Milton, Colin Loftin, and David McDowall. "Mandatory Sentencing and the Abolition of Plea Bargaining: The Michigan Felony Firearm Statute." *Law & Society Review* 13 (1979): 393–430.

Hofer, Paul J., Charles Loeffler, Kevin Blackwell, and Patricia Valentino. *Fifteen Years of Guideline Sentencing: An Assessment of How Well the Federal Criminal Justice System Is Achieving the Goals of Sentencing Reform,* November 2004. Washington, D.C.: United States Sentencing Commission, 2004. Available online at http://www.ussc.gov/15_year/15year.htm.

Holding, Reynolds. "Behind the Nationwide Move to Keep Repeaters in Prison." *San Francisco Chronicle,* December 8, 1993, sec. A.

Hong, Peter Y. "Bratton, Baca Support Attempts to Reform Three Strikes Law." *Los Angeles Times,* March 3, 2006, sec. B.

Hudson v. McMillan, 503 U.S. 1 (1992).

In re Cervera, 24 Cal.4th 1073 (2001).

Ingwerson, Marshall. "GOP Is No Longer Bastion of Tough Talk on Crime." *Christian Science Monitor,* February 1, 1994.

"It's Politics: Romero Strikes Back." *Los Angeles Times,* June 3, 2006.

Jaffe, Mark Evan, and Kaushal K. Sharma. "Malingering Uncommon Psychiatric Symptoms among Defendants Charged under California's 'Three Strikes and You're Out' Law." *Journal of Forensic Science* 43, no. 3 (1998): 549–55.

Johnson, Tracy. "Bill Would Let Some 'Three Strikes' Convicts Seek Release After 15 Years." *Seattle Post-Intelligencer,* February 9, 2005.

Judicial Council of California, Administrative Office of the Courts. *"Three Strikes" Summary.* San Francisco: Judicial Council of California, 1998.

Kannensohn, Michael. *A National Survey of Parole-Related Legislation Enacted During the 1979 Legislative Session.* Washington, D.C.: U.S. Department of Justice, Bureau of Justice Statistics, 1979.

Kershner, Vlae. "Governor Wants '3 Strikes' Plan That Is Toughest, Most Costly." *San Francisco Chronicle,* March 3, 1994, sec. A.

———. "Klaases Like Substitute 3 Strikes Bill: Polly's Kin Support Measure Excluding Nonviolent Felonies." *San Francisco Chronicle,* March 10, 1994, sec. A.

———. "Poll Shows Commanding Lead for State's '3 Strikes' Initiative." *San Francisco Chronicle,* January 26, 1994, sec. A.

Kershner, Vlae, and Carolyn Lochhead. "Politicians React with Calls for Stiffer Sentences: Wilson and Feinstein Join Cry for Less Leniency." *San Francisco Chronicle,* December 7, 1993, sec. A.

Kershner, Vlae, and Greg Lucas. "'3 Strikes' Leader Warns Assembly: He Doesn't Want Ballot Measure Softened." *San Francisco Chronicle,* January 5, 1994, sec. A.

———. "'Three Strikes' Signed into California Law." *San Francisco Chronicle,* March 8, 1994, sec. A.

Kessler, Daniel, and Steven D. Levitt. "Using Sentence Enhancements to Distinguish between Deterrence and Incapacitation." *Journal of Law and Economics* 42, no. 1 (1999): 343–63.

Kovandzic, Tomislav V., John J. Sloan III, and Lynne M. Vieraitis. "'Striking Out' as Crime Reduction Policy: The Impact of 'Three Strikes' Laws on Crime Rates in U.S. Cities." *Justice Quarterly* 21, no. 2 (2004): 207–39.

Kramer, John H., and Jeffrey T. Ulmer. "Sentencing Disparity and Departures from Guidelines." *Justice Quarterly* 13, no. 1 (1996): 81–106.

Krikorian, Greg. "Judge Slashes Life Sentence in Pizza Theft Case." *Los Angeles Times,* January 29, 1997, sec. A.

———. "More Blacks Imprisoned Under '3 Strikes,' Study Says." *Los Angeles Times,* March 5, 1996, sec. A.

Krikorian, Greg, Ann W. O'Neill, Miles Corwin, Edward J. Boyer, and Alan Abrahamson. "Front-Line Fights over 3 Strikes." *Los Angeles Times,* July 1, 1996, sec. A.

Law Enforcement Assistance Administration. *Two Hundred Years of American Criminal Justice: An LEAA Bicentennial Study* (Washington, D.C.: U.S. Department of Justice, Law Enforcement Assistance Administration, 1976).

Legislative Analyst's Office. *Status Check: The "Three Strikes and You're Out" Law—a Preliminary Assessment.* Sacramento, Calif.: Legislative Analyst's Office, 1995.

———. *The "Three Strikes and You're Out" Law: An Update.* Sacramento, Calif.: Legislative Analyst's Office, State of California, 1997.

Lewis, Neil A. "President Foresees Safer U.S." *New York Times,* August 27, 1994.

Lewis, Peter. "I-593 Strikes Out on Death Row—Worse Killers Would Not Have Been Affected." *Seattle Times,* October 28, 1993, sec. B.

———. "'Three Strikes' Initiative Gains Strength, Takes Aim at Felons—but Opponents Say Measure Will Be Drain on Taxpayers." *Seattle Times,* August 31, 1993, sec. A.

———. "'3 Strikes' Laws Have Struck Out Elsewhere—Other States See No Drop in Crime." *Seattle Times,* September 30, 1993, sec. A.

———. "'Three Strikes You're Out': Three-Fourths Yes and It's In." *Seattle Times,* November 3, 1993, sec. C.

Lindsey, Edward. "Historical Sketch of the Indeterminate Sentence and Parole System." *Journal of Criminal Law, Criminology, and Police Science* 16 (1925): 9–69.

Lockyer v. Andrade, 538 U.S. 63 (2003).

Lowenthal, Gary T. "Mandatory Sentencing Laws: Undermining the Effectiveness of Determinate Sentencing Reform." *California Law Review* 81 (1993): 61–123.

Lungren, Dan. *"Three Strikes and You're Out"—Its Impact on the California Criminal Justice System after Four Years.* Sacramento: California Attorney General's Office, 1998.

Lyons, Donna. *State Crime Legislation in 2004.* Denver, Colo.: National Conference of State Legislatures, 2005.

———. "Tough Times to Be Tough on Crime: An Edited Transcript of a Recent Discussion on Corrections and Sentencing Policy among Key State Legislators." *State Legislatures* 29, no. 6 (2003): 12–18.

Males, Mike, and Dan Macallair. "Striking Out: The Failure of California's 'Three Strikes and You're Out' Law." *Stanford Law & Policy Review* 11, no. 1 (1999): 65–74.

Martinson, Robert. "California Research at the Crossroads." In *Rehabilitation, Recidivism, and Research,* edited by Robert Martinson, Ted Palmer, and Stuart Adams, 63–74. Hackensack, N.J.: National Council on Crime and Delinquency, 1976.

———. "What Works? Questions and Answers about Prison Reform." *Public Interest* 35 (1974): 22–54.

Marvell, Thomas B., and Carlisle E. Moody. "The Lethal Effects of Three-Strikes Laws." *Journal of Legal Studies* 30 (2001): 89–106.

McAneny, Leslie. "Americans Want Tougher Action on Crime." *St. Louis Dispatch,* December 19, 1993, sec. 4.

Merritt, Nancy, Terry Fain, and Susan Turner. *Oregon's Measure 11 Sentencing Reform: Implementation and System Impact.* Santa Monica, Calif.: RAND Corporation, 2004.

Messinger, Sheldon L., and Phillip E. Johnson. "California's Determinate Sentencing Statute: History and Issues." In *Determinate Sentencing: Reform or Regression?* Proceedings of the Special Conference on Determinate Sentencing, June 2–3, 1977, Boalt Hall School of Law, University of California, Berkeley. Washington, D.C.: National Institute of Law Enforcement and Criminal Justice, Law Enforcement Assistance Administration, 1978, 13–58.

Miethe, Terance D., and Charles A. Moore. "Sentencing Guidelines: Their Effect in Minnesota." U.S. Department of Justice, Office of Justice Programs, National Institute of Justice, 1989.

———. "Socioeconomic Disparities under Determinate Sentencing Systems: A Comparison of Preguideline and Postguideline Practices in Minnesota." *Criminology* 23, no. 2 (1985): 337–63.

Misner, Robert. "Recasting Prosecutorial Discretion." *Journal of Criminal Law and Criminology* 86, no. 3 (1996): 717–77.

Monge v. California, 524 U.S. 721 (1998).

Moore, Charles A., and Terance D. Miethe. "Regulated and Unregulated Sentencing Decisions: An Analysis of First-Year Practices under Minnesota's Felony Sentencing Guidelines." *Law & Society Review* 20, no. 2 (1986): 253–77.

Morain, Dan. "Man Bankrolls Initiative to Change 3-Strikes Law." *Los Angeles Times,* May 31, 2004.

Morrissey, Jim. "Nobody Gets Life Just for Stealing a Pizza." *Los Angeles Times,* August 29, 1996.

Nagin, Daniel S. "Criminal Deterrence Research at the Outset of the Twenty-First Century." *Crime & Justice* 23 (1998): 1–42.

Nardulli, Peter F., James Eisenstein, and Roy B. Fleming. *The Tenor of Justice: Criminal Courts and the Guilty Plea Process.* Urbana: University of Chicago Press, 1988.

Newman, Donald. "The Negotiated Plea Process." In *The Invisible Justice System: Discretion and the Law,* edited by Burton Atkins and Mark Pogrebin, 187–97. Cincinnati: Anderson, 1978.

O'Neil v. Vermont, 144 U.S. 323 (1892).

"An Open Letter from Polly Klaas' Mother." *St. Petersburg Times,* December 8, 1993, sec. 8.

Parent, Dale, Terence Dunworth, Douglas McDonald, and William Rhodes. *Key Legislative Issues in Criminal Justice: Mandatory Sentencing.* Washington, D.C.: U.S. Department of Justice, Office of Justice Programs, National Institute of Justice, 1997.

People v. Garcia, 21 Cal. 4th 1 (1999).

People v. Gatson, 74 Cal. App.4th 310 (1999).

People v. Kilborn, 41 Cal. App.4th 1325 (1996).

People v. Superior Court (Romero), 13 Cal. 4th 497 (1996).

People v. Williams, 17 Cal. 4th 148 (1998).

Perez, Arturo. "States Wrangle with Corrections Budgets." *State Legislatures* 31, no. 5, 2005: 19–20.

Perry, Tony. "'Three-Strikes' Law Spawns Specialist System in San Diego County." *Los Angeles Times,* March 14, 1995, sec. A.

Perry, Tony, and Maura Dolan. "Two Counties at Opposite Poles of '3 Strikes.'" *Los Angeles Times,* June 24, 1996.

Pervear v. Massachusetts, 72 U.S. 475 (1866).

Petersilia, Joan, and Peter W. Greenwood. *Mandatory Prison Sentences: Their Projected Effects on Crime and Prison Populations.* Santa Monica, Calif.: RAND Corporation, 1977.

Petersilia, Joan, Peter W. Greenwood, and Marvin Lavin. *Criminal Careers of Habitual Felons.* Washington, D.C.: U.S. Department of Justice, National Institute of Law Enforcement and Criminal Justice, 1978.

Petersilia, Joan, and Susan Turner. "Guideline-Based Justice: Prediction and Racial Minorities." *Crime and Justice: A Review of Research* 9 (1987): 151–181.

Pound, Roscoe. *Criminal Justice in America.* Da Capo paperback, the Colver lectures, 1924. New York: Da Capo Press, reprint, 1975.

Price, Richard. "Anger and Anguish over Polly's Death: A Tragic End to California Kidnap Case." *USA Today,* December 6, 1993, sec. 3.

Price v. Georgia, 398 U.S. 323 (1970).

Ramirez, Juan R., and William D. Crano. "Deterrence and Incapacitation: An Interrupted Time-Series Analysis of California's Three Strikes Law." *Journal of Applied Social Psychology* 33, no. 1 (2003): 110–44.

Rand, Michael R., and Callie Marie Rennison. "True Crime Stories? Accounting for Differences in our National Crime Indicators." *Chance* 15, no. 1 (2002): 47–51.

Roberts, Julian V. "Public Opinion, Crime, and Criminal Justice." *Crime and Justice: A Review of Research* 16 (1992):99–180.

Rosett, Arthur. "Discretion, Severity, and Legality in Criminal Justice." *Southern California Law Review* 46 (1972): 12–50.

Rothman, David J. "For the Good of All: The Progressive Tradition in Prison Reform." In *History and Crime: Implications for Criminal Justice Policy,* edited by James A. Inciardi and Charles E. Faupel, 271–84. Beverly Hills, Calif.: Sage, 1980.

Rummel v. Estelle, 445 U.S. 263 (1980).

Schaefer, David. "NRA Backs 'Three Strikes' Initiative Campaign—Gun Lobby Puts Money, Time into Repeat-Criminal Crusade." *Seattle Times,* May 5, 1993, section E.

Schafer, John R. "The Deterrent Effect of Three Strikes Law." *FBI Law Enforcement Bulletin* (April 1999): 6–10.

Schiraldi, Vincent, Jason Colburn, and Eric Lotke. *Three Strikes and You're Out: An Examination of the Impact of 3 Strike Laws 10 Years after Their Enactment.* Washington, D.C.: Justice Policy Institute, 2004.

Schiraldi, Vincent, and Michael Godfrey. *Racial Disparities in the Charging of Los Angeles County's Third "Strike" Cases.* San Francisco: Center on Juvenile and Criminal Justice, 1994.

Serrano, Barbara A. "Life Term Sought for Repeat Felons—Initiative Proposes '3 Strikes, You're Out.'" *Seattle Times,* March 25, 1992, sec. B.

Shane-DuBow, Sandra, Alice P. Brown, and Erik Olsen. *Sentencing Reform in the United States: History, Content, and Effect.* Washington, D.C.: U.S. Department of Justice, National Institute of Justice, Office of Development, Testing, and Dissemination, 1985.

Shepherd, Joanna M. "Fear of the First Strike: The Full Deterrent Effect of California's Two- and Three-Strikes Legislation." *Journal of Legal Studies* 31 (2002): 159–201.

Simon, Stephanie. "Backers of Three Strikes Unflinchingly Defend Law." *Los Angeles Times,* July 3, 1996, sec. A.

Singer, Richard G. *Just Deserts: Sentencing Based on Equality and Desert.* Cambridge, Mass.: Ballinger, 1979.

Solem v. Helm, 468 U.S. 277 (1983).

Spolar, Christine. "California Town Cries as Polly Klaas Is Found; Twice-Convicted Suspect Faces Murder, Kidnapping Charges in Abduction of 12-Year-Old." *Washington Post,* December 6, 1993, sec. A.

Starr, Oliver Jr. "The Case of Richard Davis." *National Review,* May 30, 1994.

Stolzenberg, Lisa, and Stewart J. D'Alessio. "'Three Strikes and You're Out': The Impact of California's New Mandatory Sentencing Law on Serious Crime Rates." *Crime & Delinquency* 43 (1997): 457–69.

Sunde, Scott. "Blacks Bear Brunt of '3 Strikes' Law." *Seattle Post-Intelligencer,* February 20, 2001.

"Supreme Court Justice: Prison Terms Too Long." *USAToday.com,* August 10, 2003.

Surette, Ray. "News from Nowhere, Policy to Follow." In *Three Strikes and You're Out: Vengeance as Public Policy,* edited by David Shichor and Dale K. Sechrest, 177–202. Thousand Oaks, Calif.: Sage, 1996.

Sweeney, Anne. "Violent Crime Makes Biggest Jump Since '91." *Chicago Sun-Times,* June 13, 2006.

Thomas, Pierre. "Violent Crime Strikes a Chord Coast to Coast; '3-Time Loser' Laws Find Diverse Support." *Washington Post,* January 24, 1994, sec. A.

Tonry, Michael. "Mandatory Penalties." *Crime and Justice: A Review of Research* 16 (1992): 243–73.

———. *Sentencing Reform Impacts.* Washington, D.C.: National Institute of Justice, U.S. Department of Justice, Office of Communication and Research Utilization, 1987.

Trop v. Dulles, 356 U.S. 86 (1958).

Turner, Michael G., and Jody L. Sundt. "'Three Strikes and You're Out' Legislation: A National Assessment." *Federal Probation* 59, no. 3 (1995): 16.

Twentieth Century Fund Task Force on Criminal Sentencing. *Fair and Certain Punishment.* New York: McGraw Hill, 1976.

United States Sentencing Commission. *The Federal Sentencing Guidelines: A Report on the Operation of the Guidelines System and Short-Term Impacts on Disparity in Sentencing, Use of Incarceration, and Prosecutorial Discretion and Plea Bargaining.* Washington, D.C.: United States Sentencing Commission, 1991.

Vansickle, Abbie. "Bush Signs Jessica Lunsford Act; Parents Watch Birth of Law to Spare Others Their Agony." *St. Petersburg Times,* May 3, 2005, sec. 1.

Violent Crime Control and Law Enforcement Act of 1994. 103–322. September 13, 2004.

Vitiello, Michael. "Reforming Three Strikes' Excesses." *Washington University Law Quarterly* 82 (2004): 1–42.

———. "Three Strikes: Can We Return to Rationality?" *Journal of Criminal Law & Criminology* 87, no. 2 (1997): 395–481.

Von Hirsch, Andrew. *Doing Justice: The Choice of Punishments.* New York: Hill and Wang, 1976.

Walker, Samuel. *Taming the System: The Control of Discretion in Criminal Justice 1950–1990.* New York: Oxford University Press, 1993.

Walsh, Jennifer E. "Dismissing Strikes 'In the Furtherance of Justice': An Analysis of Prosecutorial and Judicial Discretion under the California Three-Strikes Law." Ph.D. dissertation, Claremont Graduate University, 2000.

———. *Tough for Whom? How Prosecutors and Judges Use Their Discretion to Promote Justice under the California Three-Strikes Law.* Claremont, Calif.: The Henry Salvatori Center, Claremont McKenna College, 2004.

Walters, Dan. "Apparent Flaws Mar Poll that Showed Voters Ready to Dilute 'Three Strikes.'" *Sacramento Bee,* June 25, 2004.

————. "Voter Turnaround on Proposition 66 was a Dramatic Campaign Event." *Sacramento Bee,* November 16, 2004, sec. A.

Weems v. United States, 217 U.S. 349 (1910).

Wilkerson v. Utah, 99 U.S. 130 (1878).

Williams v. Oklahoma, 358 U.S. 576 (1959).

Wilson, James Q. *Thinking about Crime.* New York: Basic Books, 1975.

Witte v. United States, 515 U.S. 389 (1995).

Wolfgang, Marvin E., Robert M. Figlio, and Thorsten Sellin. *Delinquency in a Birth Cohort, Studies in Crime and Justice.* Chicago: University of Chicago Press, 1972.

Worrall, John L. "The Effect of Three-Strikes Legislation on Serious Crime in California." *Journal of Criminal Justice* 32 (2004): 283–96.

Yoachum, Susan. "A Senseless Death, a Call to Action: Politicians at Polly's Memorial Urge Overhaul of Justice System." *San Francisco Chronicle,* December 10, 1993, sec. A.

Zalman, Marvin. "Mandatory Sentencing Legislation: Myth and Reality." In *Implementing Criminal Justice Policies,* edited by Merry Morash, 61–69. Beverly Hills, Calif.: Sage, 1982.

Zimring, Franklin E., Sam Kamin, and Gordon Hawkins. *Crime and Punishment in California: The Impact of Three Strikes and You're Out.* Berkeley: Institute of Governmental Studies Press, University of California, Berkeley, 1999.

Index

About the Author

JENNIFER E. WALSH is Associate Professor of Political Science in the Department of History and Political Science at Azusa Pacific University. She has testified before the California State Legislature as an academic expert on Three Strikes sentencing and has been interviewed by print and radio journalists about her findings.